THE TIMES

ELIZABETH

IN PHOTOS

THE TIMES

ELIZABETH

IN PHOTOS

Edited by Michael-John Jennings and Kate Mansey

"I declare before you all that my whole life whether it be long or short shall be devoted to your service and the service of our great imperial family to which we all belong."

INTRODUCTION

From Elizabeth II's earliest moments to her final acts of service, these 100 pictures, as seen by The Times, capture the life and times of Britain's longest-reigning monarch.

Spanning nearly a century, the lifetime of Her late Majesty was one which heralded a period of huge change in Britain. What began with a carriage ride, ended in the first lying-in-state to be live streamed. In between, the people of Britain witnessed huge upheaval, living through the conflict of the Second World War, the realignment of power within the Commonwealth and witnessing humanity's most rapid technological transformation.

On a personal level, her life offered an extraordinary ringside seat to history's greatest events, meeting world leaders and Hollywood stars and bearing witness to momentous occasions from the balcony of Buckingham Palace.

Throughout it all, photographers at The Times were given extraordinary access to capture the life of Elizabeth II; whether being invited into Sandringham in the year that her father George VI acceded the throne, to hand-delivering the wedding proofs to her and Philip on their honeymoon. The Queen repaid the honour, visiting the Times offices to learn more about how the paper of record was created, printed and distributed. Interested to see the long-range cameras, she was relieved to learn that, at The Times at least, they were used to capture sporting events rather than the personal lives of the royal family.

As you might expect, many of the photographs display the pomp and pageantry of the second Elizabethan era in all its glory; from the royal family's appearance with Prime Minister Winston Churchill on the Buckingham Palace balcony on VE Day in 1945 to the Queen's Coronation in 1953 and her subsequent jubilee celebrations.

Others, however, offer a tantalising glimpse of the woman behind the icon. Some of the pictures show Her Late Majesty in unguarded moments of grief and loss, whether dressed in a black veil as she follows in a car behind her father's coffin, or walking with Prince Philip through the river of floral tributes placed at the gates of Kensington Palace in memory of the late Princess Diana.

Some pictures reveal her sense of joy, particularly those images which show her with her family, her beloved pets, or both. They also show a young woman making her mark on the world stage in a way which few had seen since the days of Queen Victoria.

In doing so, she shaped not only the monarchy but the country as a whole. Unstuffy images of the Queen and Prince Philip with their young family offered a new way forward for the royal family, showing a more modern, youthful view of the Crown.

In one of many behind-the-scenes moments in the collection, we see Her late Majesty taking a break from her paperwork to offer a treat to her beloved pet corgi sitting patiently beside her chair at Buckingham Palace. We also see the bond of love she shared with her parents and rare moments of public grief and vulnerability, seen at the funerals of her father and, much later, her mother.

The pictures are proof that some of the greatest moments in history and most pivotal points in a person's life can often arrive without warning or fanfare. When Prince Philip informed his 25-year-old wife that her father King George VI had died, making her Queen, they were not in a palace or castle but on a visit to the Treetops estate in Kenya.

Her Late Majesty's extensive travels capture not just the story of the UK but the wider Commonwealth. From her first broadcast as a 21-year-old Princess in Cape Town to a visit to Tonga, a New Year's Eve visit to New Zealand and the first visit by a British sovereign to China.

There are famous faces here: members of the royal family, of course, but also stars of stage and screen and world leaders. Images featuring members of the public are no less poignant. Take, for example, the little girl handing a posy to the Queen at Charterhouse.

With the benefit of hindsight, these historic images even offer a tantalising glimpse of the future to come. Attending an aristocratic wedding in 1946, Prince Philip of Greece, a dashing young naval officer, is seen in animated conversation with the Duchess of York, better known to us now as the late Queen Mother. Within a year, he would marry her daughter, Princess Elizabeth, and go on to be Britain's longest-serving consort.

This book charts the growth of the Queen's family, and we see her obvious delight at the 2011 wedding of her grandson Prince William and his bride Kate Middleton. On her final major public outing and less than three months before her death, the 96-year-old Queen was photographed alongside their three young children as she waved from the balcony of Buckingham Palace one last time during her Platinum Jubilee celebrations in 2022.

So, this collection of 100 photographs captures and celebrates not only a reign well served but also something much more: a life well lived.

BIRTHDAY CARRIAGE RIDE

Photographer unknown

April 21, 1927

Wrapped up in a cosy white hood, Princess Elizabeth looks out of the carriage during a drive to celebrate her first birthday. The first daughter of the Duke and Duchess of York, Elizabeth was born the year beforehand in Bruton Street, Mayfair. At the time, her grandfather George V was on the throne and the young Elizabeth was not considered to be an obvious future Queen. Within a decade, that all changed when George V's death was followed by the abdication of her uncle, Edward VIII.

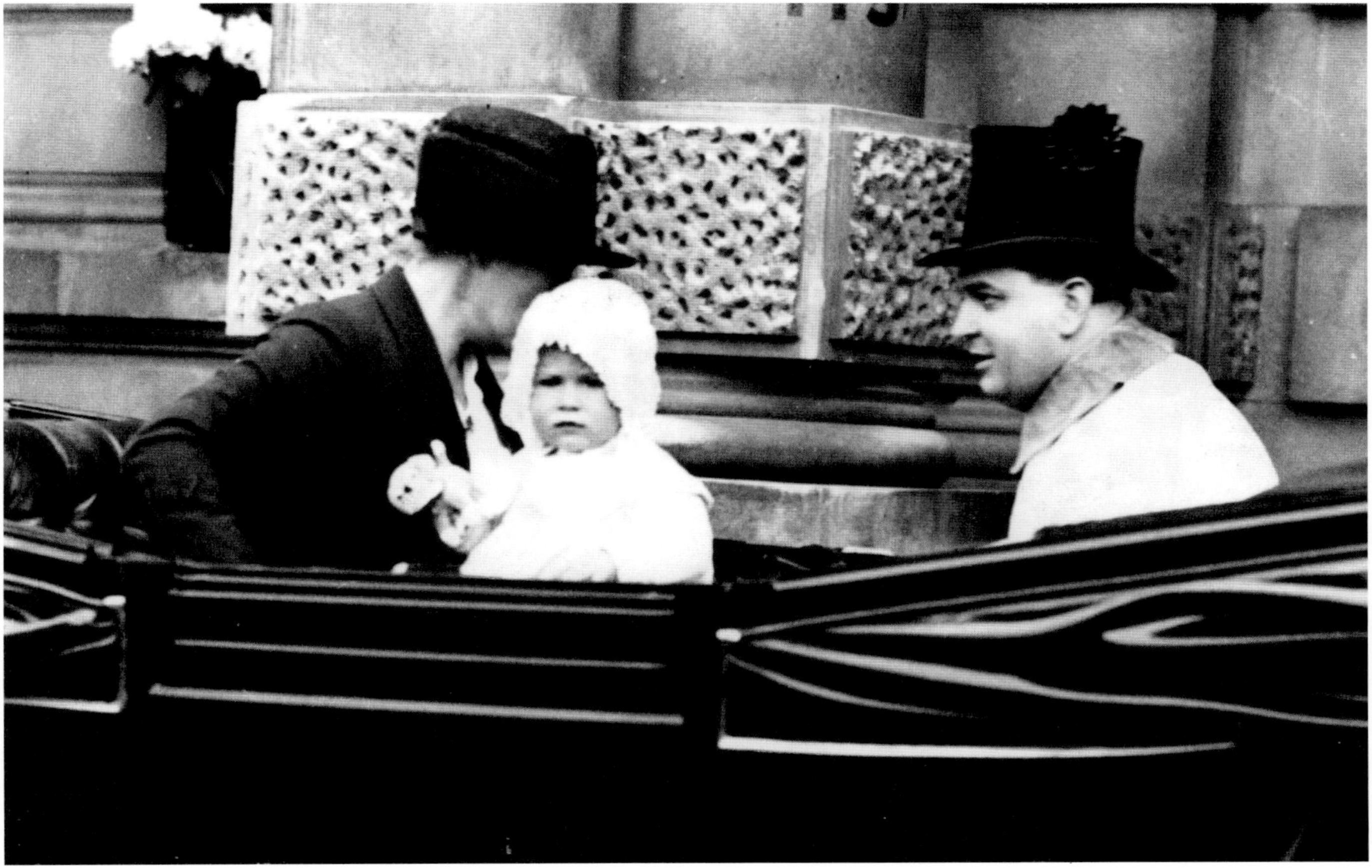

PRINCESS ELIZABETH IN HER PRAM

By Robert Field

September 12, 1927

An early introduction to the joys of Scotland; Elizabeth's gaze is directed towards an item of interest by her grandfather George V at a fete in the grounds of Balmoral Castle. As the King points with a walking stick, Elizabeth cranes her head round in her pram to get a better look. The castle is seen in the background, barely changed from Queen Victoria's time. The image, captured by Robert Field, offers a glimpse at Elizabeth's early introduction to public royal engagements. From a young age, she was often wheeled out in her pram to meet the public.

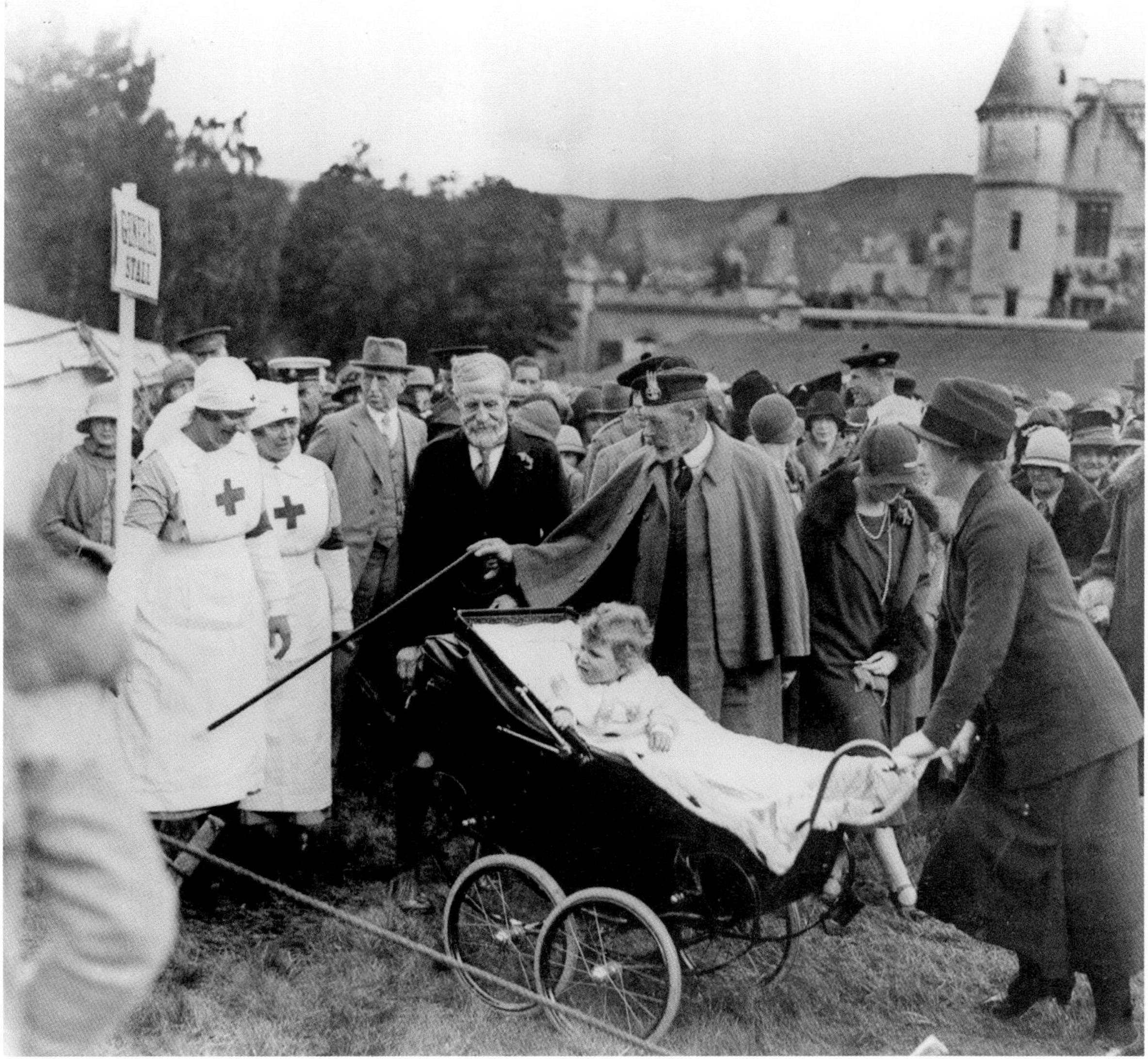
GENERAL
STALL

MAUNDY MONEY

By Herbert William "Bill" Warhurst

April 20, 1935

The Duchess of York turns to smile upon her daughter, Princess Elizabeth, after the presentation of Maundy Money at Westminster Abbey. Clutching a bouquet of flowers, the young Princess, dressed in a smart coat and hat, is seen walking with Princess Helena Victoria and Princess Marie Louise and members of the clergy as they leave the abbey. The time-honoured tradition of distributing Maundy money is an opportunity for the monarch to honour people who have provided significant Christian service to their communities.

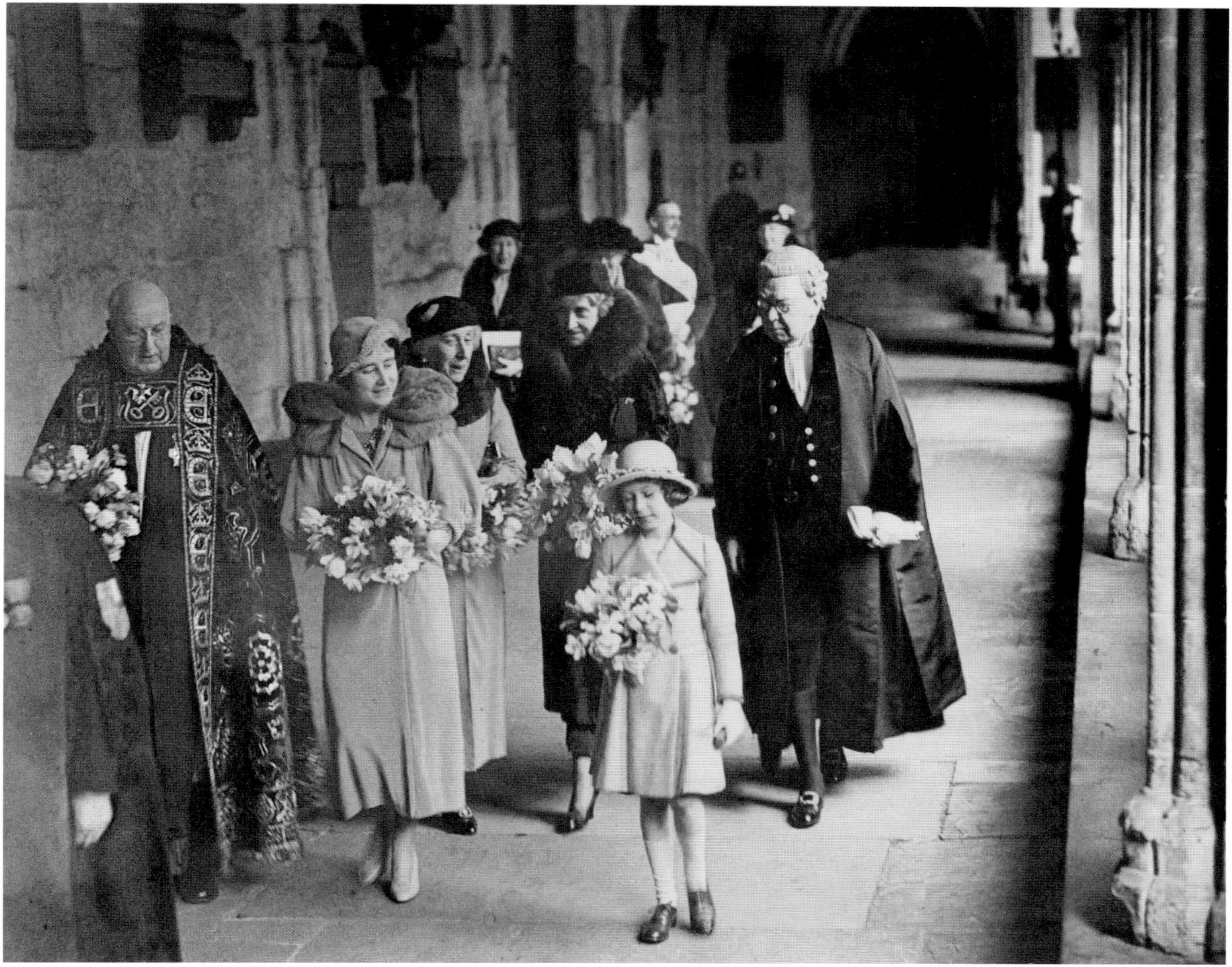

A STYLISH ENTRANCE AT THE ROYAL TOURNAMENT

By Jack Barker

May 15, 1935

With pristine white gloves and perfectly coiffed hair, a young Princess Elizabeth follows her mother, the Duchess of York, and sister, Princess Margaret, as she steps from a car during a visit to the Royal Tournament at Olympia. The event, held annually between 1880 and 1999, was the world's largest military tattoo and pageant and a notable date in the royal calendar. In the interwar years, the tournament grew in popularity with competitions involving the British Army, RAF and Royal Navy.

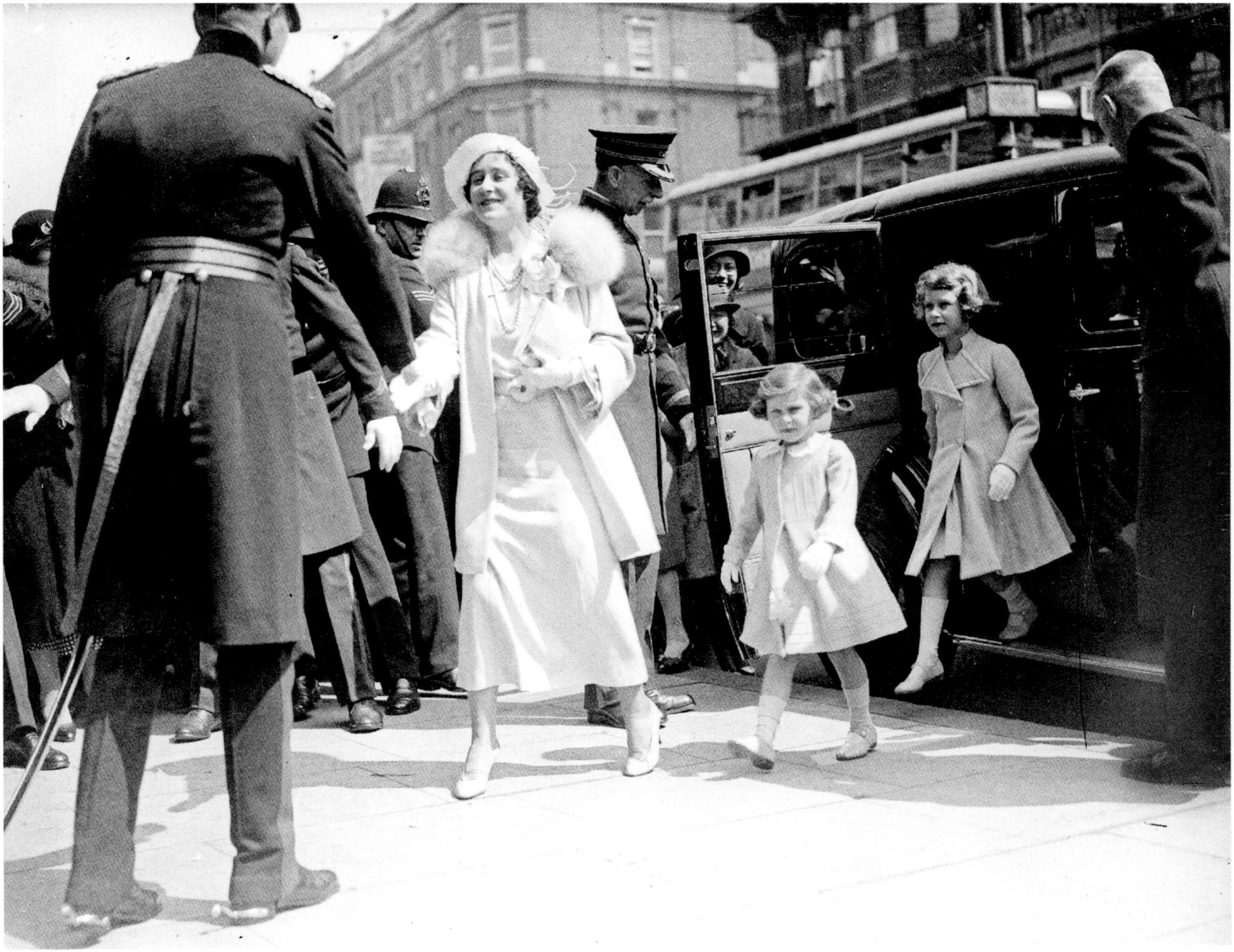

A ROYAL HOME PORTRAIT

By Eric Greenwood

March 12, 1936

A rare and intimate glimpse of life within the royal family in a year of great upheaval. Following the death of George V in January, he was succeeded by Edward VIII who abdicated at the end of the year. This almost ethereal portrait of Queen Mary with her grandchildren Princesses Elizabeth and Margaret was taken by Eric Greenwood, a staff photographer of The Times, who was invited into the main house at Sandringham. George V had been fond of his granddaughters and gave Elizabeth the nickname "Lilibet". His death may offer an explanation as to the trio's sombre expressions.

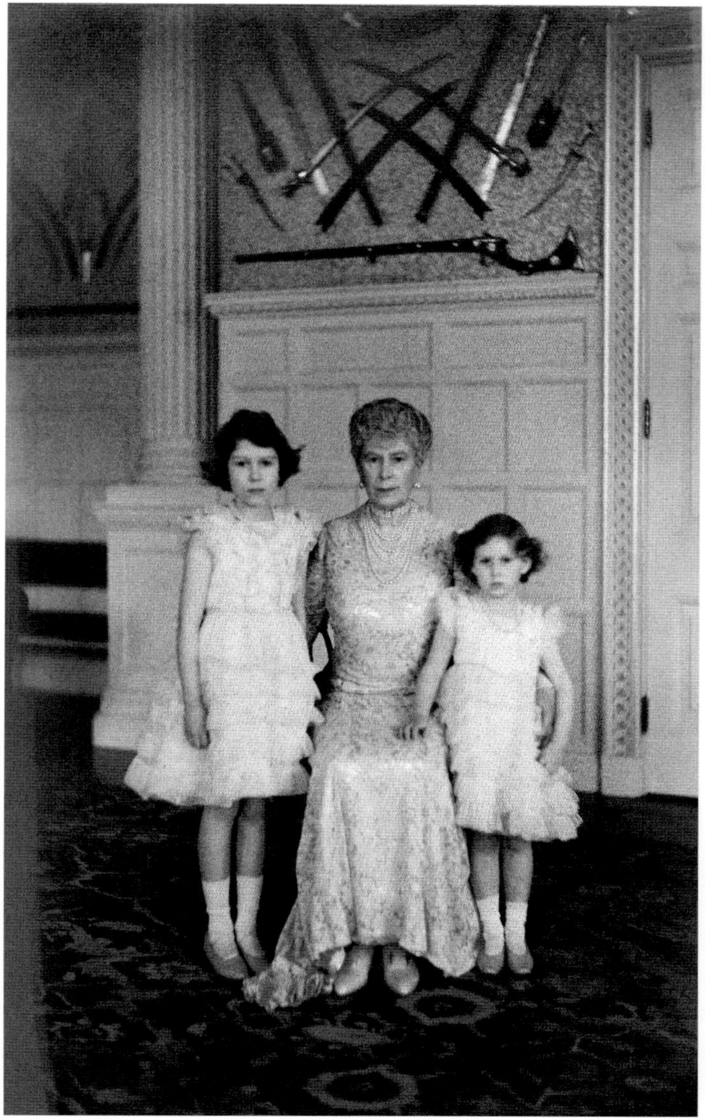

PLAYING HOUSE

Photographer unknown

July 28, 1936

A keen family man, the Duke of York, later King George VI, referred to his nuclear family as "we four". Shown here in the gardens of Royal Lodge in Windsor, his delight is clear to see as he lifts one of the family's pets over a little wall while Princess Margaret cradles another dog on her lap. Princess Elizabeth looks on while her mother leans out of a window. Over the door is the sign Y Bwythn Bach, meaning "Little House"; the two-storey thatched cottage was a gift from the people of Wales and presented to the Yorks to mark Princess Elizabeth's sixth birthday.

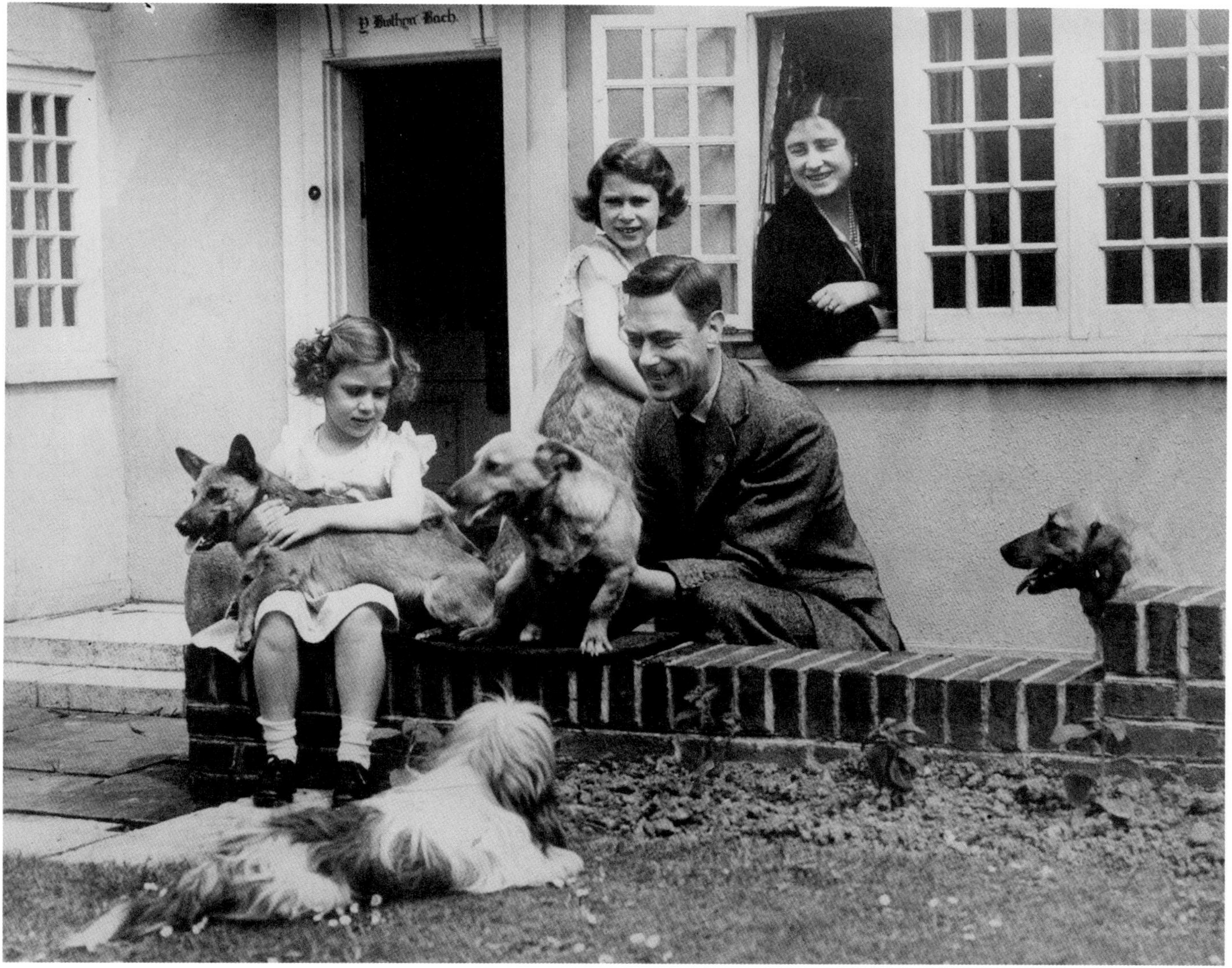

OFF TO A WEDDING

By Robert Chandler

1936

Dressed in matching outfits with double-breasted coats, flower-embroidered hats and white gloves, Princesses Elizabeth and Margaret are smartly presented for a wedding. Their mother, the Duchess of York, wears a fashionable cap-sleeved dress embellished with flowers on the sleeves and hem as she walks hand-in-hand with her younger daughter. The Duke of York, meanwhile, stands tall in morning suit with his top hat in hand.

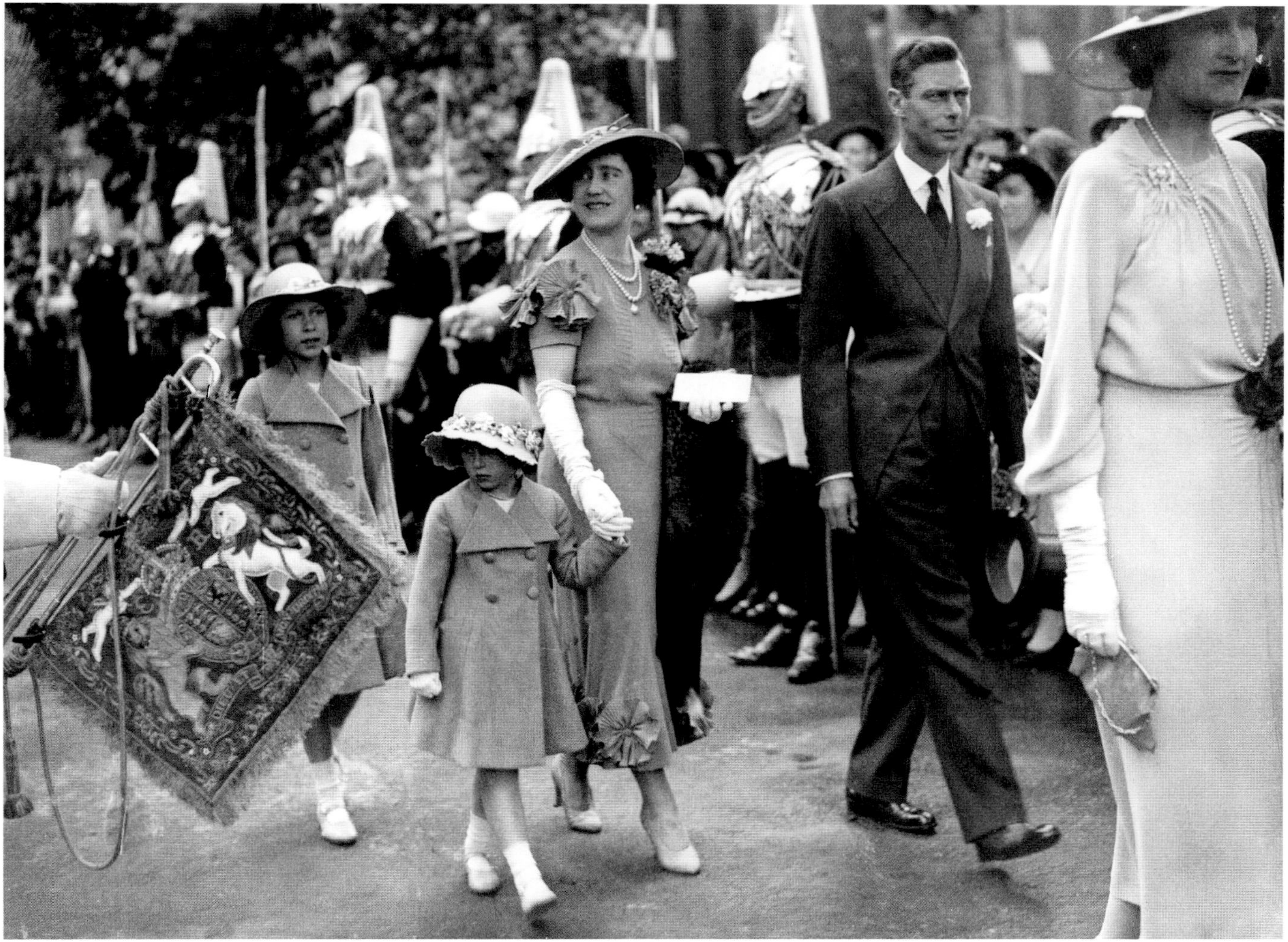

AT THE THEATRE

By Herbert William "Bill" Warhurst

March 29, 1937

With hands clasped together and her face lit by the glow from the stage, this majestic image of a young Princess Elizabeth shows the heir apparent smiling down at a performance. The image captures the magic of the theatre and the rapture of the future Queen, who wore a single string of pearls to the event. Sitting between her parents, Elizabeth was attending a show at the London Coliseum in aid of the King George's Pension Fund for actors and actresses.

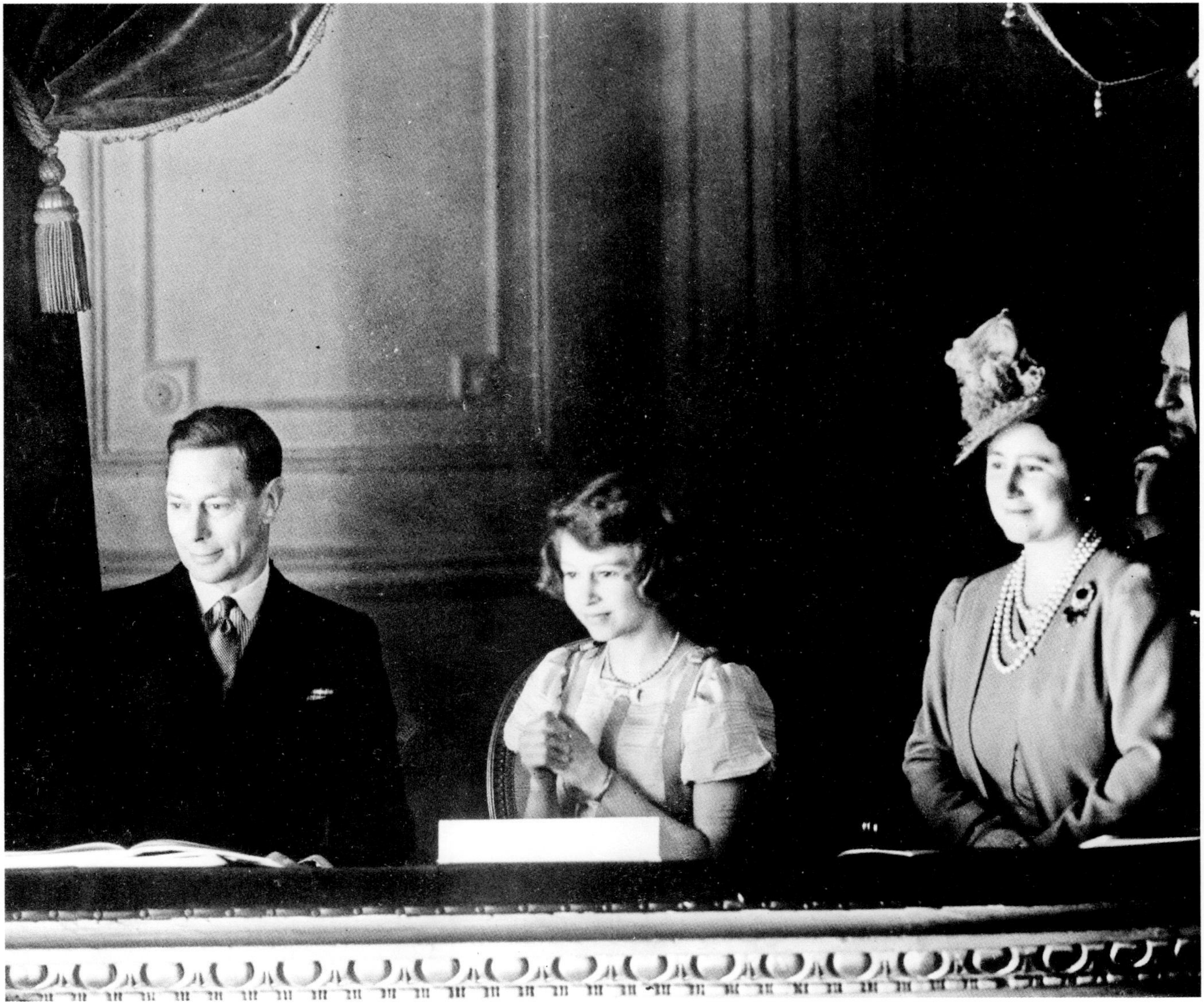

KING GEORGE VI CORONATION

By Jack Barker

May 12, 1937

When the day was set for a coronation, it had initially been intended for Edward VIII. Following his abdication, however, his brother King George VI presented a new future for the monarchy with his Queen Consort and two daughters, Princesses Elizabeth and Margaret. In this striking image, the King is seen wearing the Imperial Crown on the day of his Coronation as his ermine robes flow down the steps inside Buckingham Palace. His Queen Consort, later the Queen Mother, wears a bespoke crown modelled on one used by Queen Mary, while Princesses Elizabeth and Margaret have lightweight silver-gilt coronets delicately placed on their heads.

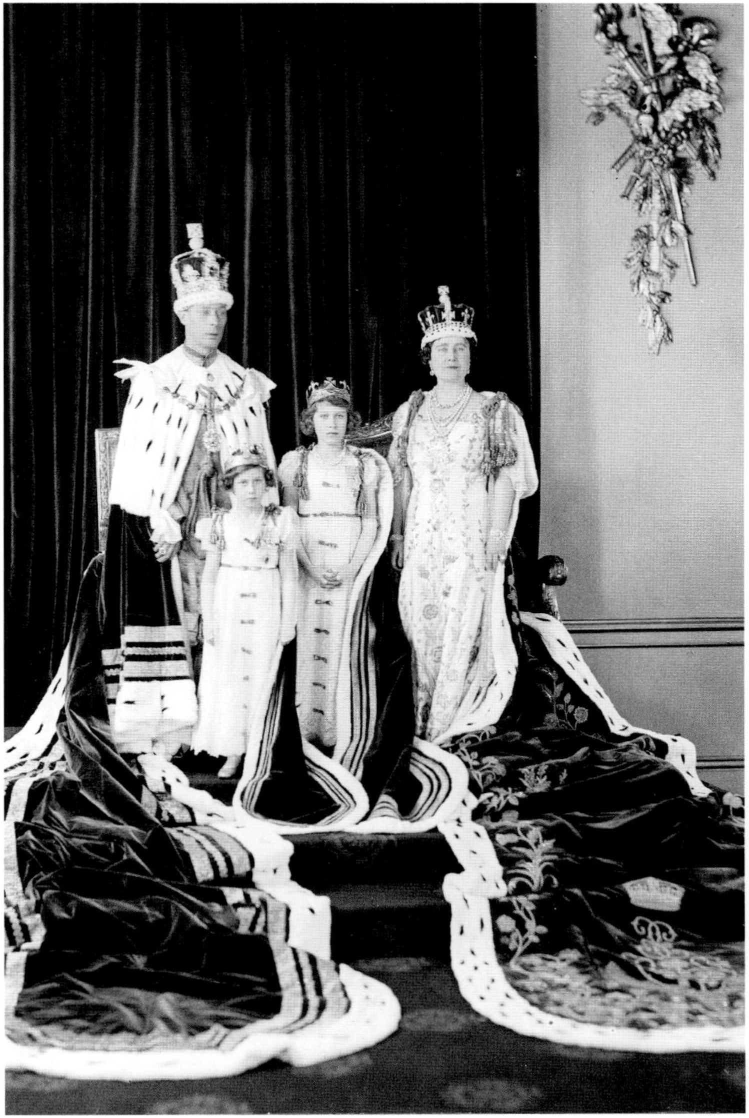

BIRTHDAY GIRL

Photographer unknown

April 21, 1940

This wartime family portrait was released in 1940 to mark Princess Elizabeth's 14th birthday. In a tweed skirt with shiny shoes and a smart blazer, Elizabeth gently clasps her hands in front of her with a self confidence that belies her years. Her younger sister, Princess Margaret, is dressed in the same outfit while their father and mother stand protectively behind them. The image, first published in The Sunday Times, was taken at Windsor Castle where Elizabeth and Margaret stayed during the Second World War.

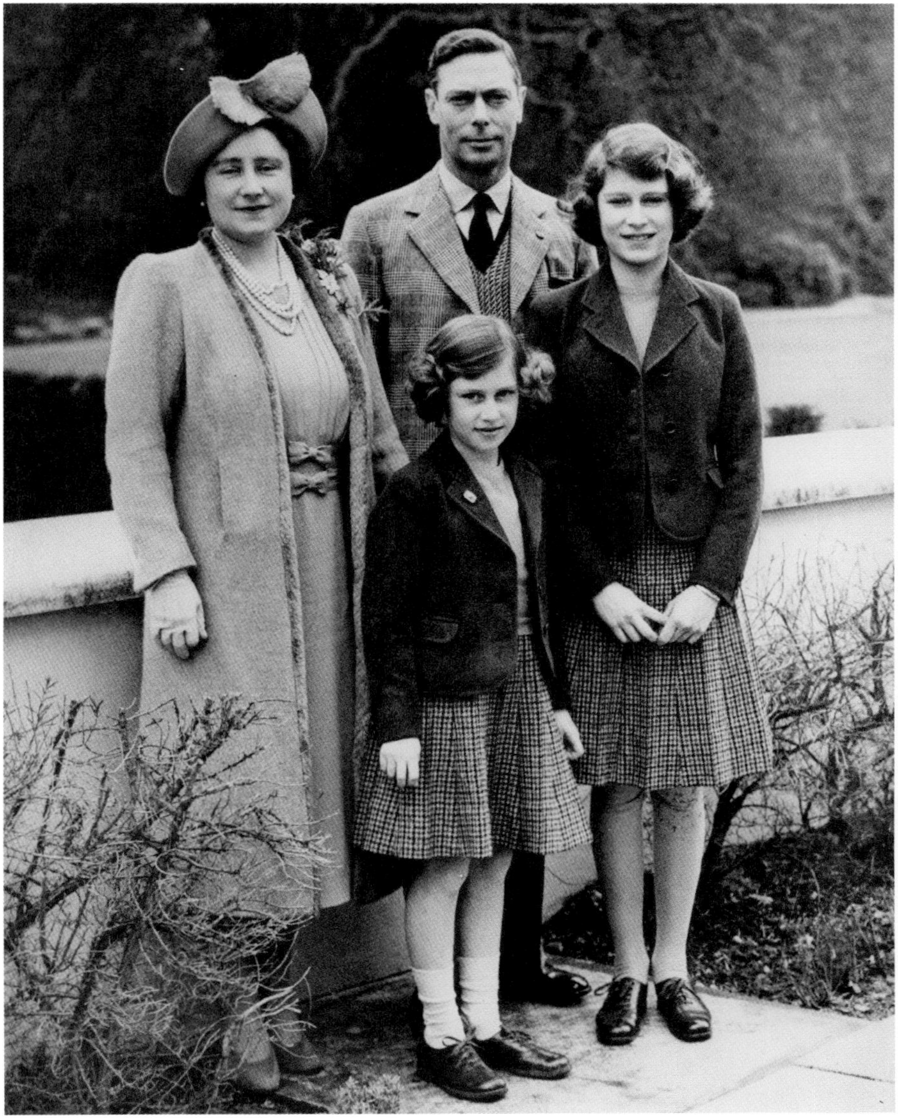

HARVEST TIME

By Jack Barker

August 26, 1940

Few occasions elicited such a generous and genuine smile from Princess Elizabeth than when she was confronted with animals. Beaming towards the camera, Princess Elizabeth, aged 14, poses with one of the King's horses during harvest time at Sandringham. An animal lover from a young age, Her Late Majesty found succour in the outdoors. With the wind in her hair and wearing a button-down dress delicately embroidered with birds, she gives every sense of being at ease in the countryside.

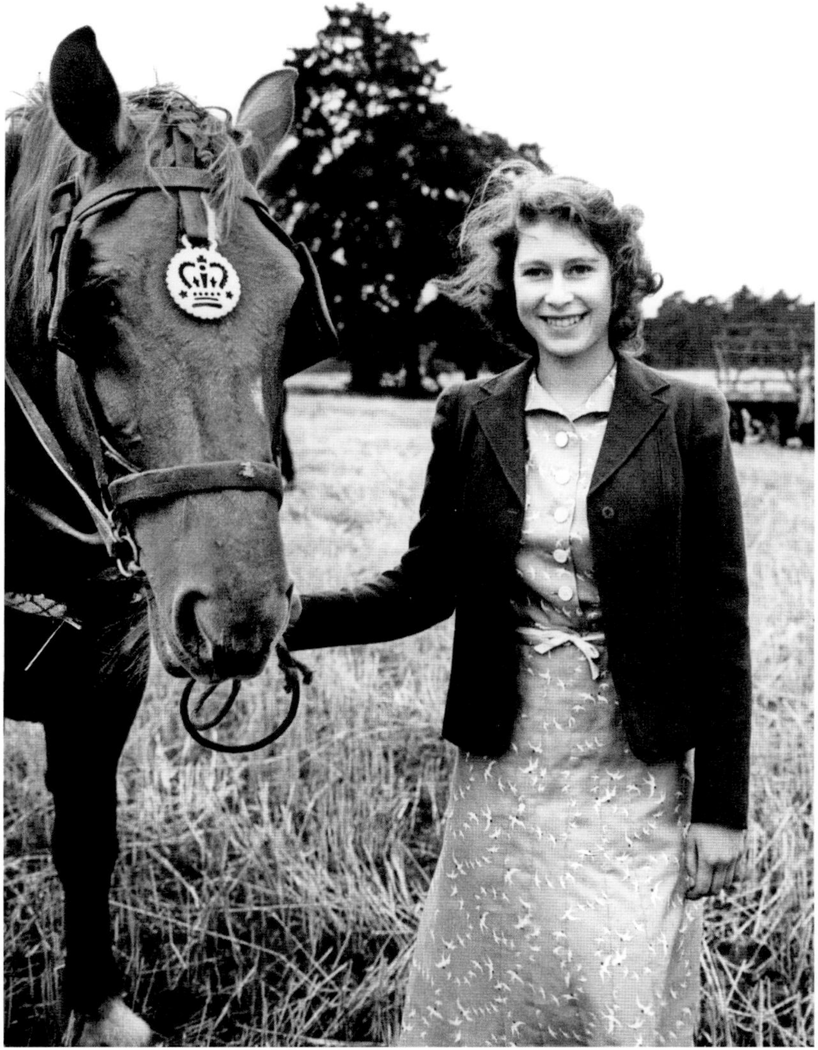

SAVING PETROL IN WARTIME

By Jack Barker

August 26, 1940

Everyone was called upon to do their bit for the war effort and the royal family was no exception. Here, King George VI and Princesses Elizabeth and Margaret are seen inspecting the harvest at Sandringham using bicycles, to save on the petrol required to carry out the task by motorcar. Meanwhile, Queen Elizabeth, later the Queen Mother, holds the reins of a horse-drawn carriage. The methods were used as a means of saving petrol, which was sorely needed for the war effort.

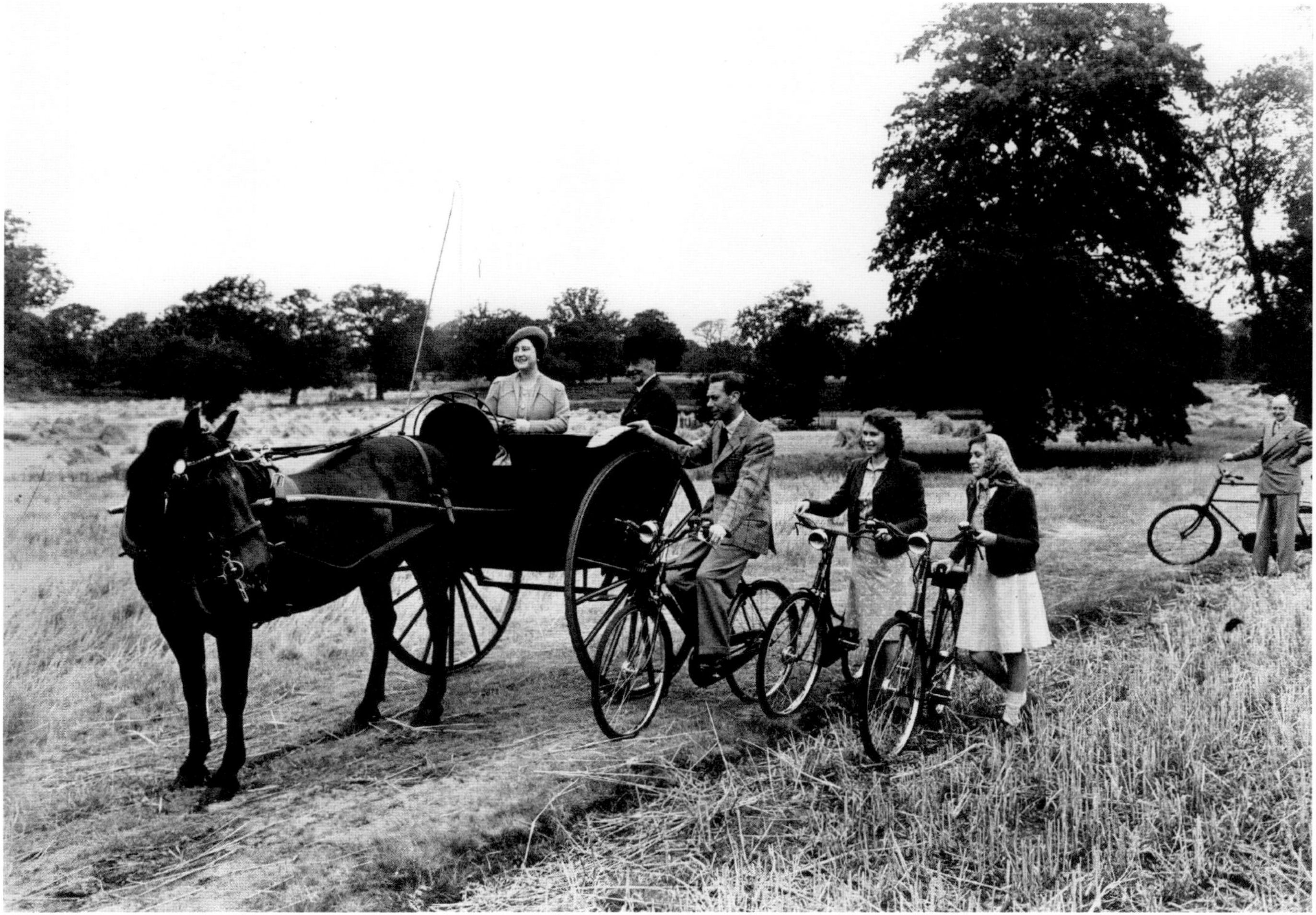

FIRST PUBLIC BROADCAST

By Cathal O'Gorman

October 13, 1940

In her first public speech, Princess Elizabeth gives a wartime address to children of the Commonwealth, many of whom had been evacuated from their homes. Joined by "my sister Margaret Rose", Elizabeth expressed "a message of true sympathy" to the "thousands of you in this country" who "have had to leave your homes and be separated from your fathers and mothers". "When peace comes, remember it will be for us the children of today, to make the world of tomorrow a better and happier place," she said. The message was broadcast on the BBC's Children's Hour from Windsor Castle.

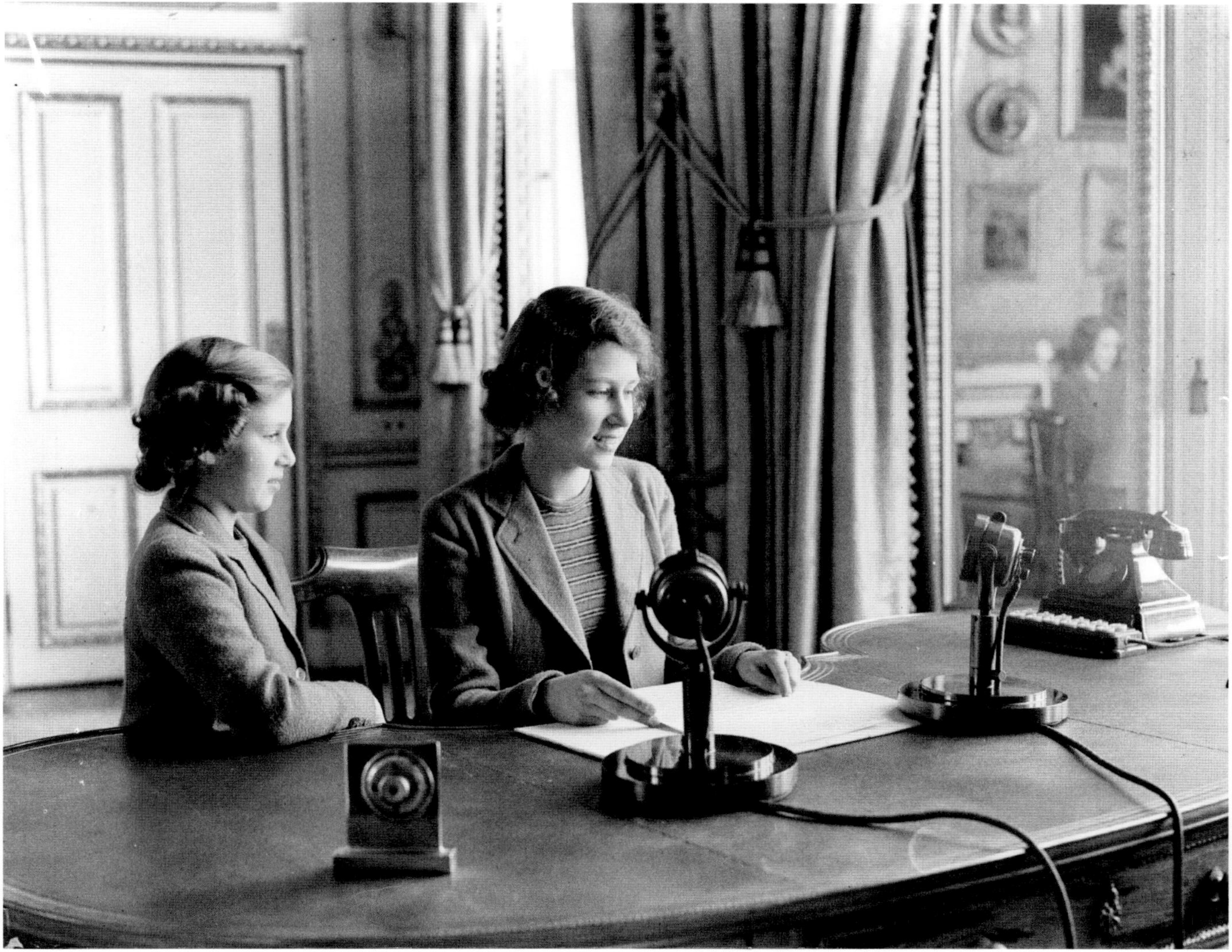

A MESSAGE FROM A GIRL GUIDE

By Robert Chandler

February 20, 1943

As patrol leader of the Girl Guides, Princess Elizabeth was often seen in her uniform. Here, she writes a message to be sent by carrier pigeon to Lady Baden Powell, the first Chief Guide for Britain and the wife of Robert Baden Powell, founder of the Scouting movement. Princess Margaret looks on as Elizabeth writes out her message and helps her older sister by holding the pigeon carrier. The message was sent to mark the annual Girl Guide tradition of Thinking Day and included a greeting to Lady Baden Powell on the occasion of her birthday.

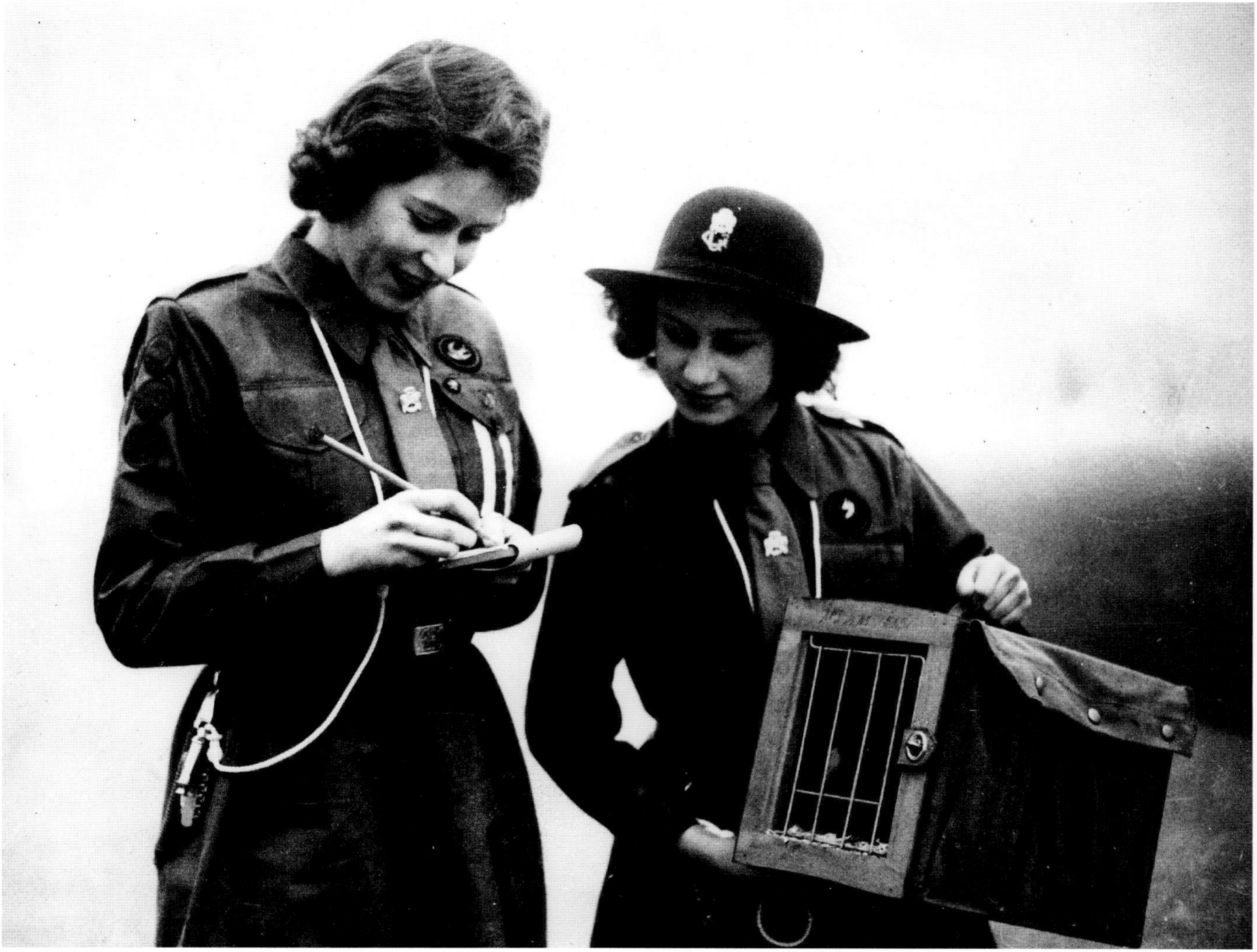

18TH BIRTHDAY

By Herbert William "Bill" Warhurst

April 21, 1944

Princess Elizabeth was 13 when war broke out and her teenage years were dominated by news of bombardments and conflict. As she grew older she was keen to play her part. Elizabeth was appointed Colonel of the Grenadier Guards two years beforehand in 1942, and is seen here on her 18th birthday proudly wearing the diamond brooch in the shape of the regimental badge, which was presented to her upon her appointment. Her proud parents are beside their daughter, supporting her as she transitions into adulthood.

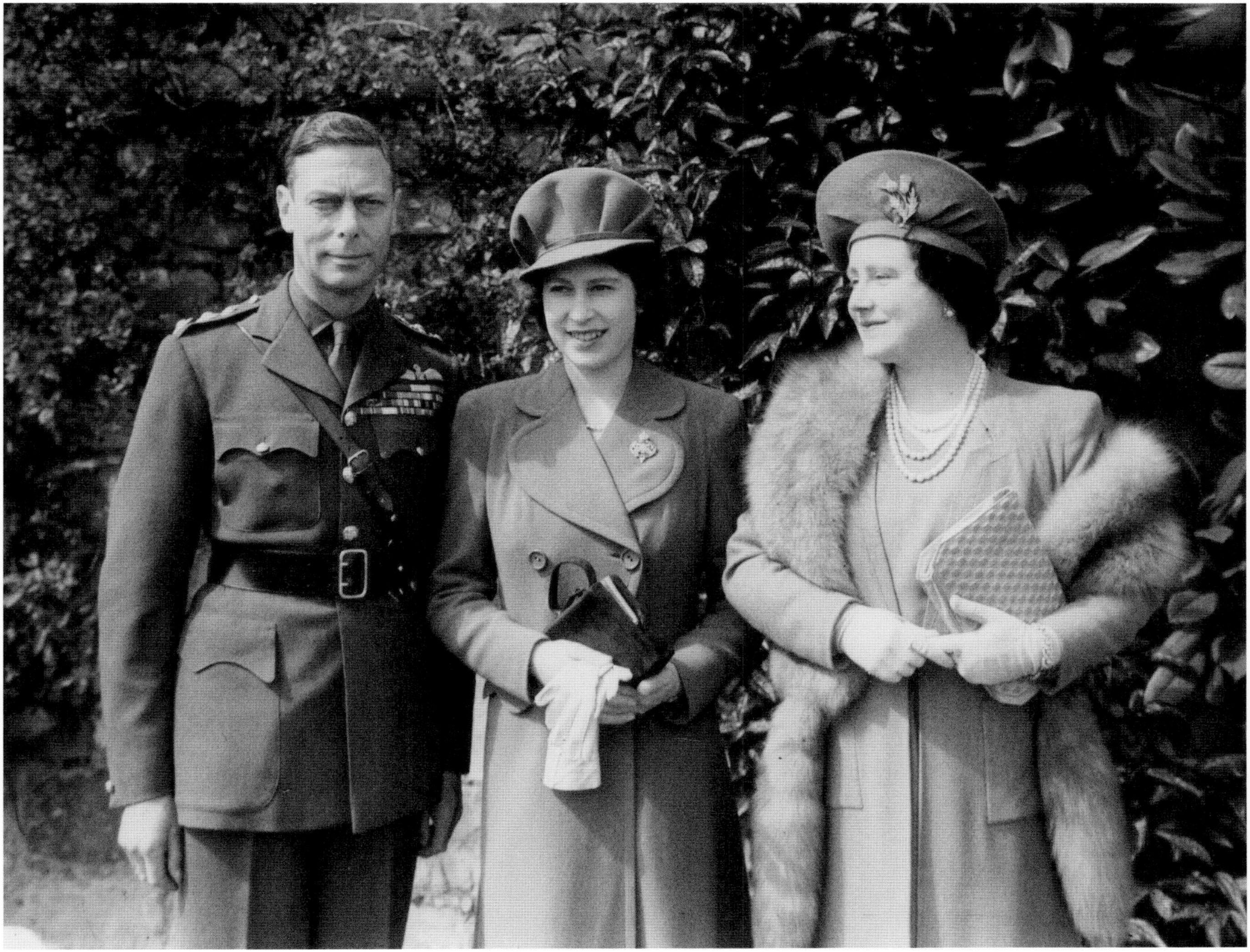

THE ROSE OF YORK

By Robert Chandler

July 6, 1944

During a military-themed engagement, Princess Elizabeth performs the naming ceremony of “Rose of York”, a B-17G Flying Fortress of 367th Bombardment Squadron, at Thurleigh in Bedfordshire. Originally called the “Princess Elizabeth”, the aircraft was renamed amid concerns of the propaganda value for the Nazis if it were to be shot down. The Rose of York refers to her parents’ former titles of the Duke and Duchess of York. The bomber, from the 8th Air Force, was lost on its 63rd mission.

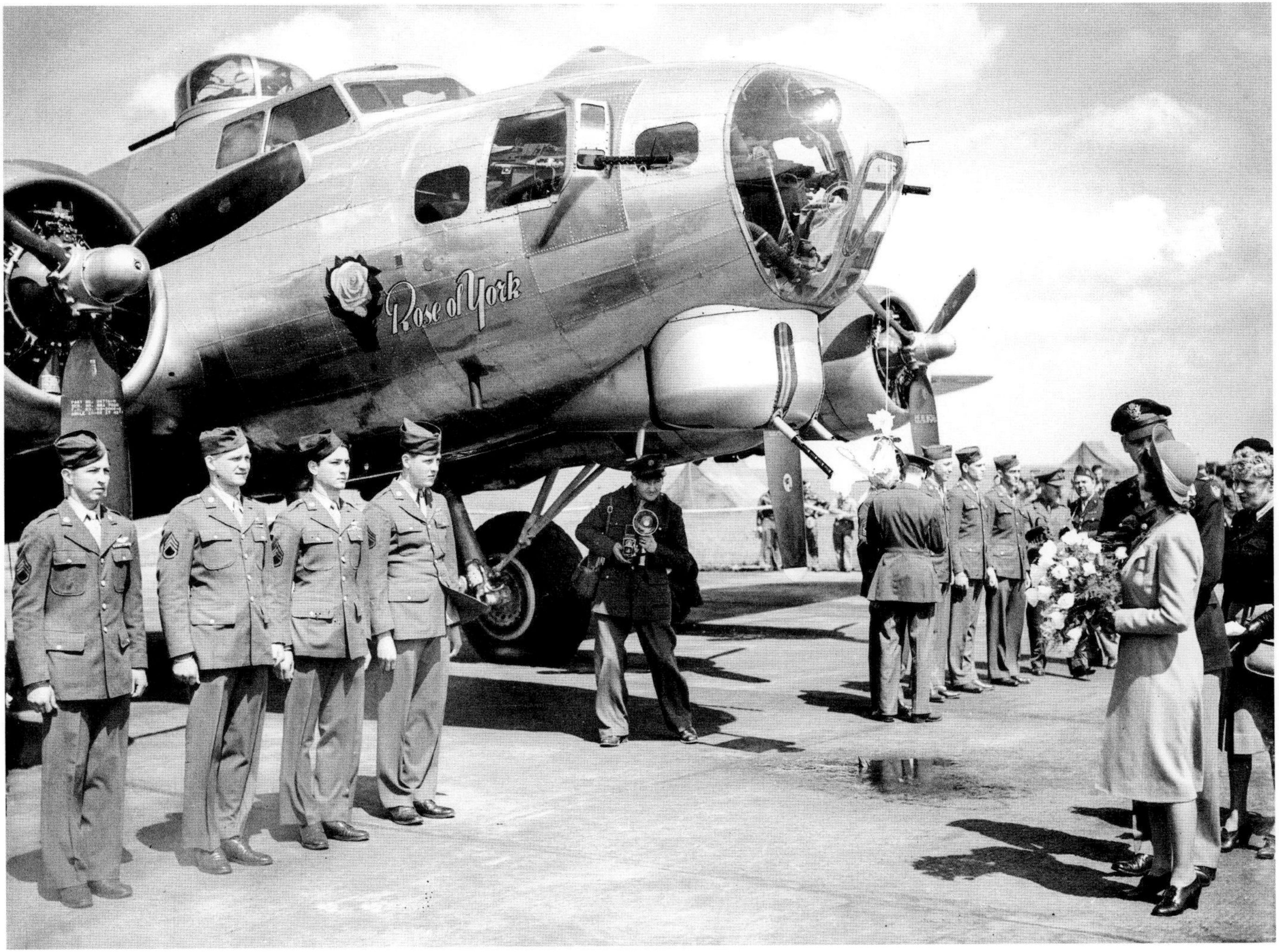
Rose of York

VE DAY

By Cathal O'Gorman

May 8, 1945

With Prime Minister Winston Churchill in the centre of the Buckingham Palace balcony, Princess Elizabeth joins the royal family amid the celebrations to mark VE Day, Victory in Europe. While it was an extraordinary moment for the nation and the Commonwealth, it was also a personal milestone for the future Queen. Dressed in the khaki uniform of the Auxiliary Territorial Service (ATS), the Princess waved down to vast crowds that had gathered on the Mall. Princess Elizabeth, then aged 19, had also been able to join the throngs on the streets, slipping out into the city with her 14-year-old sister, Princess Margaret.

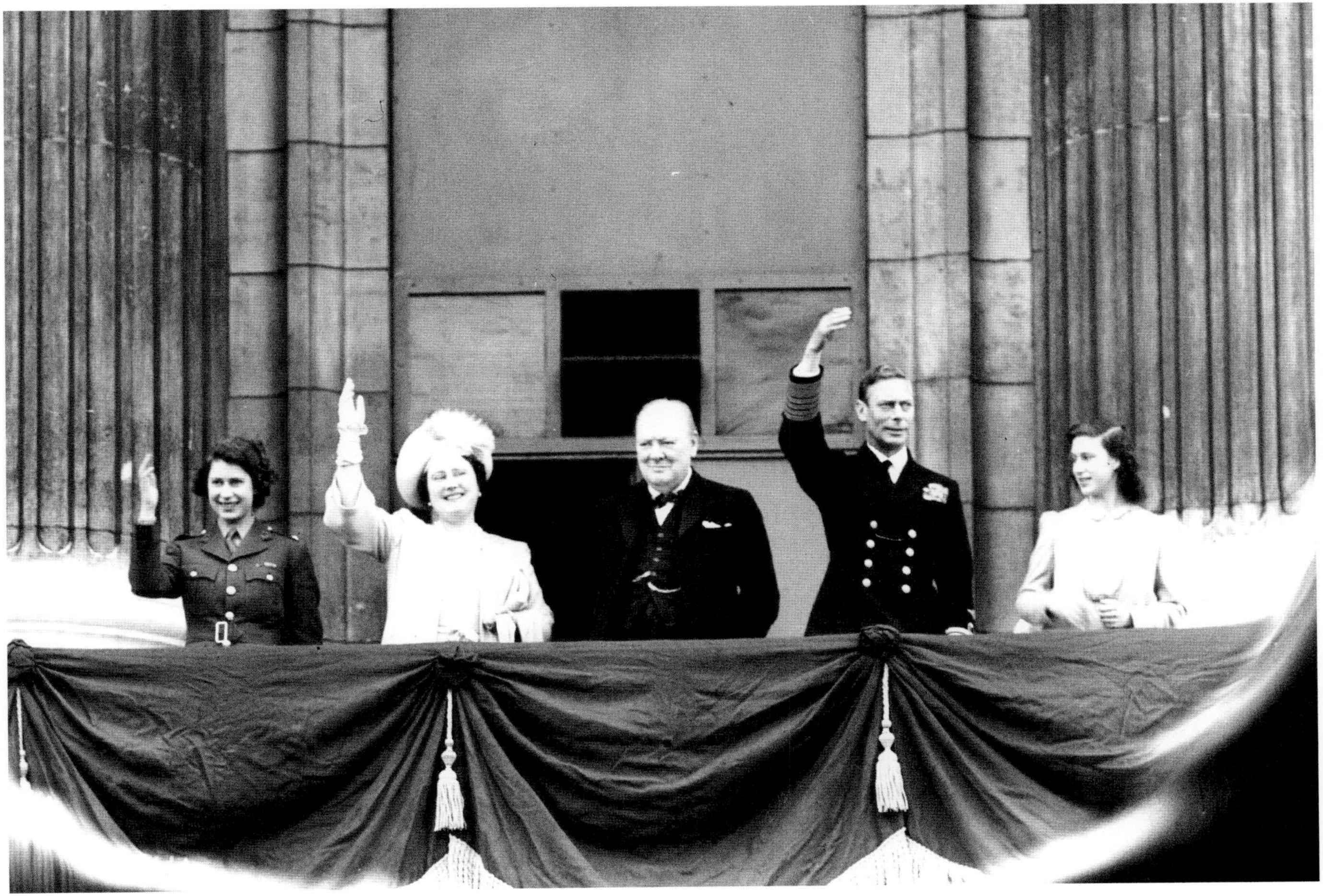

A WELSH INITIATION

By Herbert Muggeridge

August 6, 1946

Dressed in emerald bardic robes, Princess Elizabeth takes part in a traditional bardic ceremony where she was invested as an honorary bard at the National Eisteddfod in Mountain Ash, Glamorgan, in August 1946. The experience would inspire a lifelong love of the Welsh language. During the ceremony, druids raised the sacred sword above their heads and gave the Princess the bardic name of “Elizabeth o Windsor”. Elizabeth visited the Eisteddfod again as Queen in 1960, making history as the first reigning monarch to attend the bardic festival.

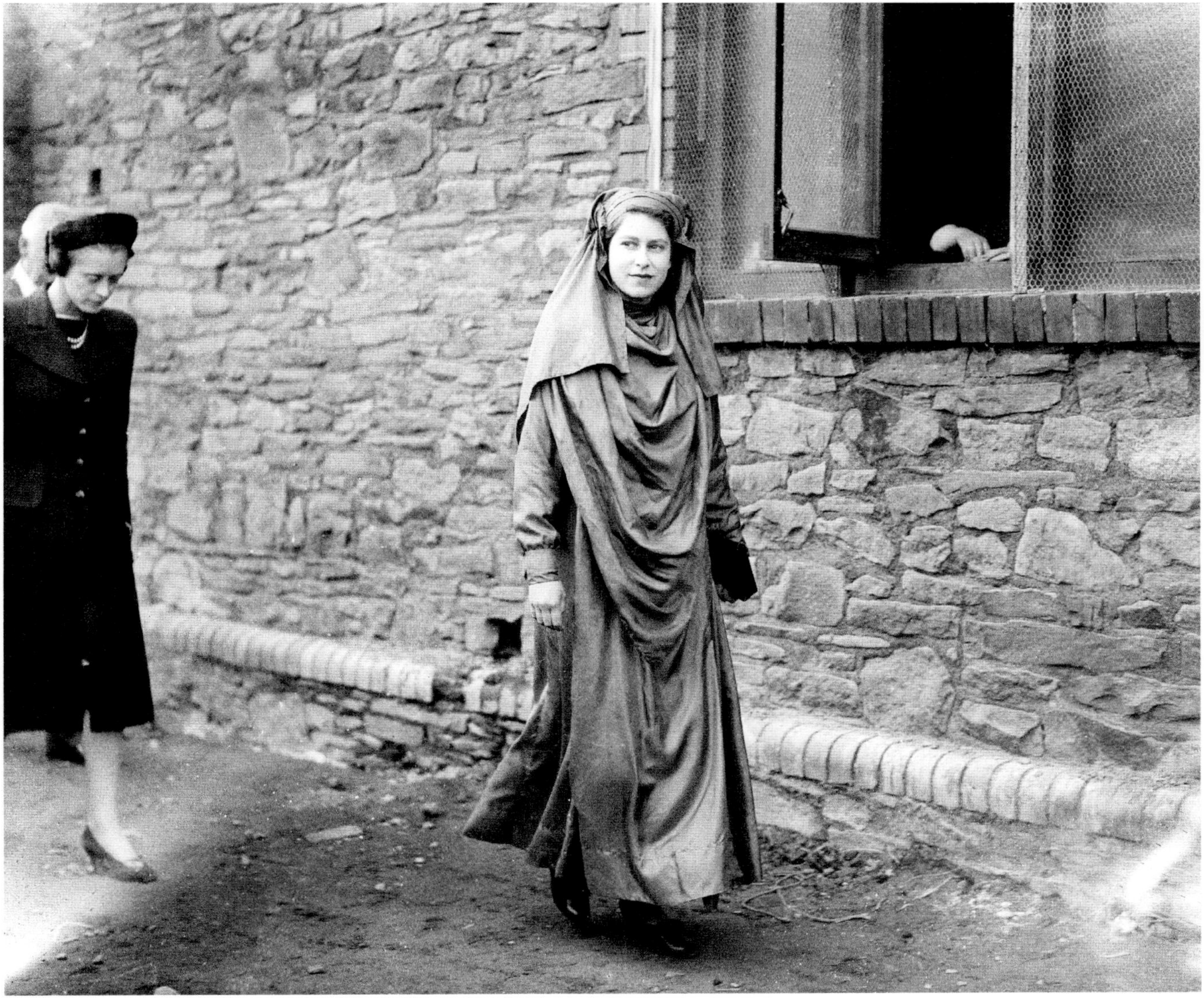

A WEDDING WITH A PRINCE

By Herbert Muggeridge

October 26, 1946

Following a downpour on a bright and blustery autumn day, Princess Elizabeth lifts her skirts as she walks towards Romsey Abbey in Hampshire for the wedding of Lord Brabourne and the Honourable Patricia Mountbatten. Another romance, however, is already underway. Elizabeth is joined by her father, King George VI (left) and her sister Princess Margaret (centre), although someone else has captivated her mother: Prince Philip of Greece, a cousin of the bride, who was an usher at the wedding. A little over a year later, Princess Elizabeth and Prince Philip would be married at Westminster Abbey.

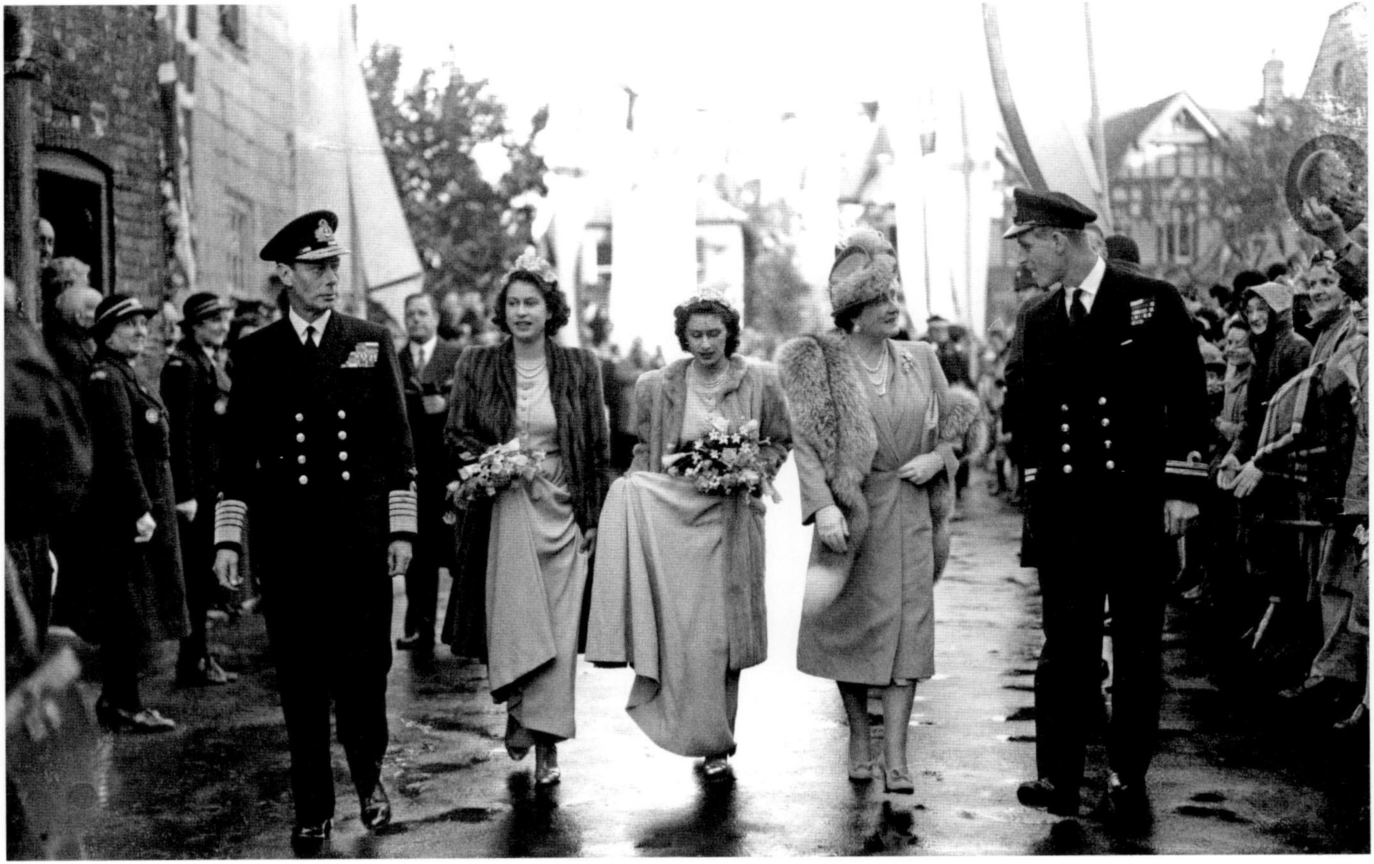

ROYAL FILM PERFORMANCE

By Herbert Muggeridge

November 5, 1946

With a beaming smile, Princess Elizabeth appears to relish the film premiere of *A Matter of Life and Death*, a picture by Michael Powell and Emeric Pressburger. The attendance of senior members of the royal family at the Empire Theatre in Leicester Square not only raised the status of the British film industry, but also helped its benevolent fund. Known at first as the Royal Command Film Performance, it later changed its name to the Royal Film Performance to make it clear that the royal family had not dictated which film should be screened.

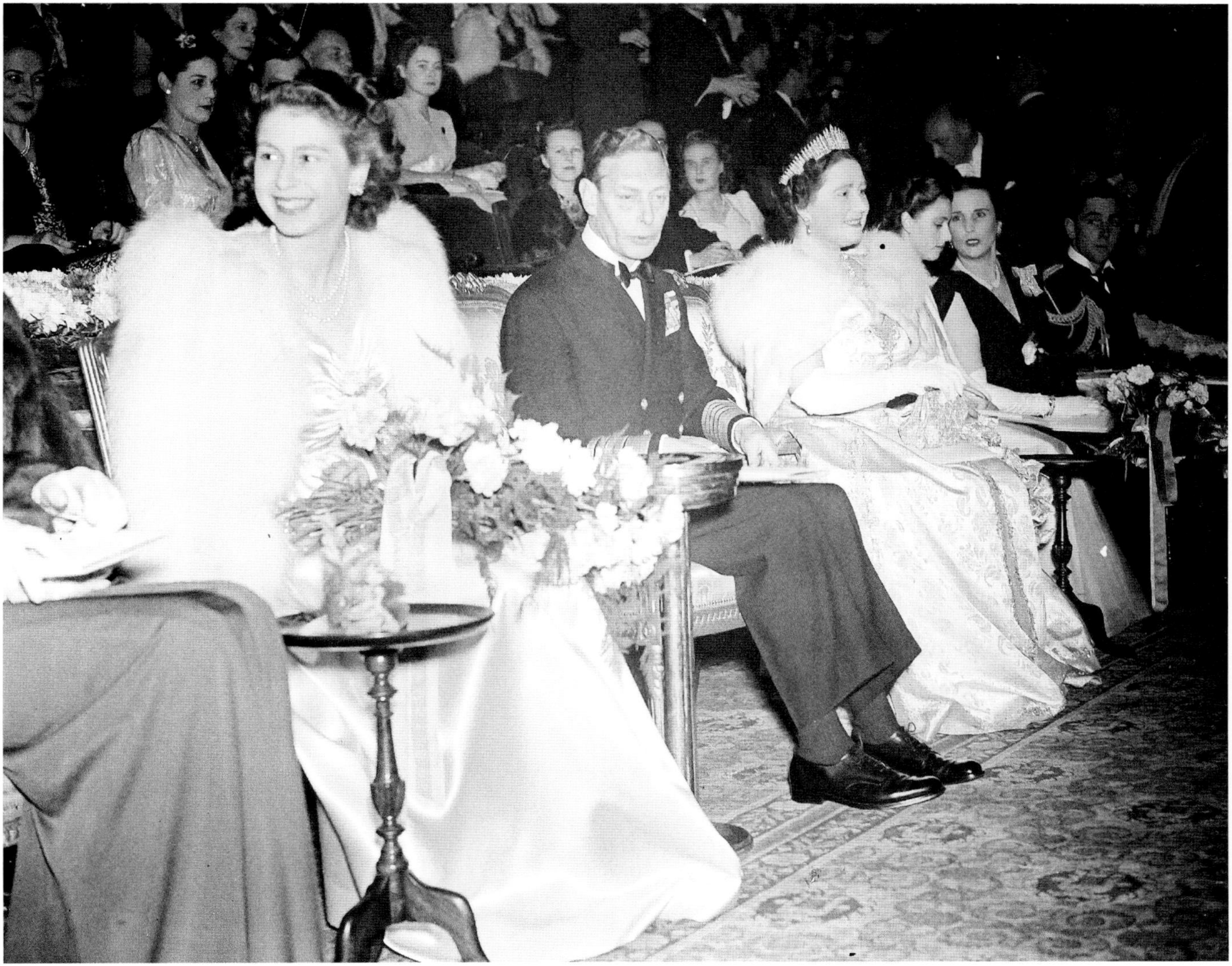

TAKING AIM

By William Horton

February 7, 1947

When George VI made a three-month visit to South Africa with his Queen Consort, he took both his daughters, Princesses Elizabeth and Margaret, with him. The length of the tour, which included ceremonial events and many meetings with foreign dignitaries, also afforded time for other pursuits. Here, the two princesses take part in a rifle-shooting competition on HMS Vanguard. As an officer offers words of encouragement, Elizabeth is seen lying on the deck as she takes aim.

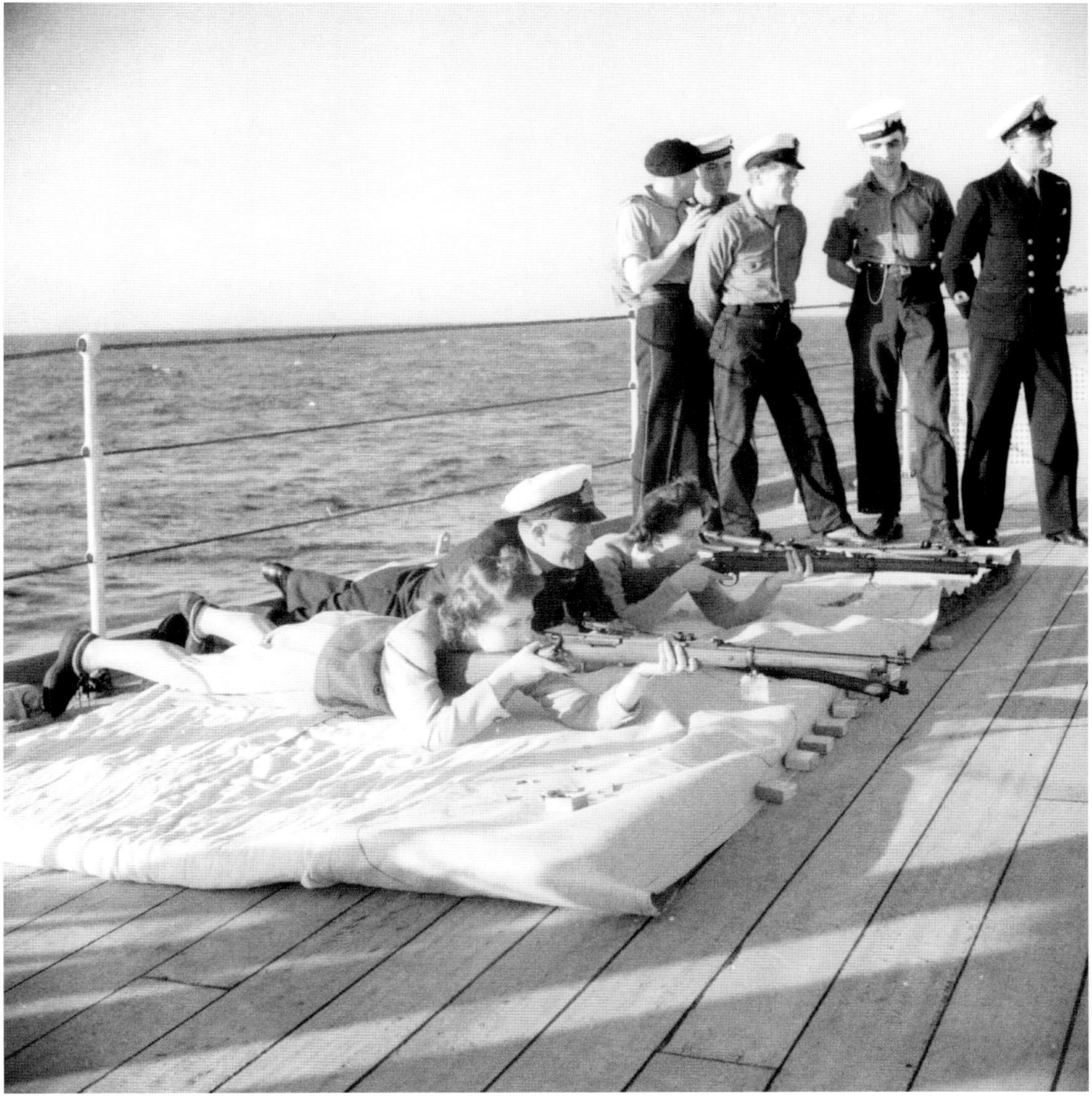

I DEVOTE MY WHOLE LIFE TO YOUR SERVICE

By William Horton

April 21, 1947

"I declare before you all that my whole life whether it be long or short shall be devoted to your service and the service of our great imperial family to which we all belong." So pledged Princess Elizabeth in a prescient and historic address which was broadcast on her 21st birthday in Cape Town, South Africa. Elizabeth was in the city on an official visit with her family and made the statement in the soft dappled light of Government House. Her stirring speech was written by Dermot Morrah, The Times journalist who was reporting on the royal visit. Sir Alan Lascelles, private secretary to George VI, later told Morrah that the speech was so beautifully penned that it made Elizabeth "cry" when she first read it.

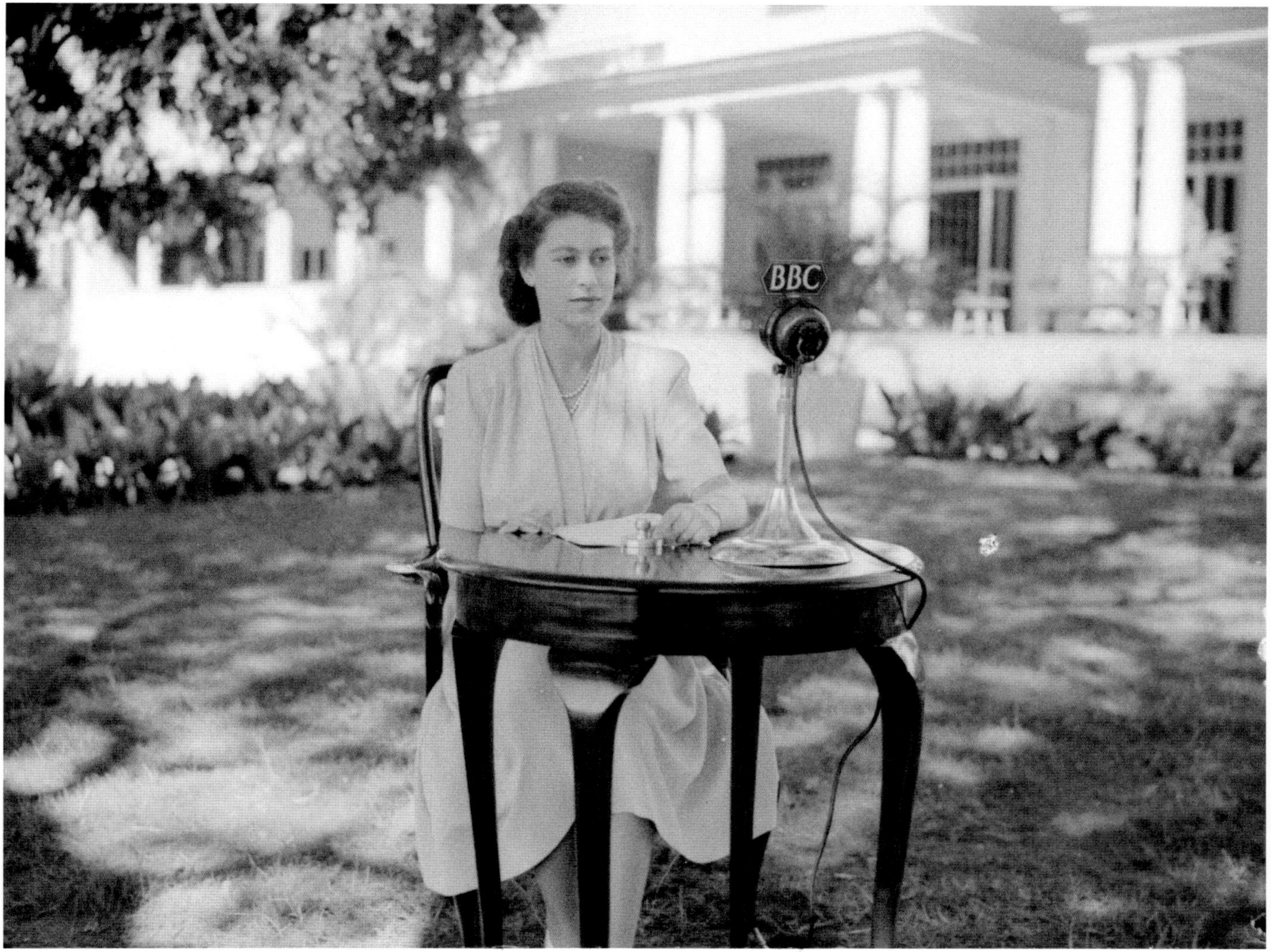
BBC

LAUNCHING THE 'CARONIA'

By Stanley Devon

October 30, 1947

Weeks before their wedding day, Princess Elizabeth and Prince Philip seem perfectly at ease in their royal roles as they launch the 30,000-ton Cunard liner Caronia from the shipyards of John Brown & Company in Clydebank. Dubbed "The Green Goddess", on account of her distinctive livery of four different shades of green, the Caronia was the largest ship to be built after the war. The Princess is being handed a bouquet from a young girl while Philip looks on with pride. According to a local newspaper report, Princess Elizabeth and Lieutenant Philip Mountbatten were greeted "in wild fashion" by a crowd of 30,000 spectators.

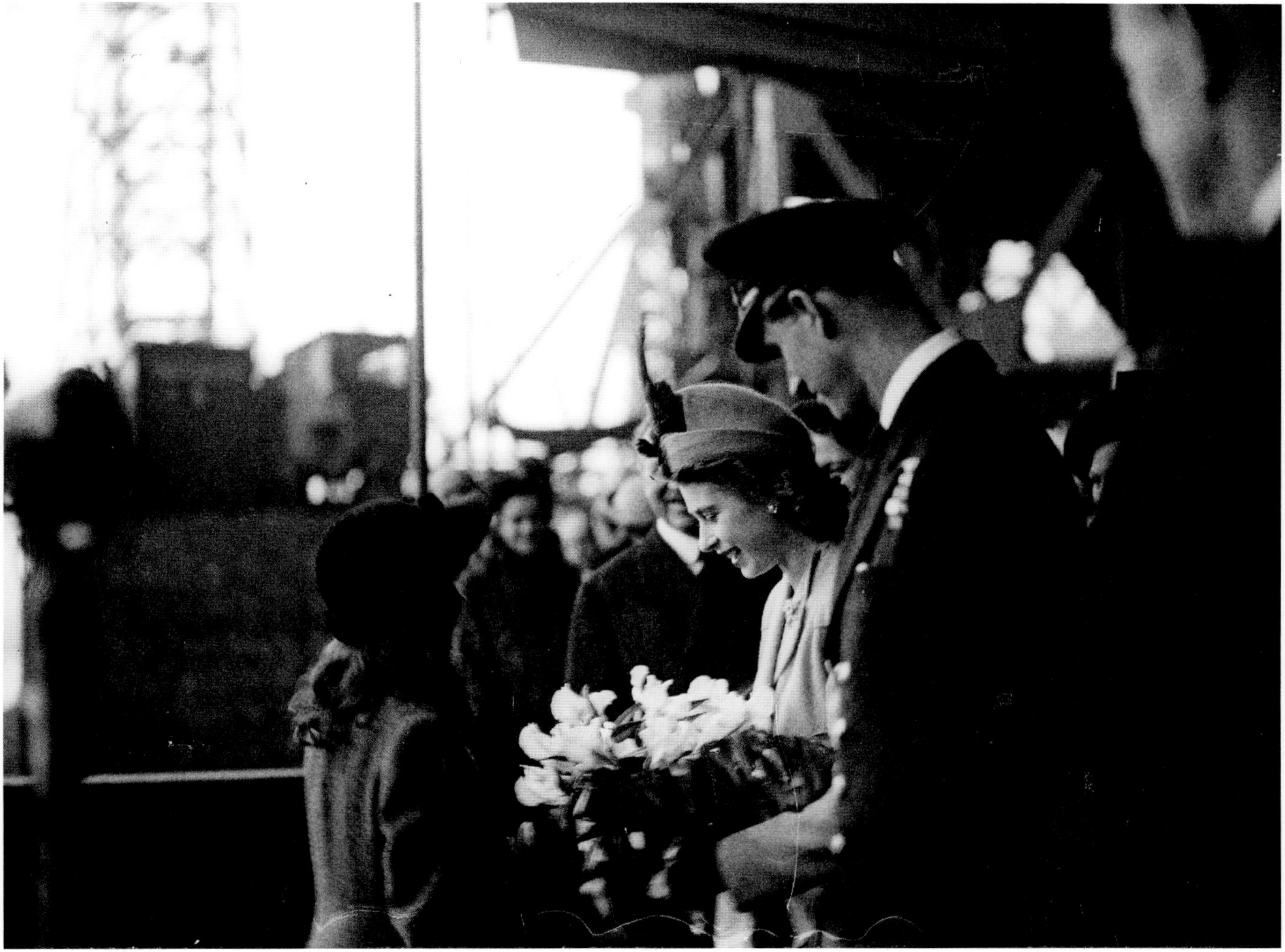

A ROYAL WEDDING

By Jack Barker

November 20, 1947

A historic moment is witnessed inside Westminster Abbey as Princess Elizabeth marries Prince Philip in a service officiated by Geoffrey Fisher, the Archbishop of Canterbury, and Cyril Garbett, the Archbishop of York. Before the wedding Philip, a prince by birth, was created Duke of Edinburgh, Earl of Merioneth and Baron Greenwich of Greenwich in the County of London. King George VI had been keen for the couple to delay the announcement of their engagement at first but finally agreed to go ahead with their wedding at Westminster Abbey four months later. This followed the wedding of Elizabeth's parents there in 1923, and made her the tenth member of the royal family to marry there.

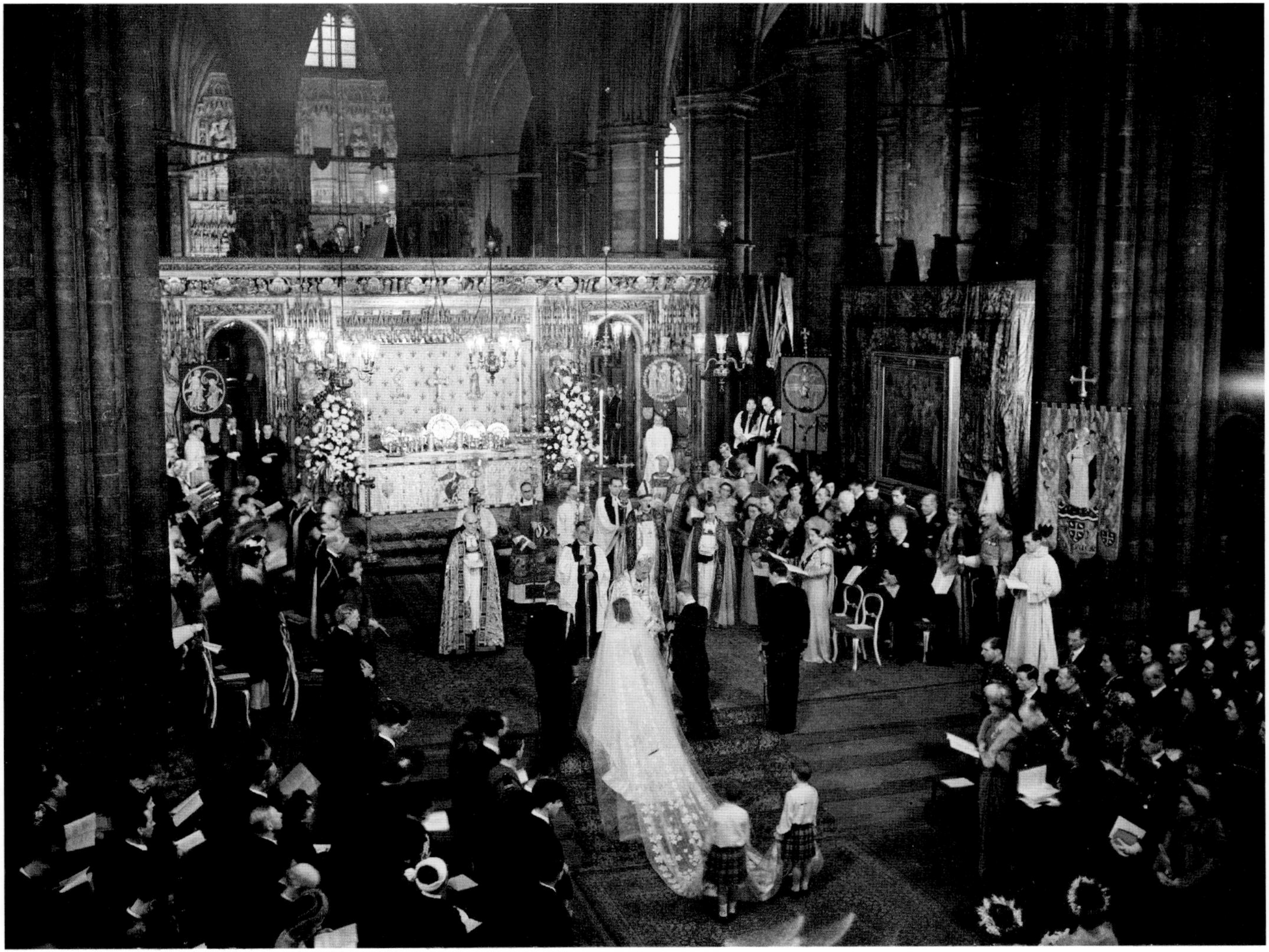

THE GLASS COACH

Photographer unknown

November 20, 1947

Following the marriage ceremony the couple are driven to Buckingham Palace in the Glass Coach, which was built in 1881 and bought for King George V's Coronation in 1911. Queen Mary's fringe tiara was lent to Elizabeth on her wedding day as her "something borrowed", and her dress, embroidered with leaves, was created by the designer Sir Norman Hartnell who later said that he had been inspired by Botticelli's famous painting, *Primavera*, about the coming of spring.

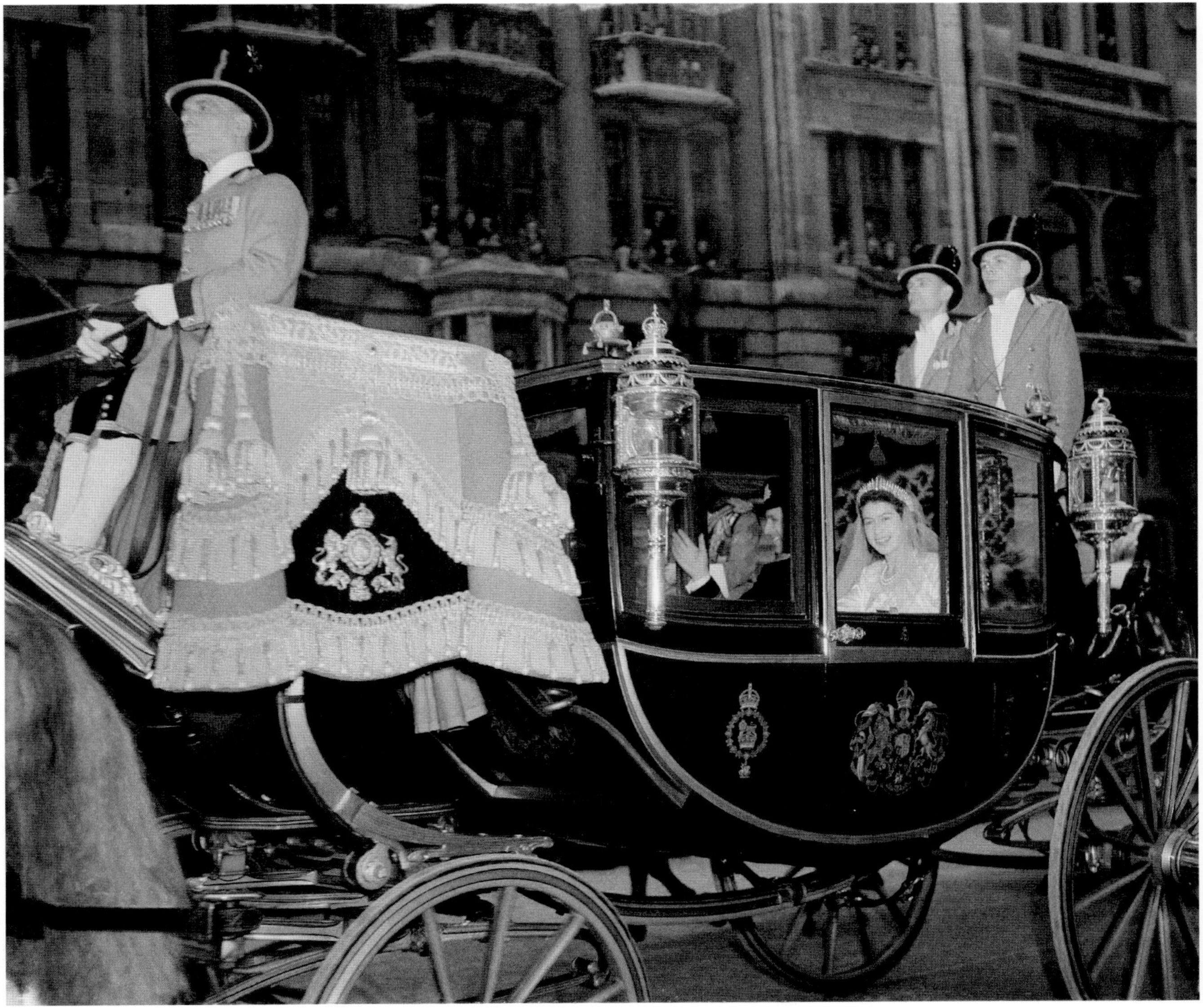

A YOUNG COUPLE IN LOVE

By William Horton

November 24, 1947

With an easy intimacy that is hard to ignore, Prince Philip, now the Duke of Edinburgh, leans close to his wife as they pore over photographic proofs four days after their wedding. The image shows Elizabeth sitting on a bench at Broadlands in Hampshire where the couple spent their honeymoon. William Horton, a photographer with The Times who had accompanied the Princess and her family on their royal tour of South Africa earlier in the year, had delivered the proofs of the wedding pictures and was able to capture their response. Extending a little finger, the newlywed Princess indicates one image that has caught her eye.

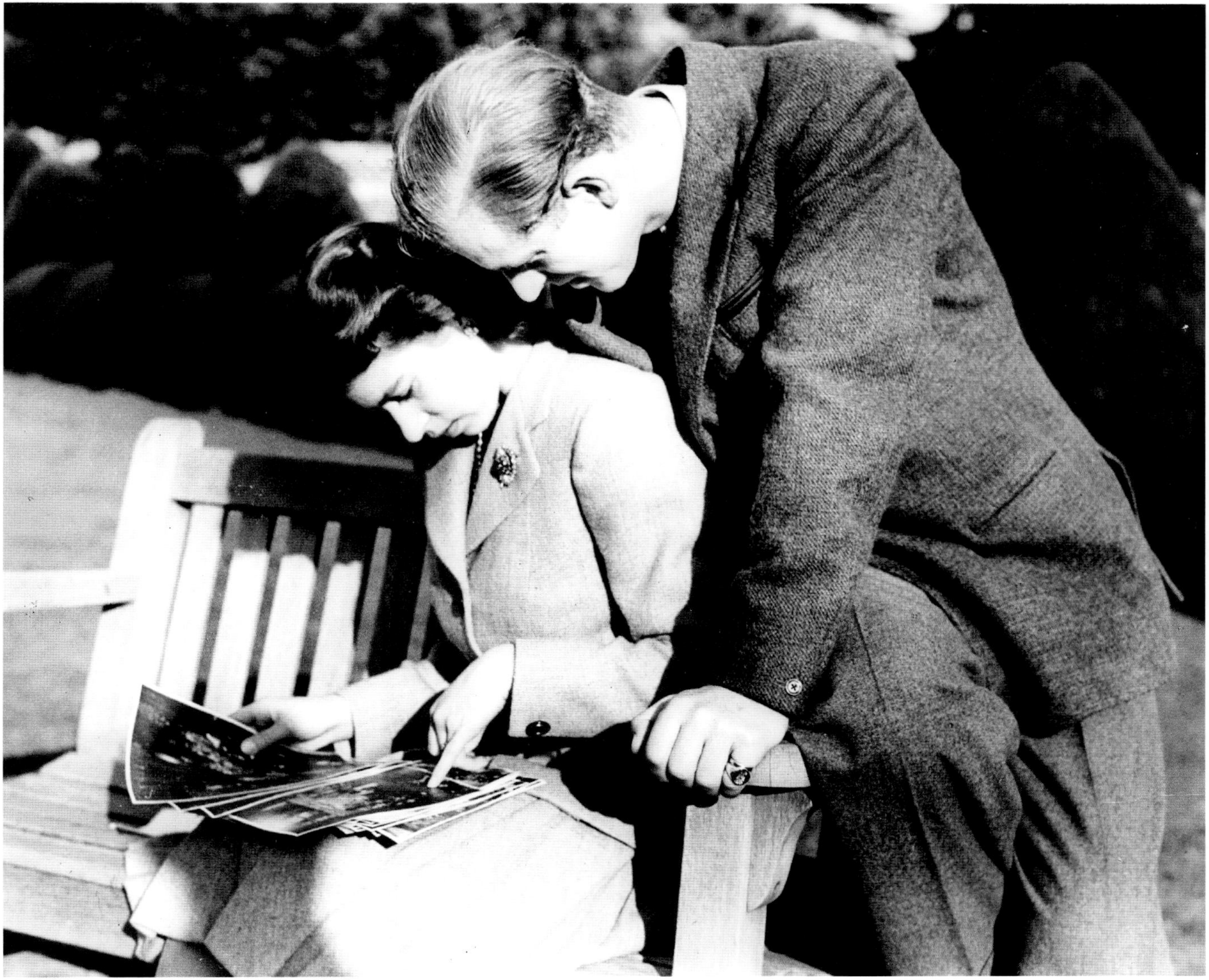

PRINCESS ANNE'S CHRISTENING

By Stanley Devon

October 21, 1950

When his younger sister is christened, a young Prince Charles successfully attempts to steal the limelight from his new sibling. To the delight of his grandmother the Queen, and his great-grandmother Queen Mary, Charles parades around with his hands on his hips. But Charles only has eyes for his father, Prince Philip, who is seen beaming proudly in the background. Meanwhile, Princess Elizabeth glances over at the scene as the infant Princess Anne, then two months old, is oblivious to all the fuss.

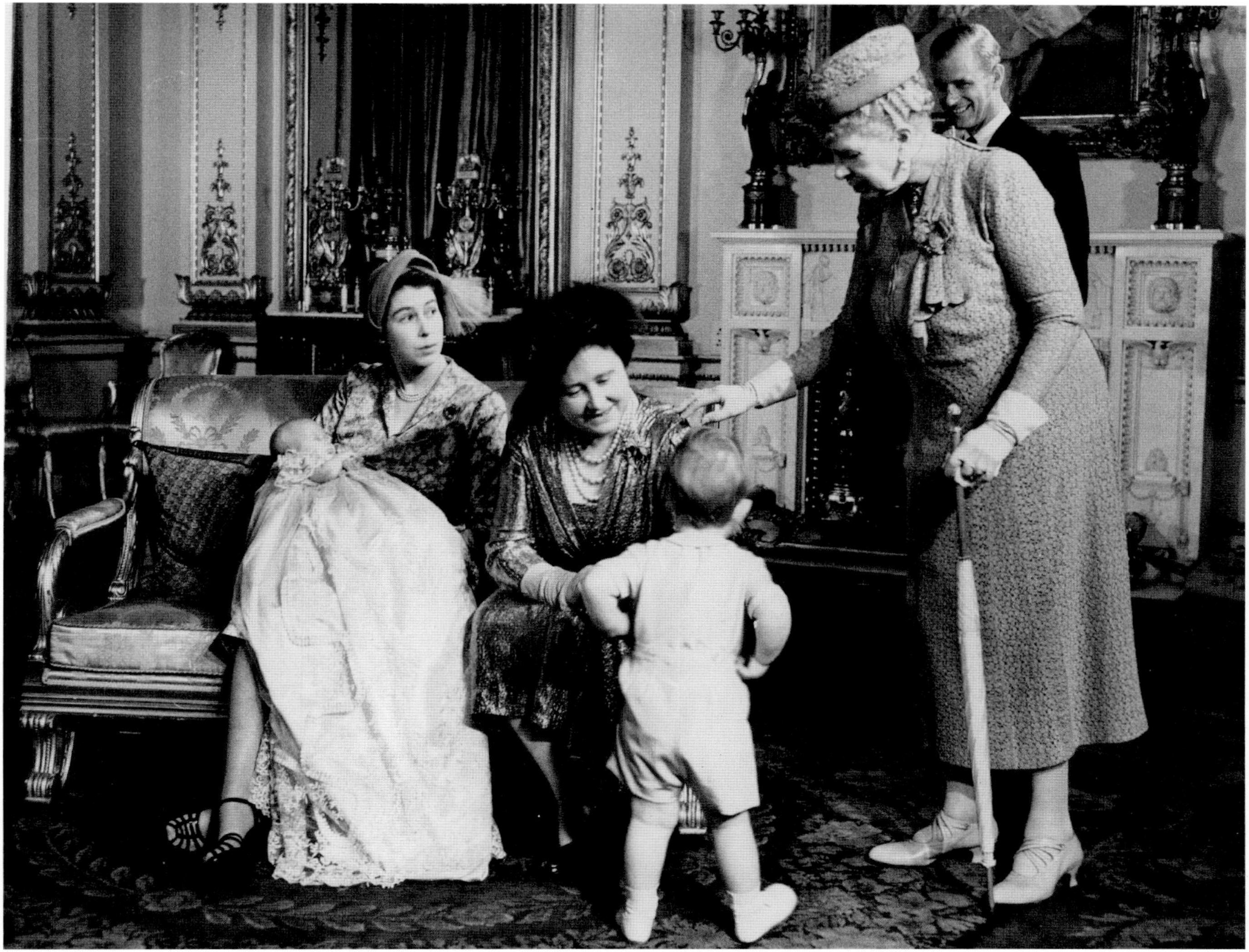

TROOPING THE COLOUR

Photographer unknown

June 7, 1951

A key point of the royal calendar, Trooping the Colour marks the monarch's official birthday with all the pomp and pageantry that a sovereign could and should expect. Princess Elizabeth is seen here on horseback taking part in the annual parade, riding side-saddle down the Mall from Buckingham Palace to Horse Guards Parade. In 1951, King George VI was unwell and unable to attend, leaving Elizabeth to take the salute in his place. By this point his symptoms had been identified as Buerger's disease and he was later diagnosed with lung cancer.

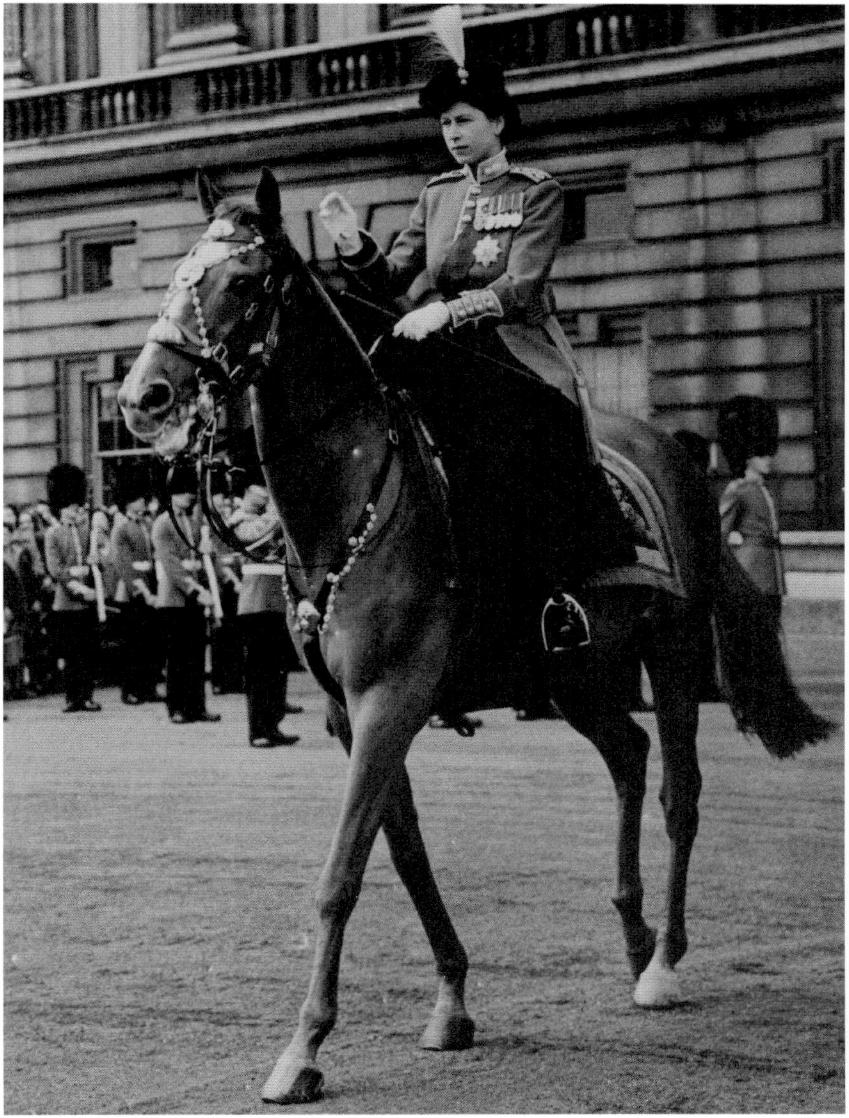

DANCING SOON-TO-BE-QUEEN

By Stanley Devon

October 18, 1951

During a tour of Canada, Princess Elizabeth is seen taking part in a square dance at Rideau Hall, Government House, in Ottawa. During her visit to the Commonwealth realm with Prince Philip, Elizabeth was keen to get into the swing of local customs. During the tour Elizabeth made a speech, in which she switched easily between English and French, saying that it had been her "cherished dream" to visit Canada, a place where she felt "very much at home".

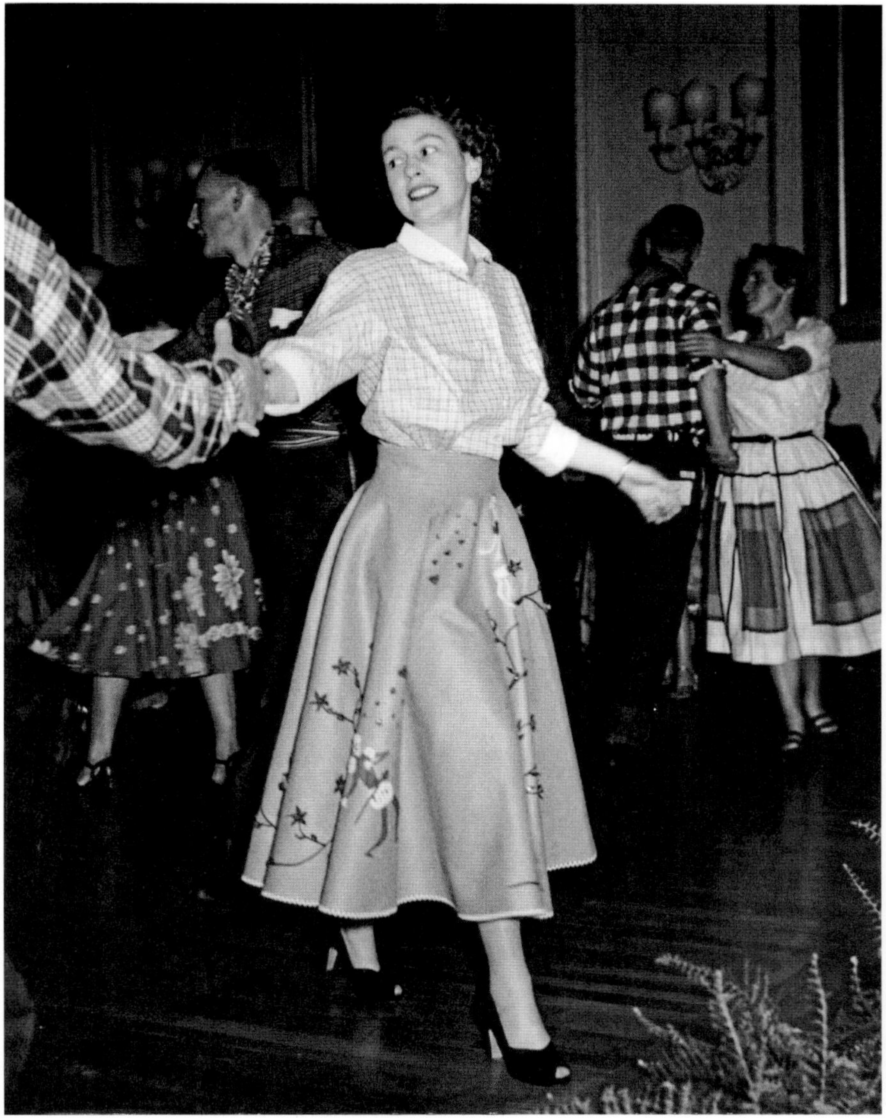

A ROYAL TRAIN WITH A DIFFERENCE

By Stanley Devon

October-November, 1951

It was her radiance and youth that first endeared her to the people of the Commonwealth, bolstered by her willingness to get involved in all manner of tasks. Having stepped aboard a train to Edmonton, Alberta, Princess Elizabeth certainly looks the part as she is shown how the steam engine works. With the help of engineer Mr A McPhail she even had a go at driving the train during her royal tour of Canada.

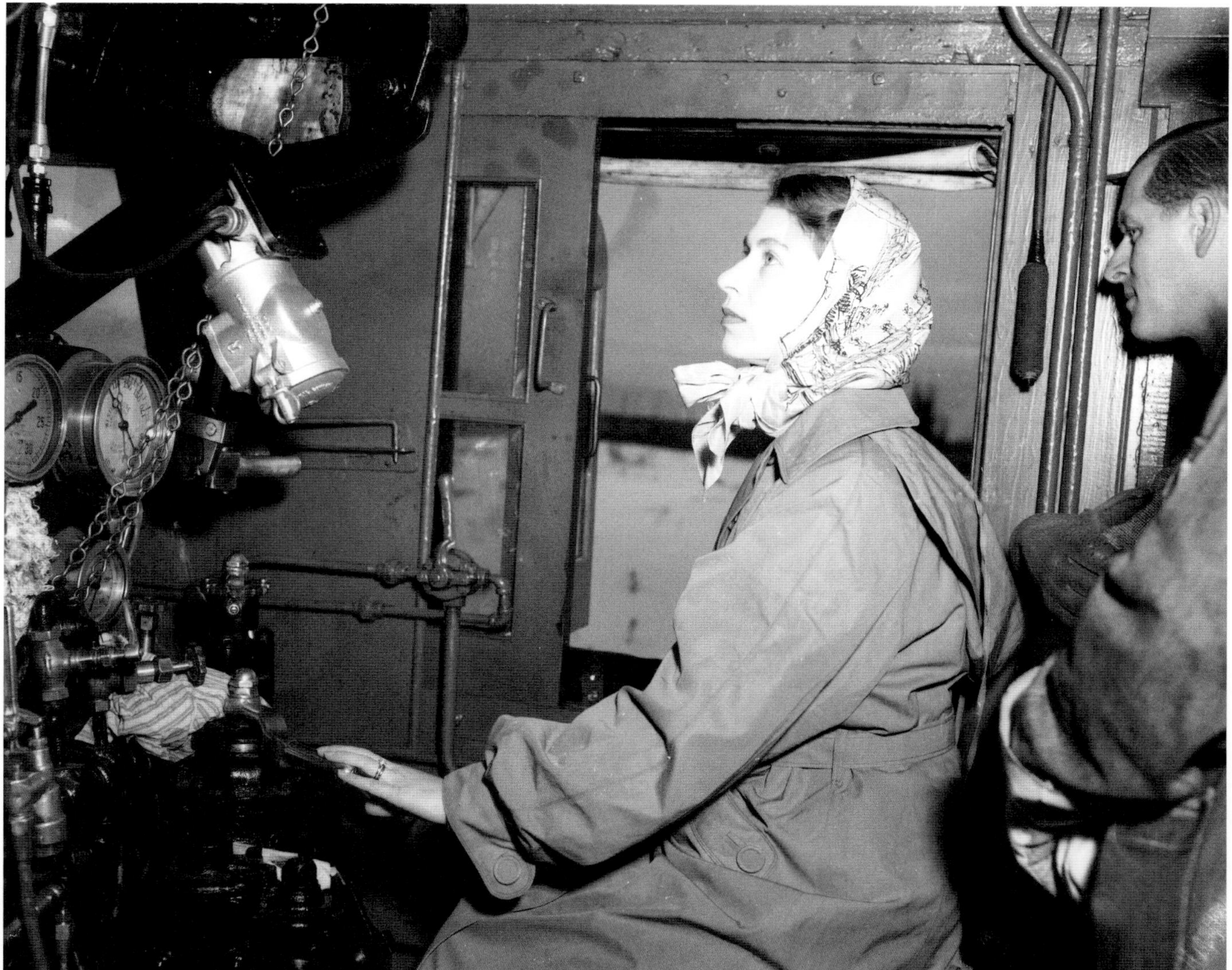

A FAMILY OF FOUR

By Stanley Devon

1951

From the comfort of her mother's arms, a young Princess Anne places a pudgy little finger firmly on her father's lips as he holds her brother Prince Charles. Princess Elizabeth and the Duke of Edinburgh were happy to be pictured with their young family in a more informal setting than seen in royal portraits of the past, here in the grounds of Clarence House, London.

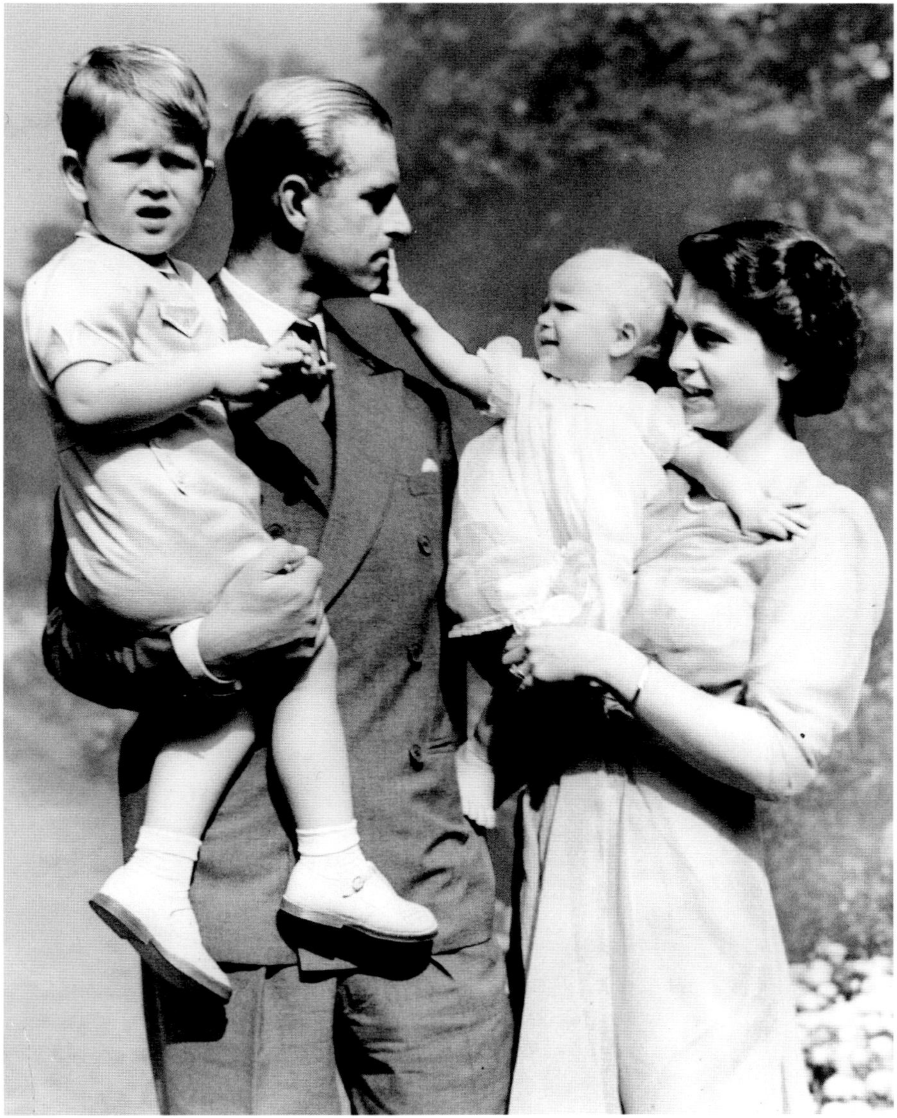

TREETOPS

By Stanley Devon

February, 1952

Unaware of the momentous events that are about to unfold, Princess Elizabeth and Prince Philip are seen here on a visit to a game-viewing lodge at the Treetops estate, around 100 miles north of Nairobi, during an official tour of Kenya. It was an unforgettable moment for all concerned when Elizabeth, aged 25, went up a treehouse a Princess, and came down a Queen after the news came that the King had died in his sleep on February 6. The couple had been waved off by the King and, while he was known to have been unwell, the news was unexpected.

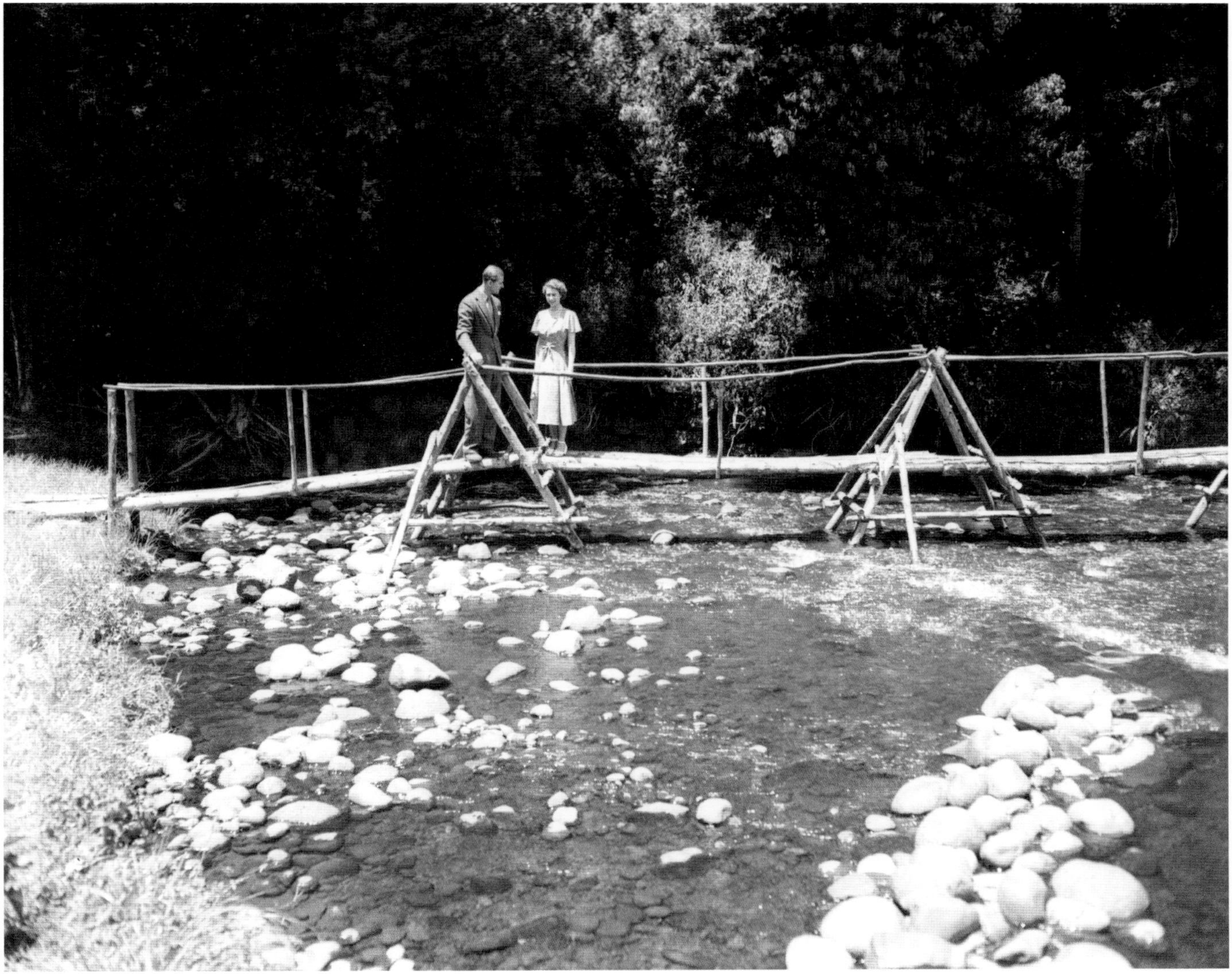

A QUEEN SETS FOOT ON BRITISH SOIL

By Geoffrey White

February 7, 1952

After sending letters of regret to her hosts and cancelling plans to continue on to Australia and New Zealand, Queen Elizabeth II returns to the UK with the Duke of Edinburgh. Touching down at London Airport dressed in black, the new Queen steps onto British soil for the first time since acceding the throne. The scene is sombre; a Queen mourning her beloved father and embracing a new role as sovereign. Among the dignitaries who have arrived to greet the Queen on her return from Kenya is Prime Minister Winston Churchill, who has removed his hat as the Queen descends the steps towards him.

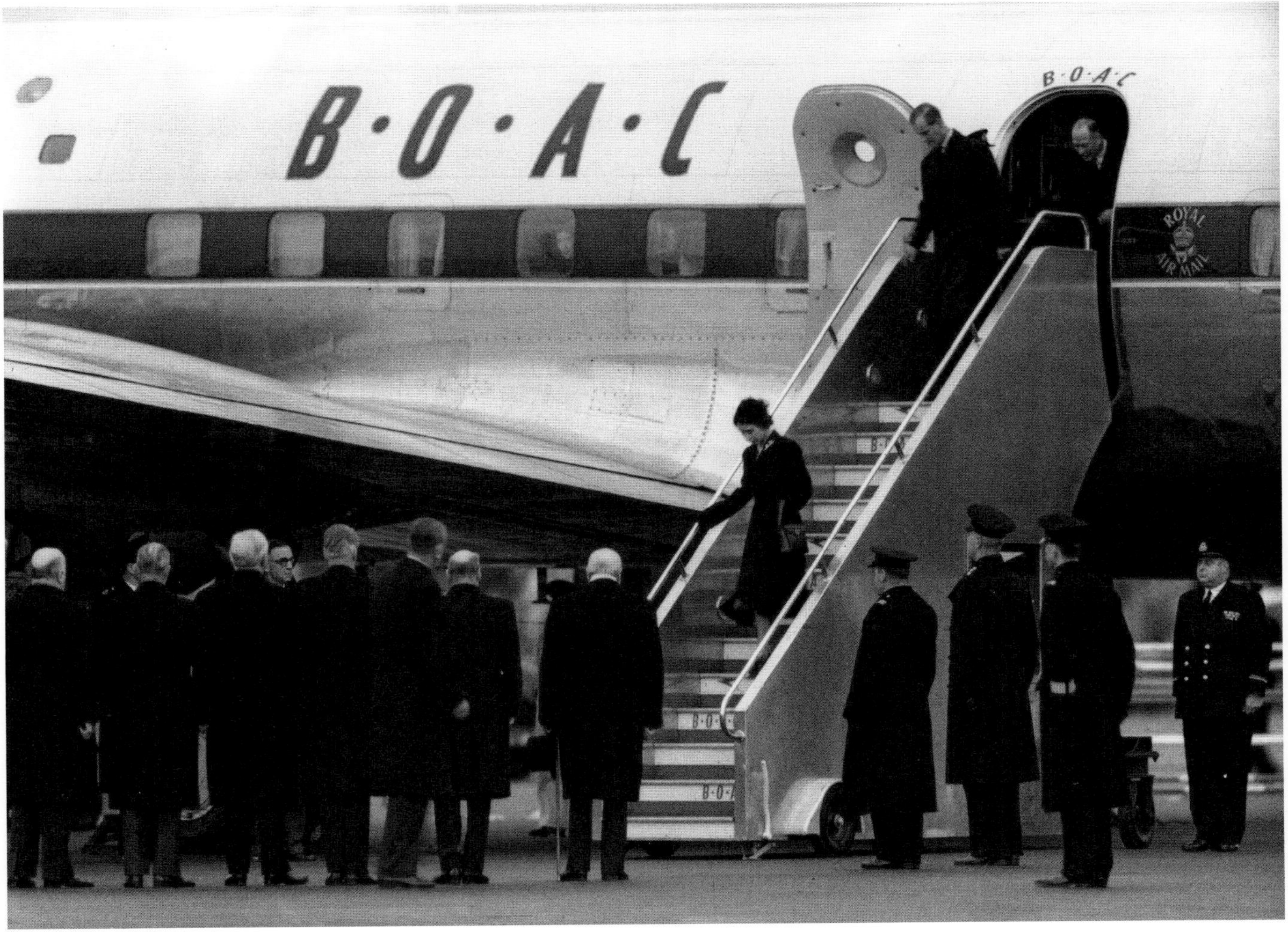

B·O·A·C
B·O·A·C
ROYAL AIR MAIL

THE FUNERAL OF KING GEORGE VI

By Sidney Beadell

February 11, 1952

Wearing a black mourning veil over her face, Queen Elizabeth II stares from the window of the car as she takes part in the funeral procession of her father, King George VI. Amid the huge personal upheaval, the new Queen, sitting behind her sister, Princess Margaret, travels behind the gun carriage bearing their father's coffin. The funeral procession went from Sandringham Church to Wolferton station. The King's body was later taken to lie in state at Westminster Hall.

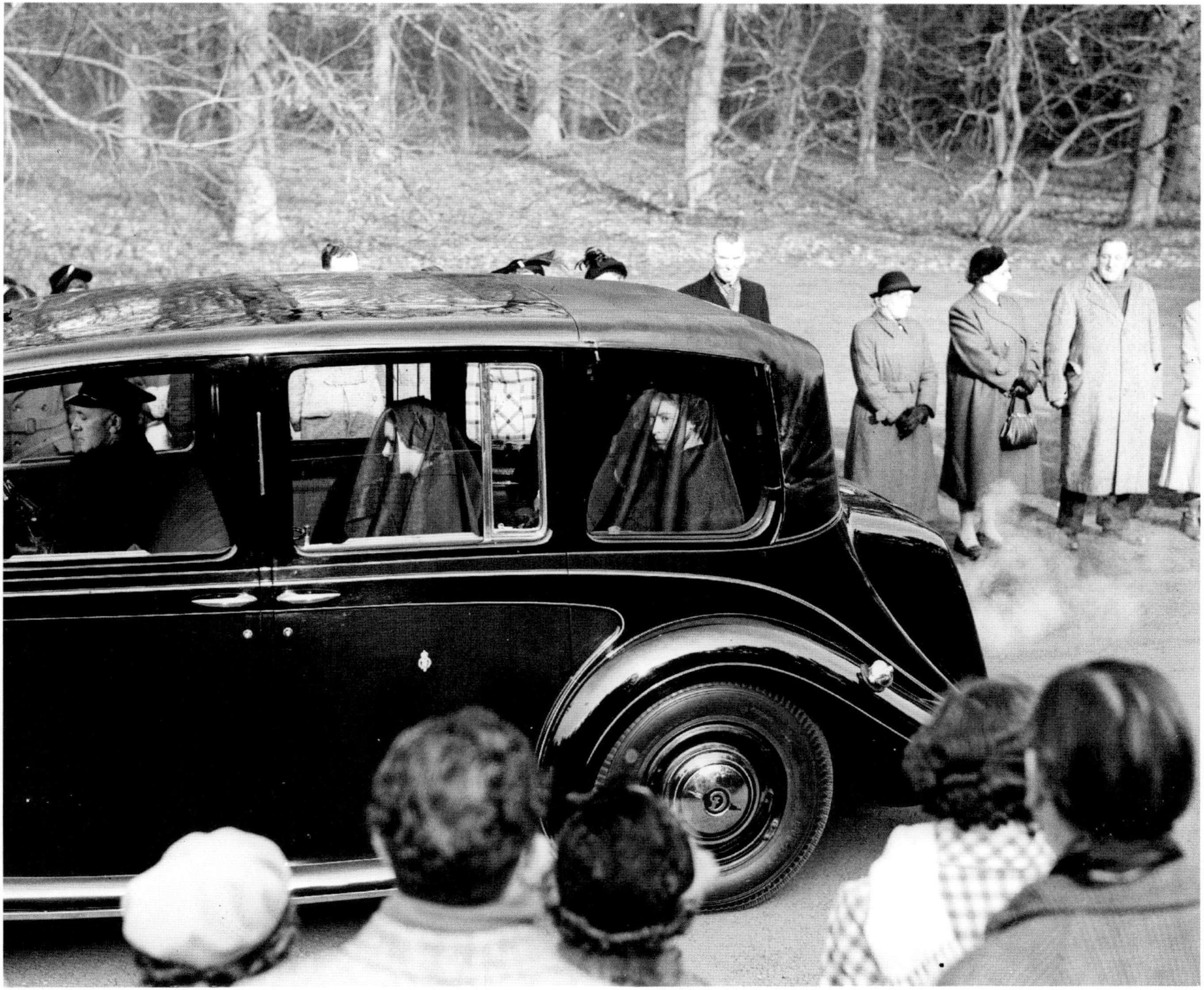

A NEW HEAD OF THE COMMONWEALTH

By William Horton

December 15, 1952

With a new vision for the family of countries, the Queen led the Commonwealth into the modern era. In doing so, she met with the Commonwealth prime ministers, including Winston Churchill, at the Commonwealth Prime Ministers' Economic Conference in December 1952, ahead of her Coronation in 1953. In her Christmas message that followed the Coronation she said: "The Commonwealth bears no resemblance to the Empires of the past. It is an entirely new conception, built on the highest qualities of the spirit of man: friendship, loyalty and the desire for freedom and peace. To that new conception of an equal partnership of nations and races I shall give myself, heart and soul, every day of my life."

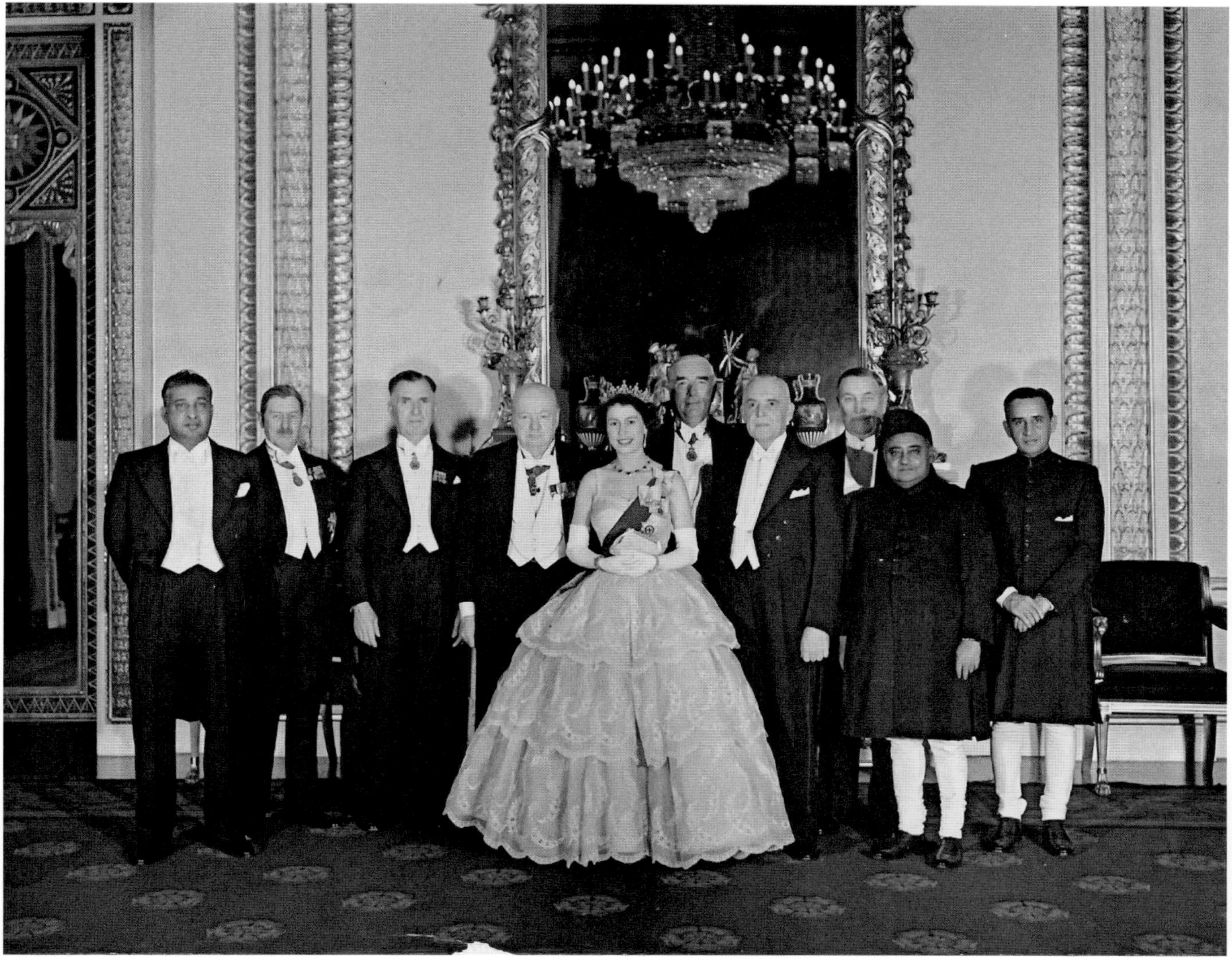

THE CORONATION VIEW FROM THE MALL

By Alfred Harris

June 2, 1953

Long to reign over us: the newly crowned Queen Elizabeth II appears on the balcony of Buckingham Palace alongside six maids of honour and members of the royal family after her Coronation at Westminster Abbey. During the service she swore an oath, saying, "The things which I have here before promised, I will perform and keep. So help me God." Extra seating was erected in the abbey to accommodate 8,251 guests for the service. It was the first coronation to be filmed, with families crowding round television sets all around the world to witness the pomp and pageantry of the historic occasion.

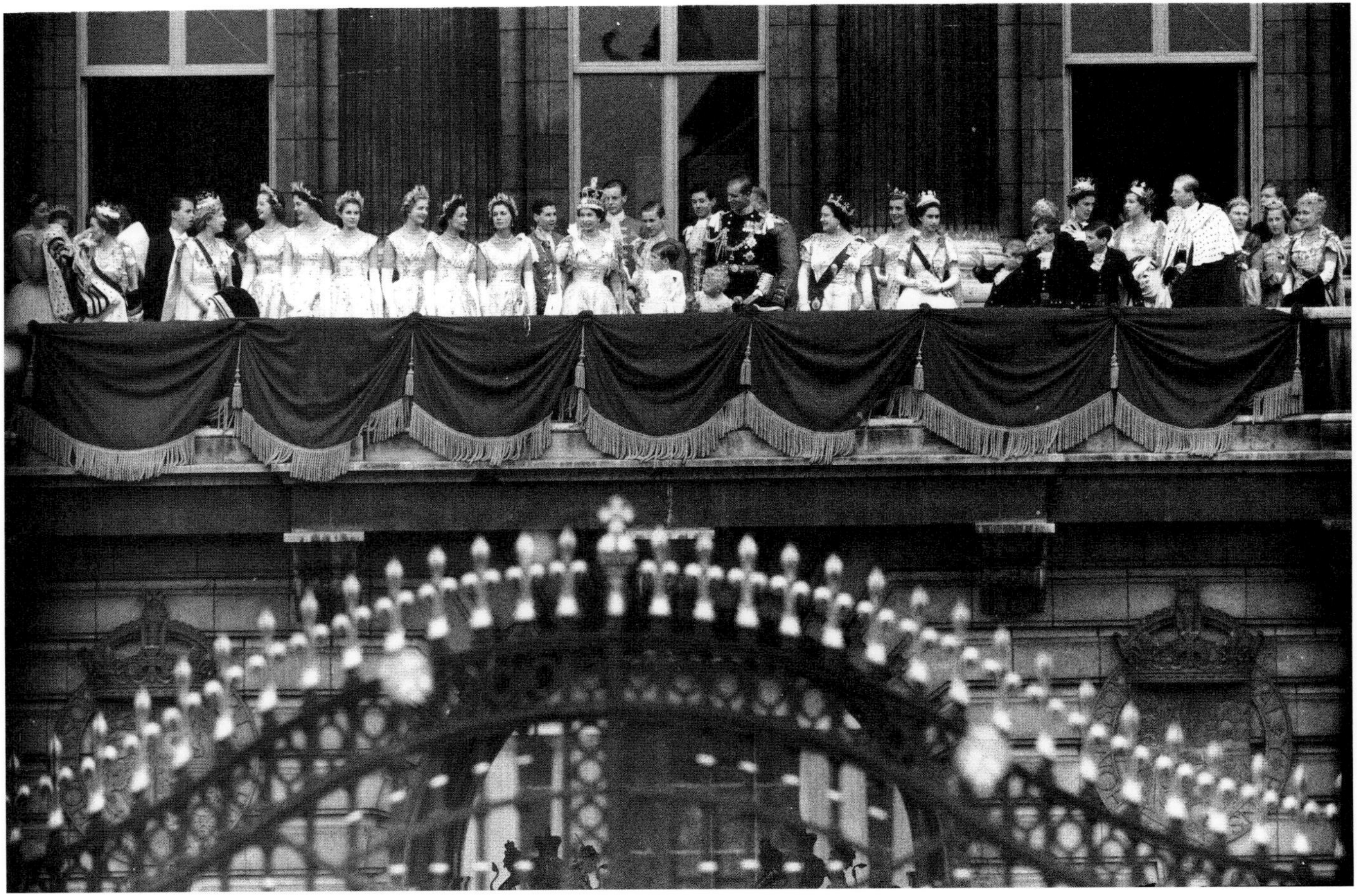

A KEEN EYE FOR A PICTURE

By Jack Barker

December 12, 1953

Exuding grace and style, the young Queen and her dashing husband Prince Philip set off on a six-month round-the-world tour, leaving behind their two young children in the name of duty. Here, the Queen is seen filming the arrival of HMNZS Black Prince as she takes over escort duty from HMS Sheffield. It was a rare opportunity to be on the other side of the camera for a change.

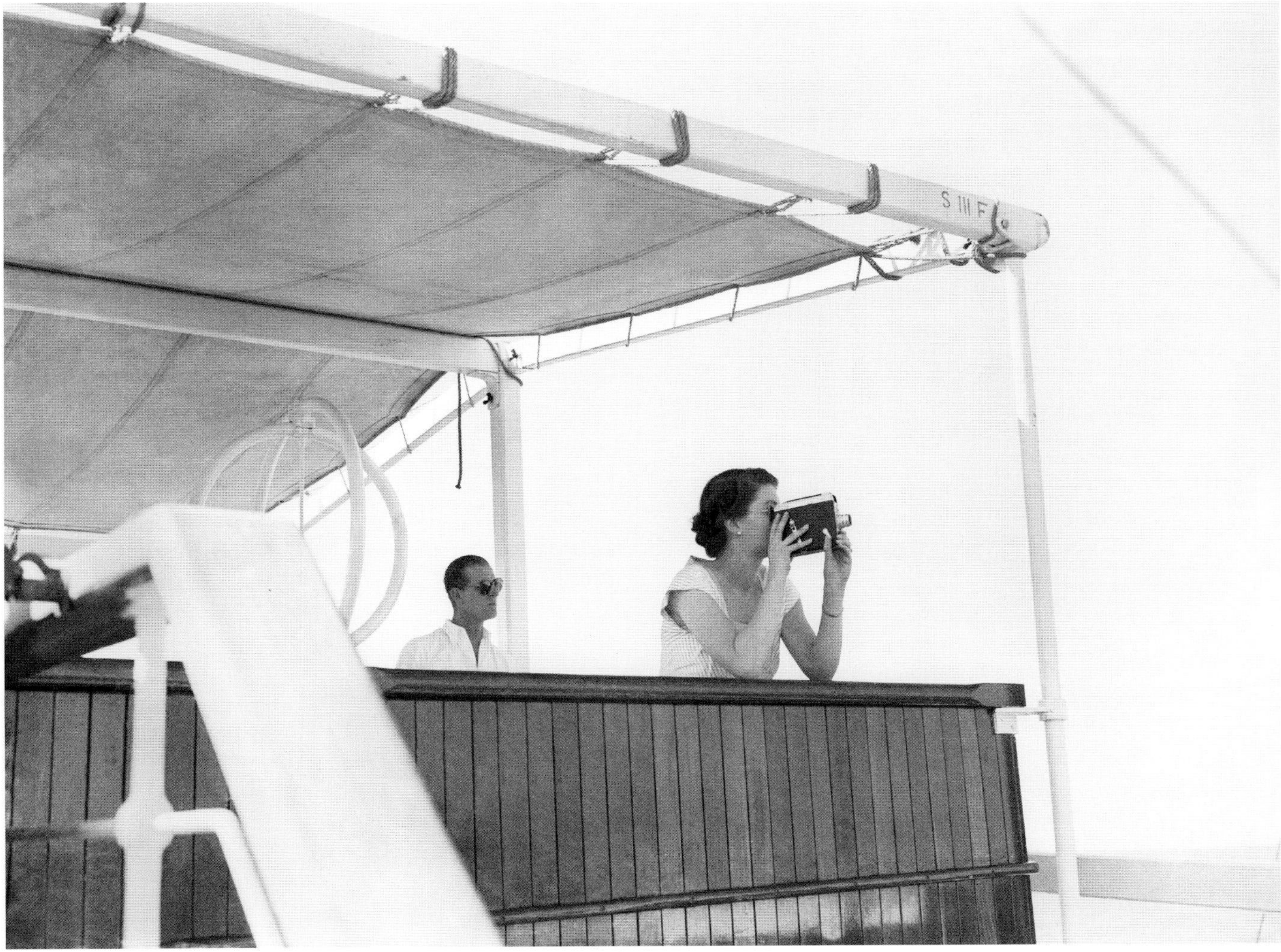
S III F

A SPECIAL TONGA WELCOME

Photographer unknown

December 20, 1953

When Queen Salote of Tonga smiled and waved in the pouring rain after refusing to put the hood up on her carriage during Elizabeth II's Coronation procession, she won the affection of the British public. Now, it was time for Queen Elizabeth to visit Tonga and delight the people there. Six months after the Coronation at Westminster Abbey, the Queen and Prince Philip join Queen Salote where they are the guests of honour at a magnificent feast. A roasted pig has been placed in front of every guest and the Duke is seen chatting amiably with Queen Salote.

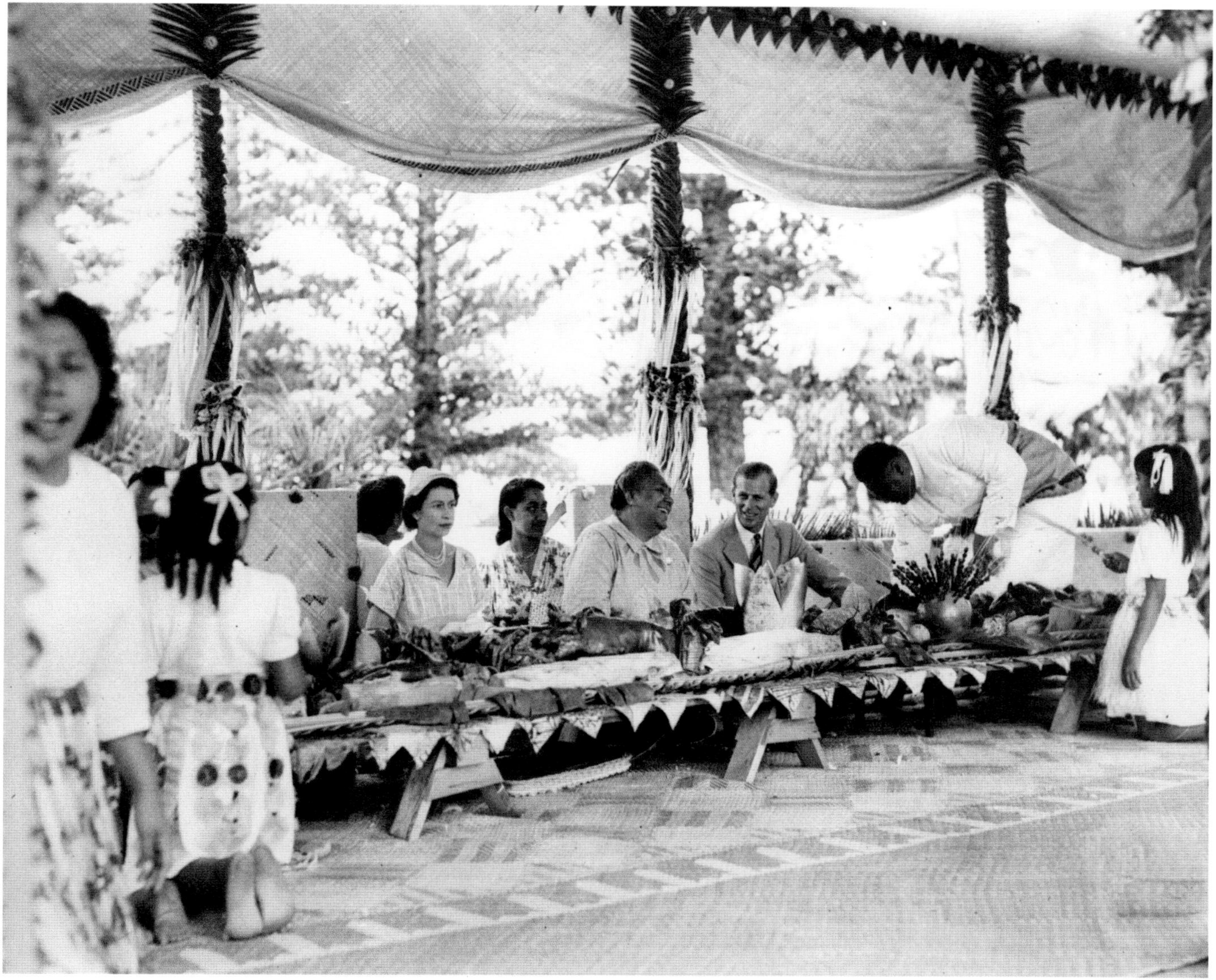

ARANUI CAVE

By Jack Barker

December 31, 1953

Looking up at the stalactites, the Queen takes in the wonder of Aranui Cave in Waikato, New Zealand, during the Royal Commonwealth Tour of 1953-54. The Queen and Prince Philip marked New Year's Eve with a visit to the spectacular limestone caves, steeped in Maori myth and legend, which was explained by chief tour guide George Sear, seen on the Duke's left. The Queen and the Duke welcomed the New Year with a meal at the Waitomo Hotel which included whitebait fritters, iced asparagus, and a choice of roast lamb, pork, beef or duckling. Elizabeth II's visit to New Zealand marked the first time that a reigning monarch had set foot in the country.

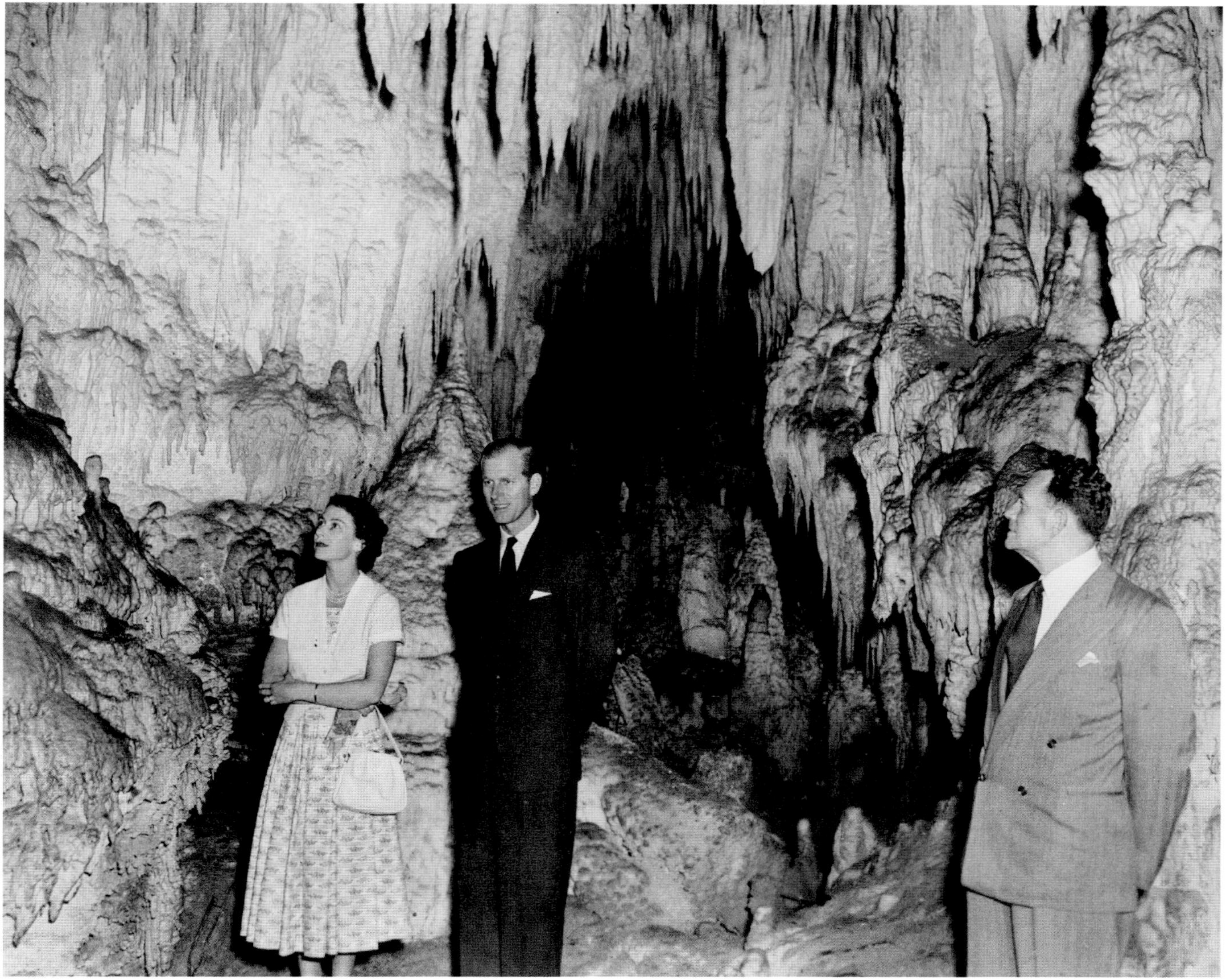

CHURCH FETE

Photographer unknown

August 20, 1955

Standing by a trestle table laden with jam and local produce, three generations of royal women attend a church fete at Abergeldie Castle, near Balmoral. On the left, the Queen Mother, Queen Elizabeth and a young Princess Anne have their attention diverted across the marquee as volunteers busy themselves at the event to raise funds for Crathie Kirk, the royal family's local church in Scotland. Princess Margaret, on the right, waits to engage her mother in conversation.

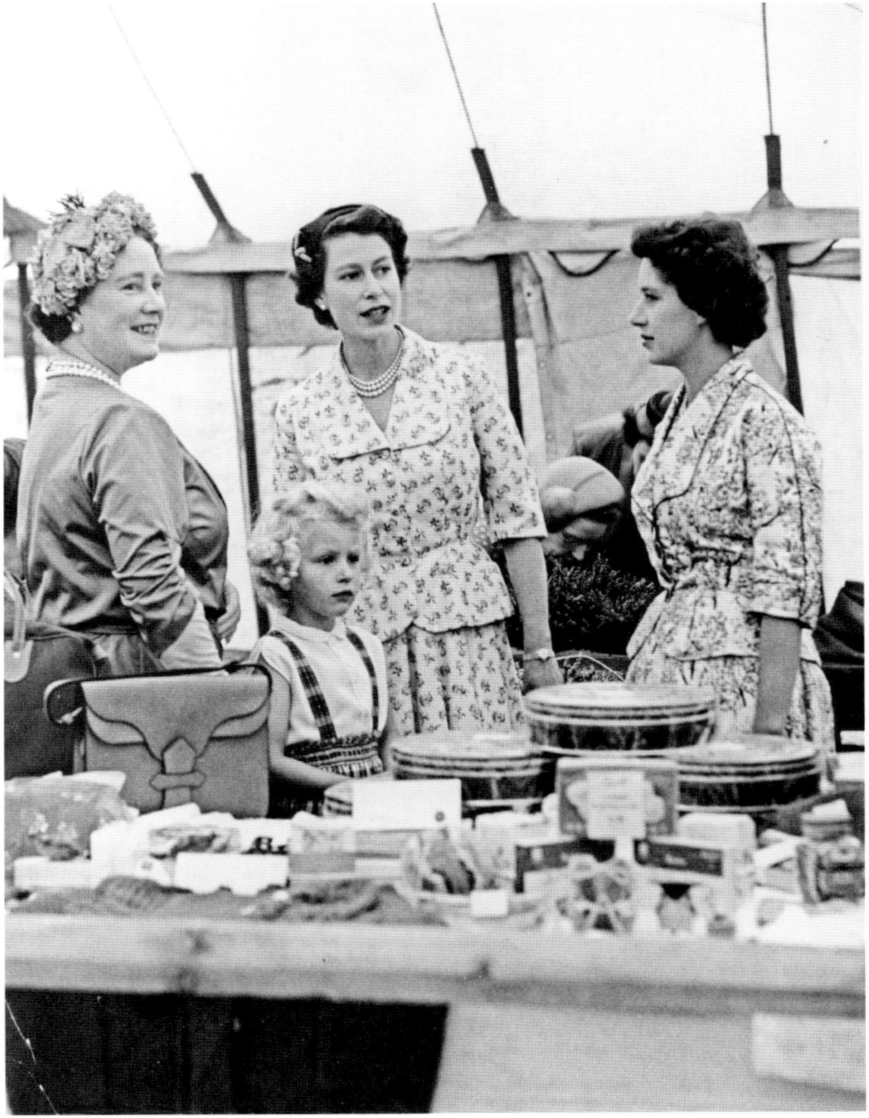

A VISIT TO A LEPER COLONY

By Horace Tonge

February 2, 1956

When most people think of the royal family pushing boundaries, the late Princess Diana is brought to mind. Long before Diana's birth, however, a young Queen Elizabeth did much to change perceptions and eradicate taboos. Here, she tours a leper colony in Nigeria. Upon her return, the Queen's visit was commended in the Houses of Parliament by Prime Minister Anthony Eden, who said that Her Majesty "did that act of visiting the leper settlement, showing thereby her understanding sympathy with the unhappy people who suffer from that disease."

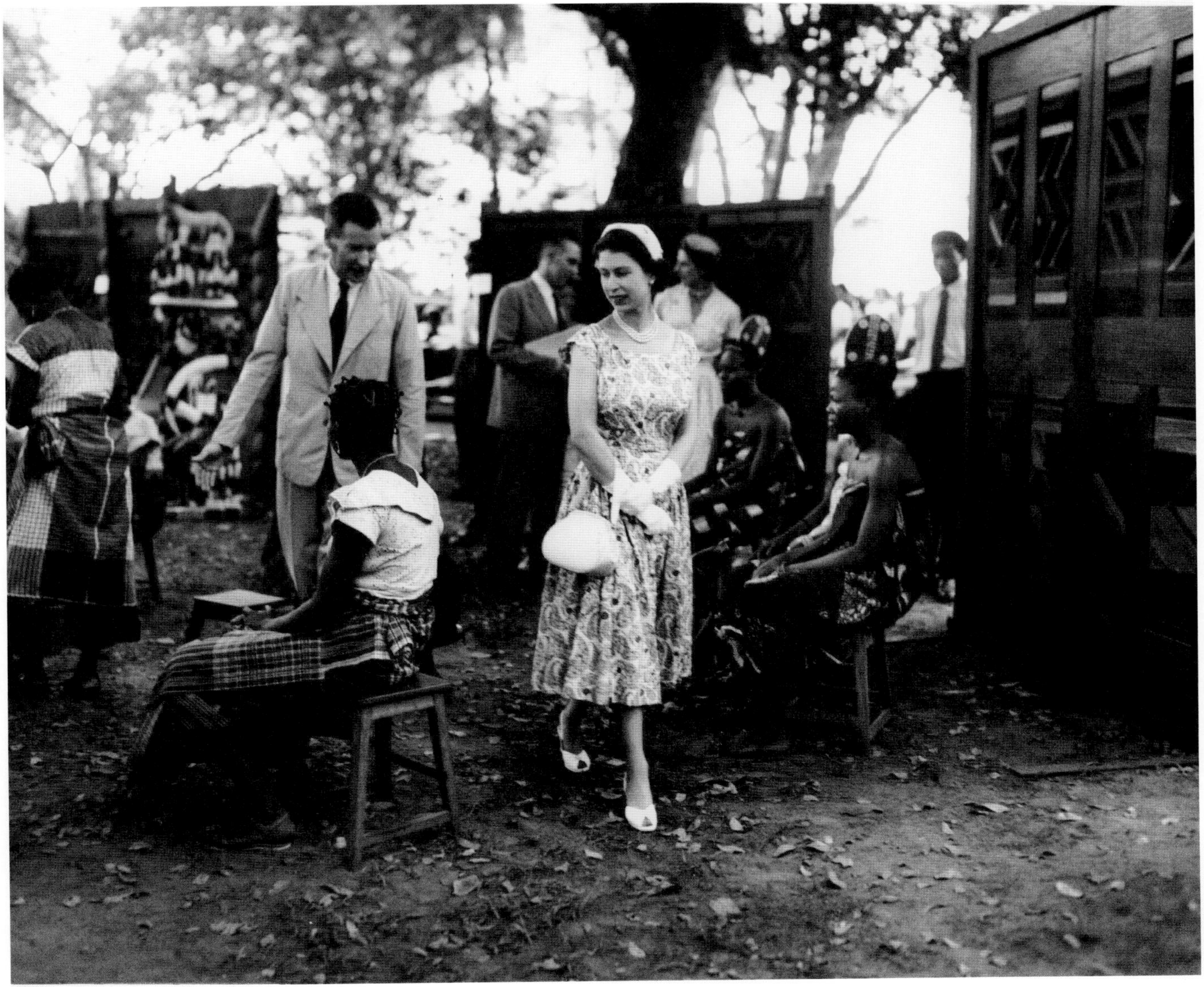

POLO, THE SPORT OF KINGS

By Martin Beddall

June 23, 1956

Chewing thoughtfully on a fingernail, a young Prince Charles looks on as he watches his father, Prince Philip, compete in a polo match at Windsor. From an early age, Charles was captivated by the game, known as the sport of Kings, and later proved to be an adept player. With hands clasped, the Queen looks towards the action. Meanwhile, Princess Anne seems determined to gain her mother's attention.
A love of horses was something the Queen shared with her husband, although she preferred riding in the countryside and watching the races, while he preferred polo and carriage riding.

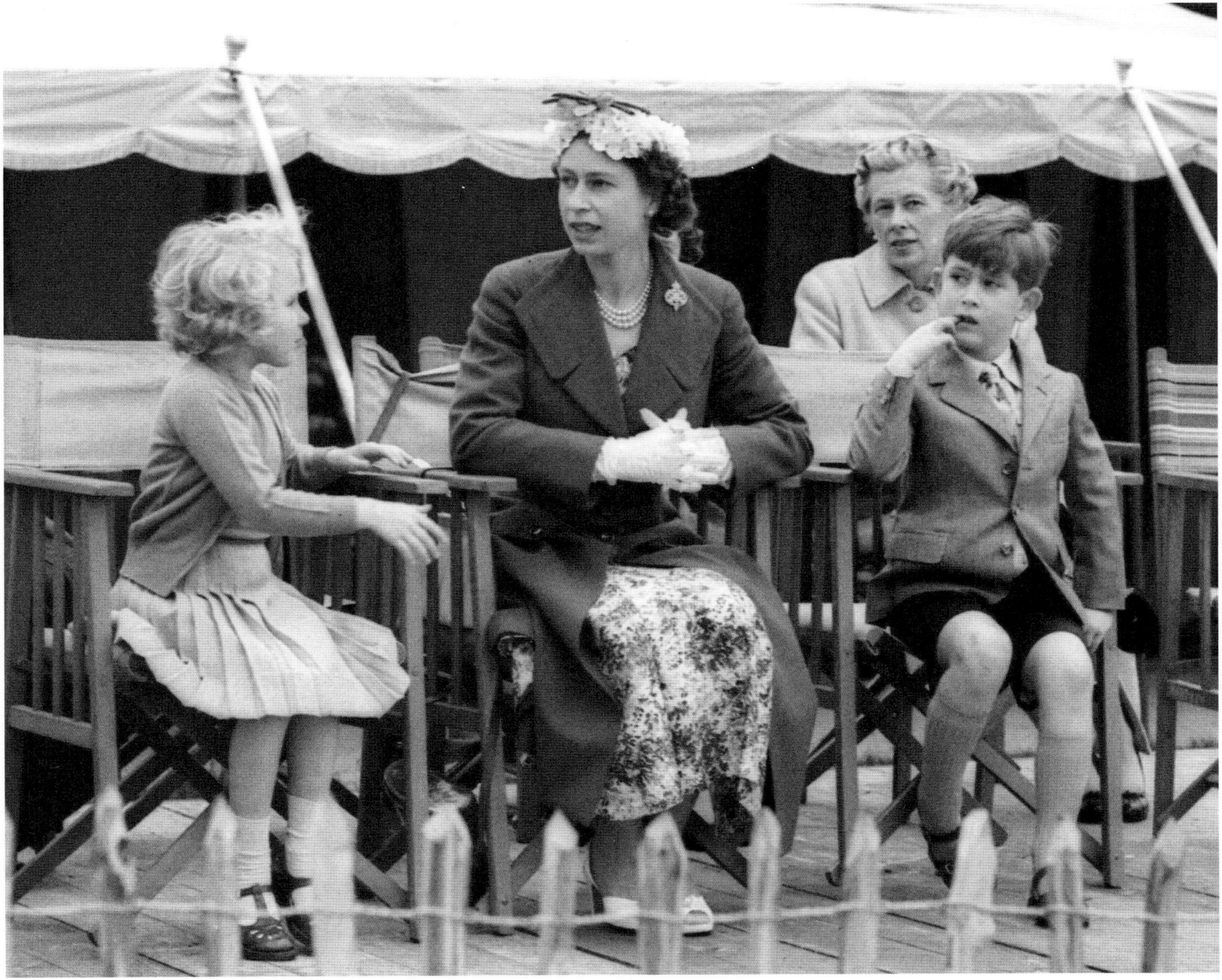

A ROYAL DOG WALK

Photographer unknown

November 19, 1956

Enjoying a stroll with their dogs, the Queen and the Queen Mother take a tour of the Sandringham estate while their pet corgis follow obediently behind. Her Majesty's love of corgis began as a child. When her parents, King George VI and Queen Elizabeth, acquired the family's first corgi in 1933, a dog named Dookie, Elizabeth was smitten. It led to a lifelong passion for the breed which became synonymous with her reign.

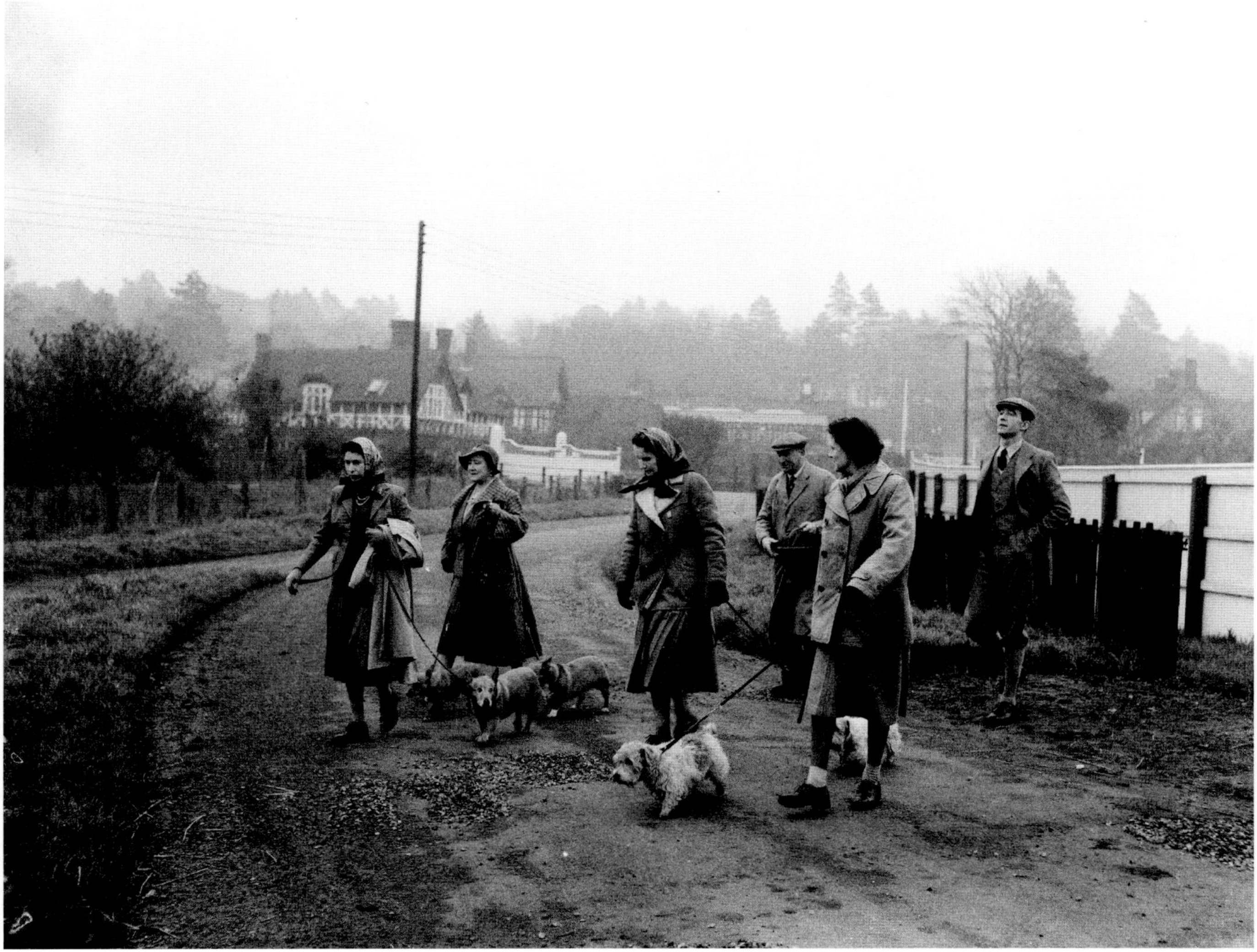

PRESENTING A TROPHY

By Stanley Devon

June 23, 1957

Fancy seeing you here! The Queen and Prince Philip share a smile as the Queen presents her husband with the gleaming winner's trophy cup at a polo match in Windsor. Often held to raise money for charity, polo matches have been a tradition of the royal family for years and is one continued by King Charles III and his son, Prince William.

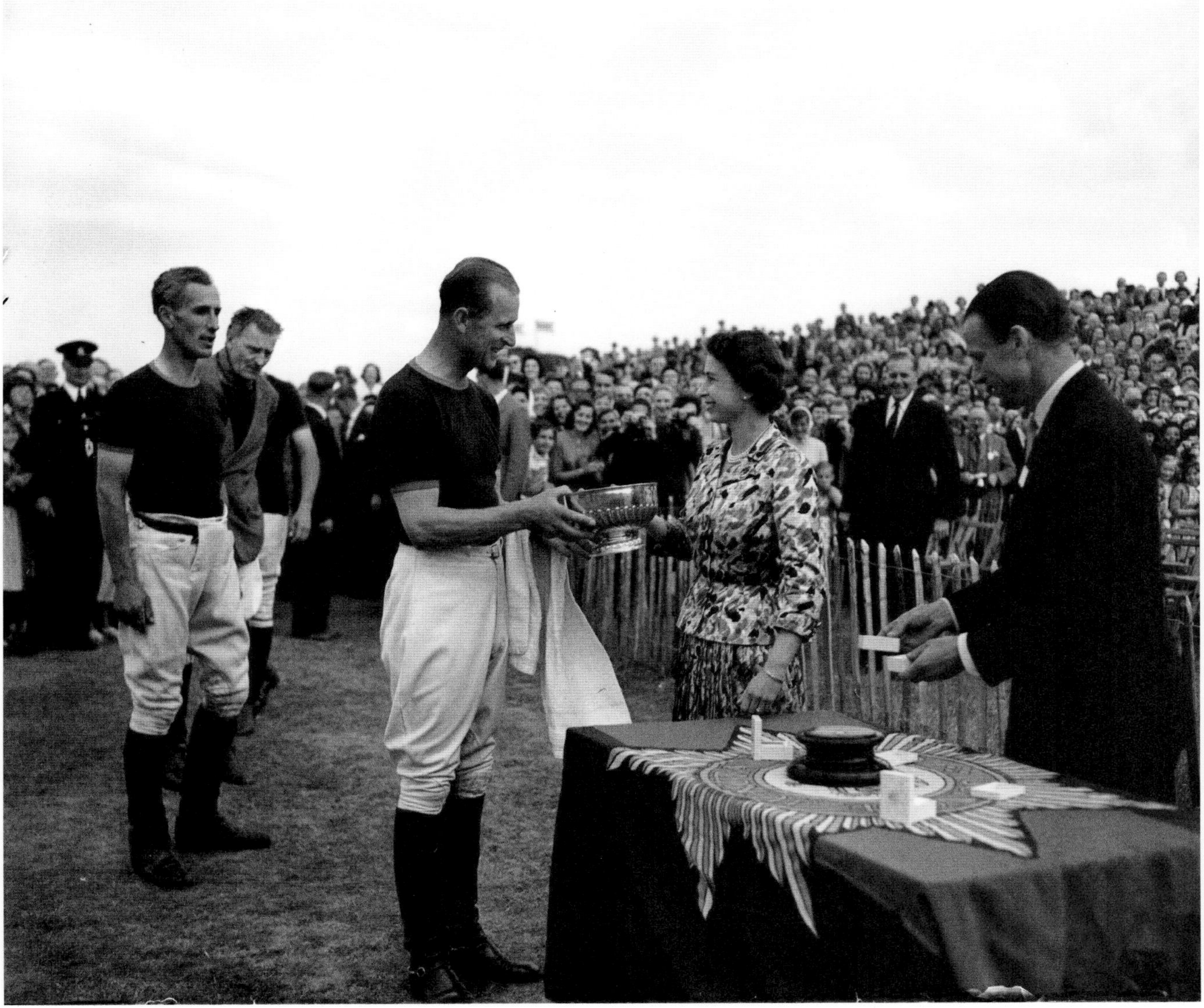

STROLL WITH MOTHER

By Jack Easton

April 19, 1958

There are no greater pictures of Elizabeth II than those in which she is celebrating her love of animals and this is no exception. With a headscarf tied elegantly beneath her chin, Her Majesty cradles her pet dachshund dog on a day out to watch the Badminton Horse Trials in Gloucestershire with the Queen Mother. Prince Philip had stayed away from the event while suffering with a cold and the Queen appears glad to have the company of her mother. On this occasion, Elizabeth II presented the winning cup to Sheila Willcox who rode High and Mighty.

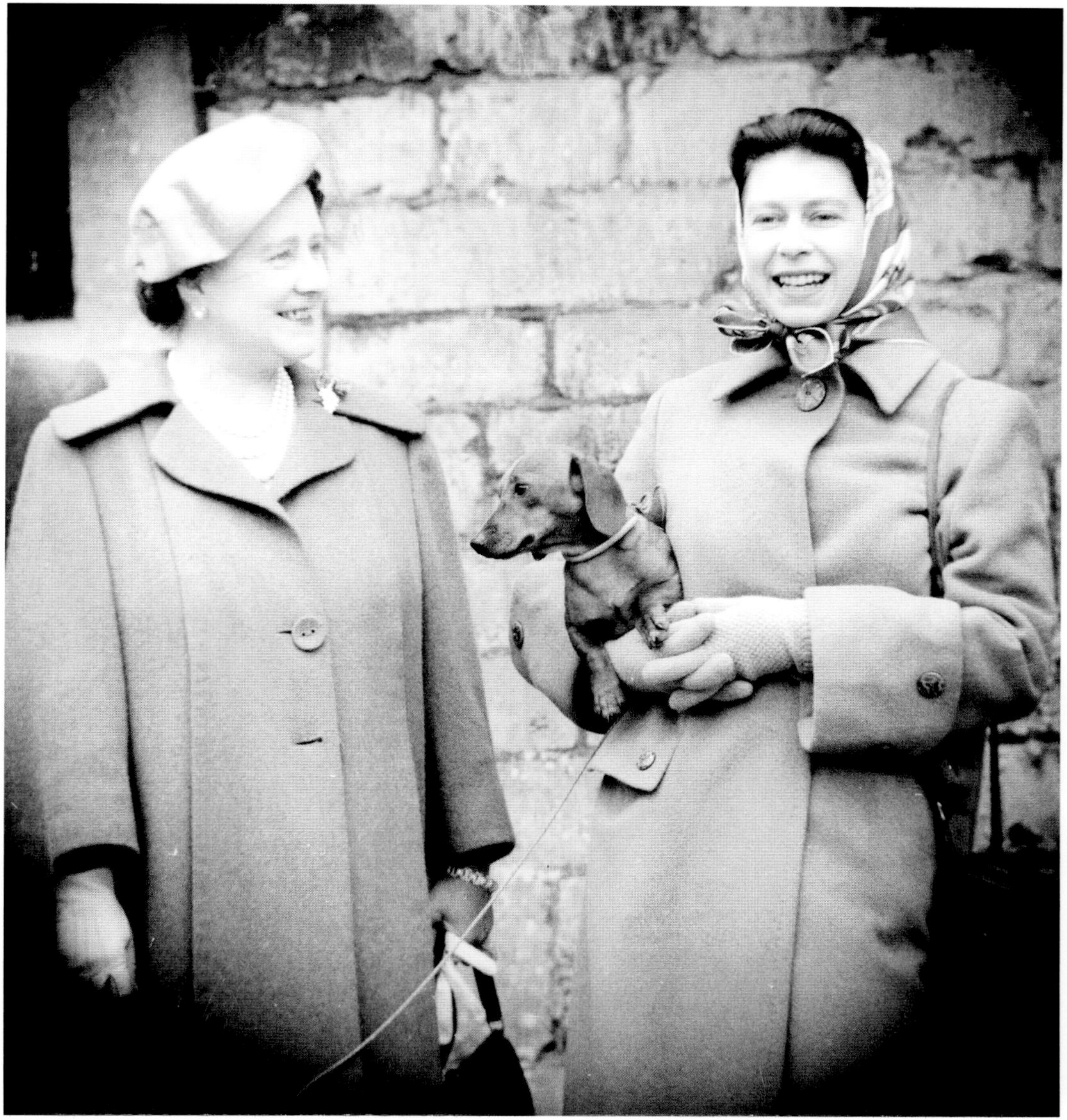

A LITTLE HELP FROM A 'FRIEND'

By Stanley Devon

January 25, 1959

The Queen gets a little help with her daily red box of government papers from Susan, one of her corgis. Elizabeth II received the official documents every day and was happy to take a break from time to time to pass a dog biscuit to her pets who frequented the royal palaces. Over the years, hapless government ministers recounted anecdotes whereby they had inadvertently helped themselves to trays of biscuits which turned out to be dog treats. Here, Elizabeth II is seen at her desk in Buckingham Palace, which is adorned with fresh flowers and family photographs.

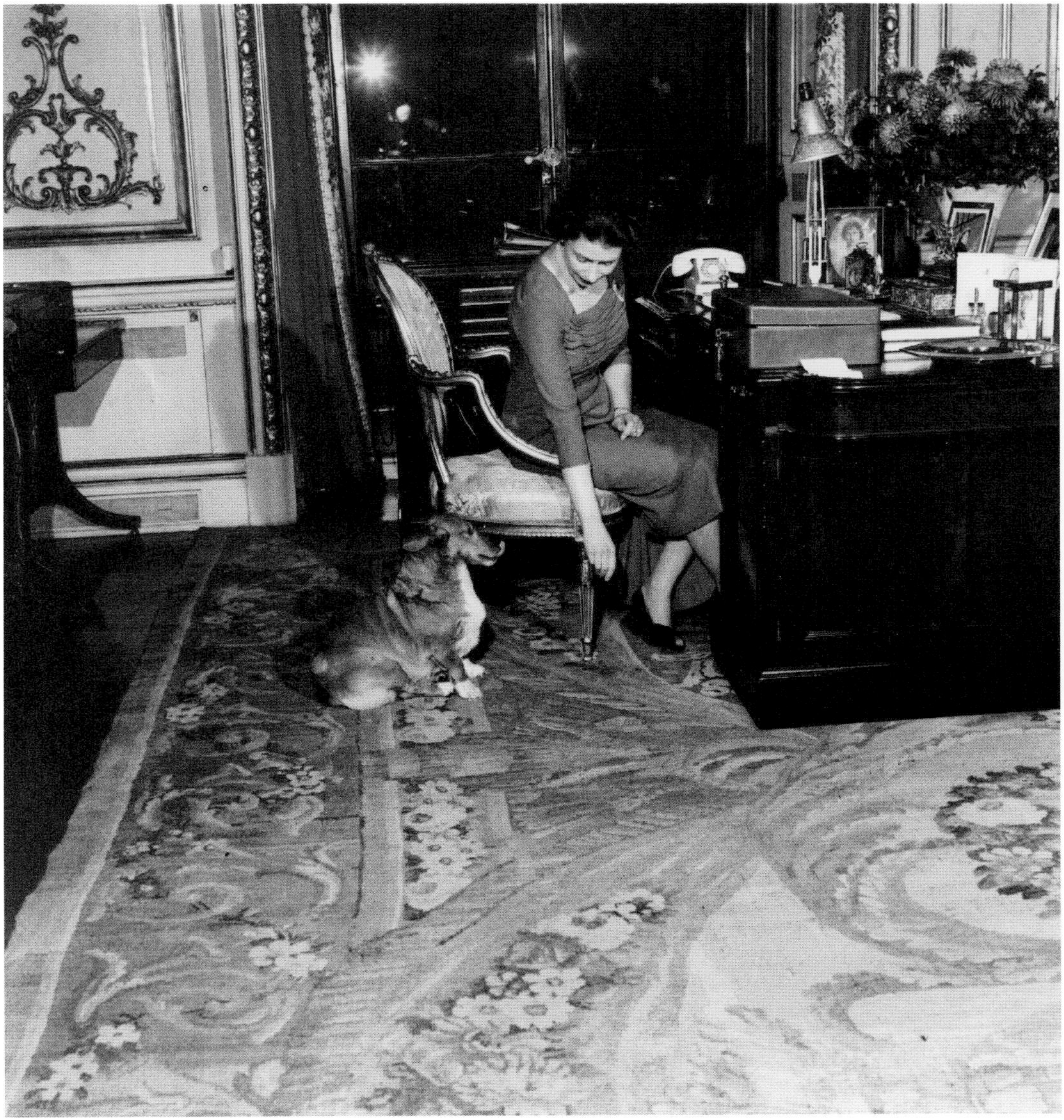

VISIT TO KEW

By Tom Dixon

June 2, 1959

Amid the flora and fauna of the reconstructed Palm House at the Royal Botanic Gardens in Kew, the Queen stands out in a light-coloured dress and hat with white gloves. During their visit, which was made as part of the gardens' 200th anniversary celebration, the Queen and Prince Philip planted a commemorative walnut tree within the grounds and attended a garden party. As well as seeing the new Palm House, the Queen, an enthusiastic gardener, marked the bicentenary by touring the Waterlily House and The Orangery.

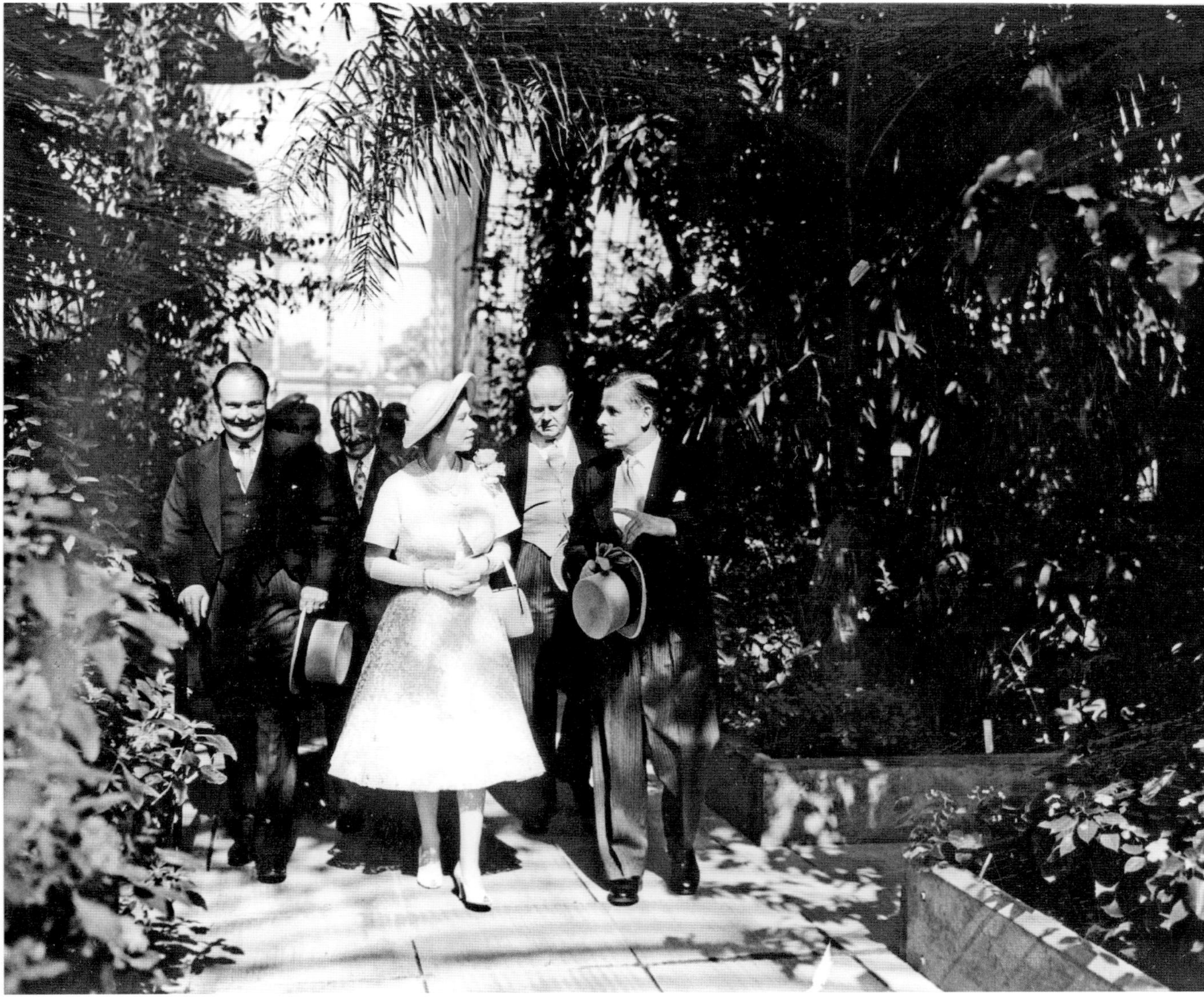

BADMINTON HORSE TRIALS

By Gerrard Herbert "Bill" Warhurst

April 23, 1960

A keen photographer, the Queen often recorded events for her own amusement. Wearing warm gloves Elizabeth II is seen talking to Prince Charles, then aged 11, at the Badminton Horse Trials. Her Majesty also attended the event with her daughter, Princess Anne, who became an accomplished equestrian and who would later compete at the event. In the years to come Anne's daughter, Zara, would also take part.

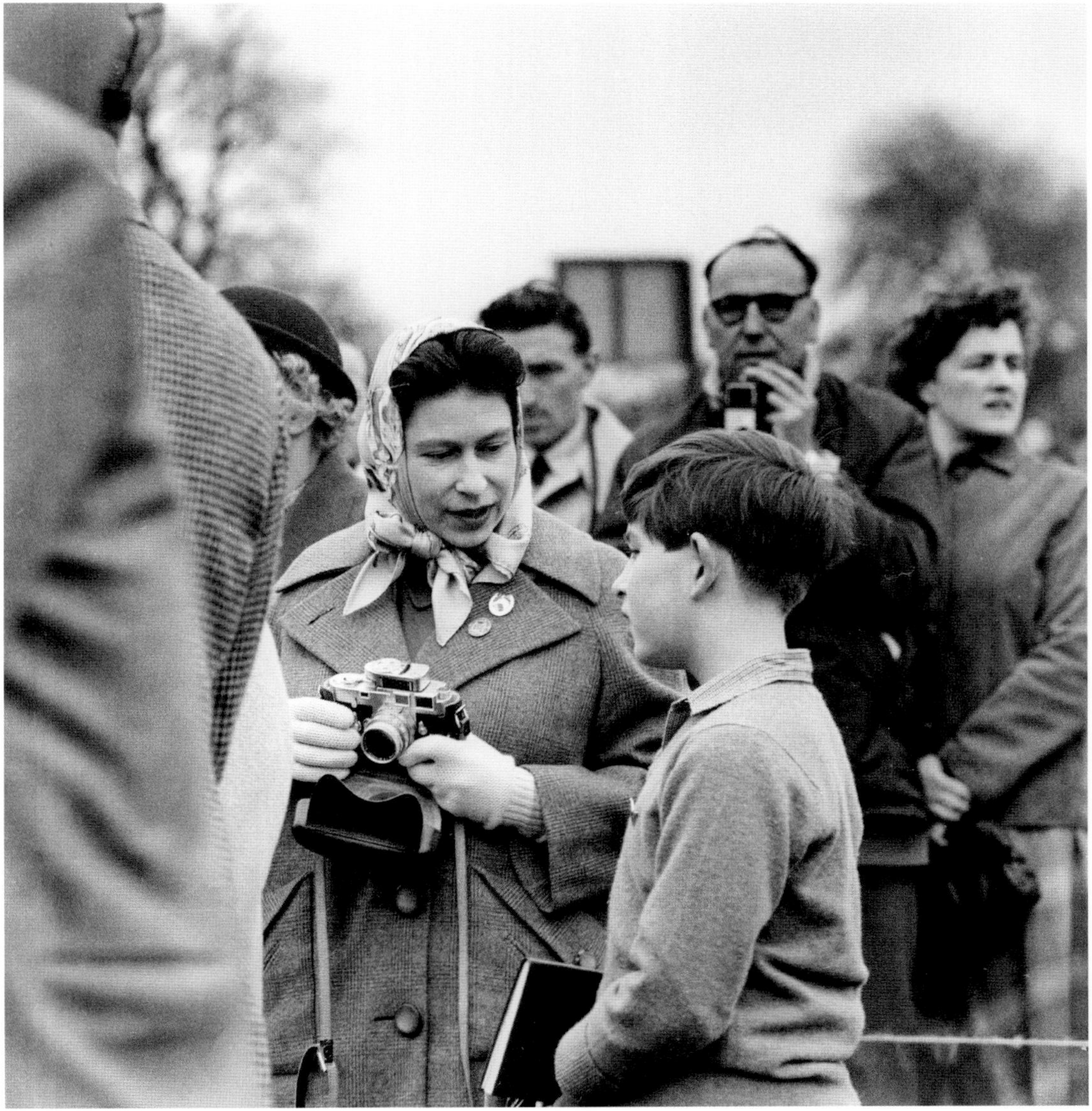

ON THE LAWN AT BALMORAL

By Jack Barker

September, 1960

And then there were five. The Queen and Prince Philip welcomed their third child, Andrew. The young family are sitting on a picnic blanket on the lawn in front of Balmoral Castle with their family pets. Now secure in her reign, the Queen was said to dote on her second son. In a letter to her midwife after the birth, Elizabeth wrote that the baby was “adorable and … very good, and putting on weight well. Both the older children are completely riveted by him and all in all, he’s going to be terribly spoilt by all of us, I’m sure!”

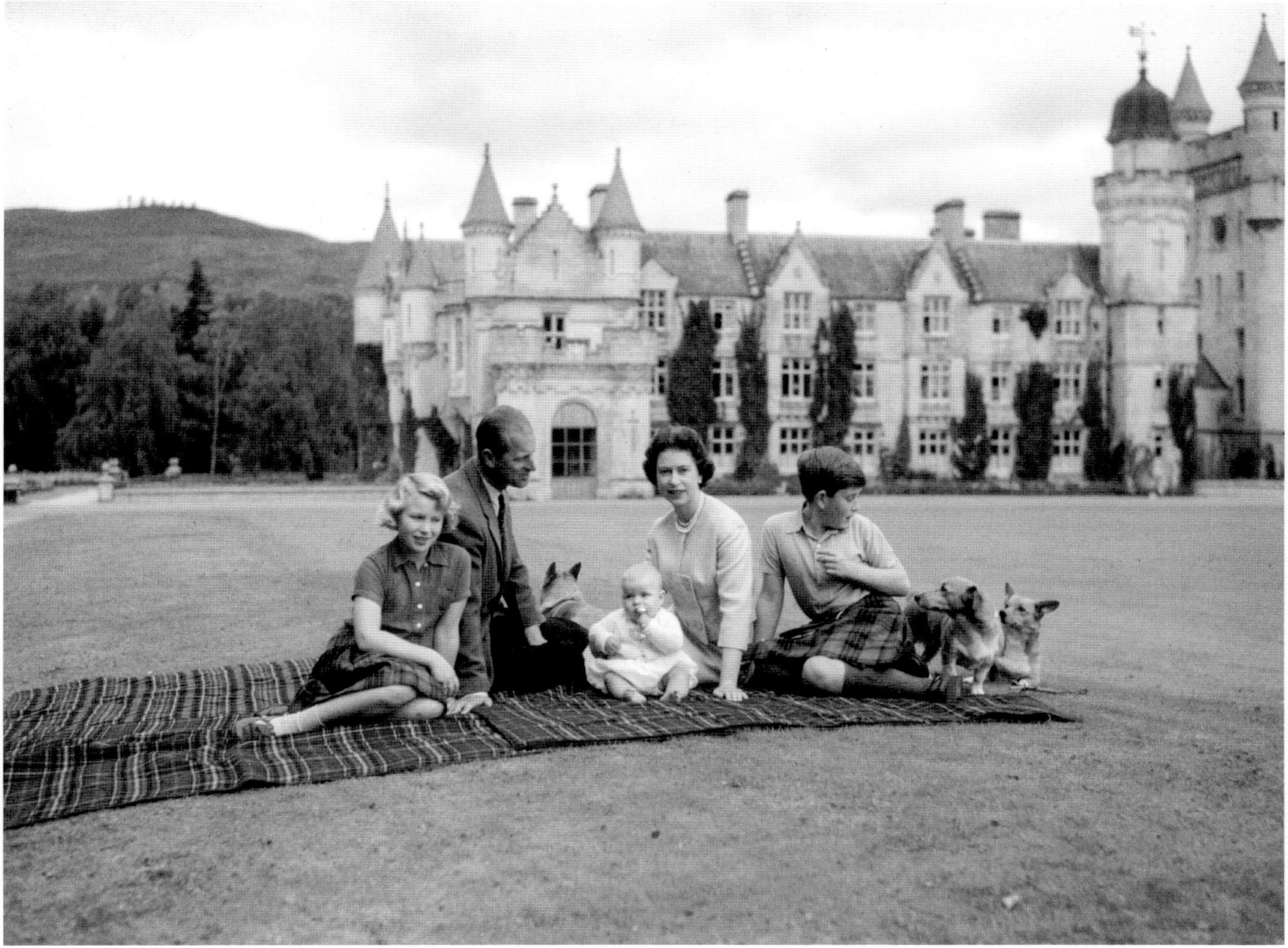

ROYAL TOUR OF INDIA AND PAKISTAN

Photographer unknown

February, 1961

Deep within the lush undergrowth of Nepal, Queen Elizabeth II rides on an elephant as she watches a tiger hunt. The Queen and Prince Philip were the guests of King Mahendra of Nepal and had been asked to join in the local tradition in the Terai region of the country. It involved hundreds of elephants being used to drive a tiger into an area where hunters were waiting. While the Queen and Prince Philip were merely spectators, their involvement proved controversial as tigers were listed as an endangered species.

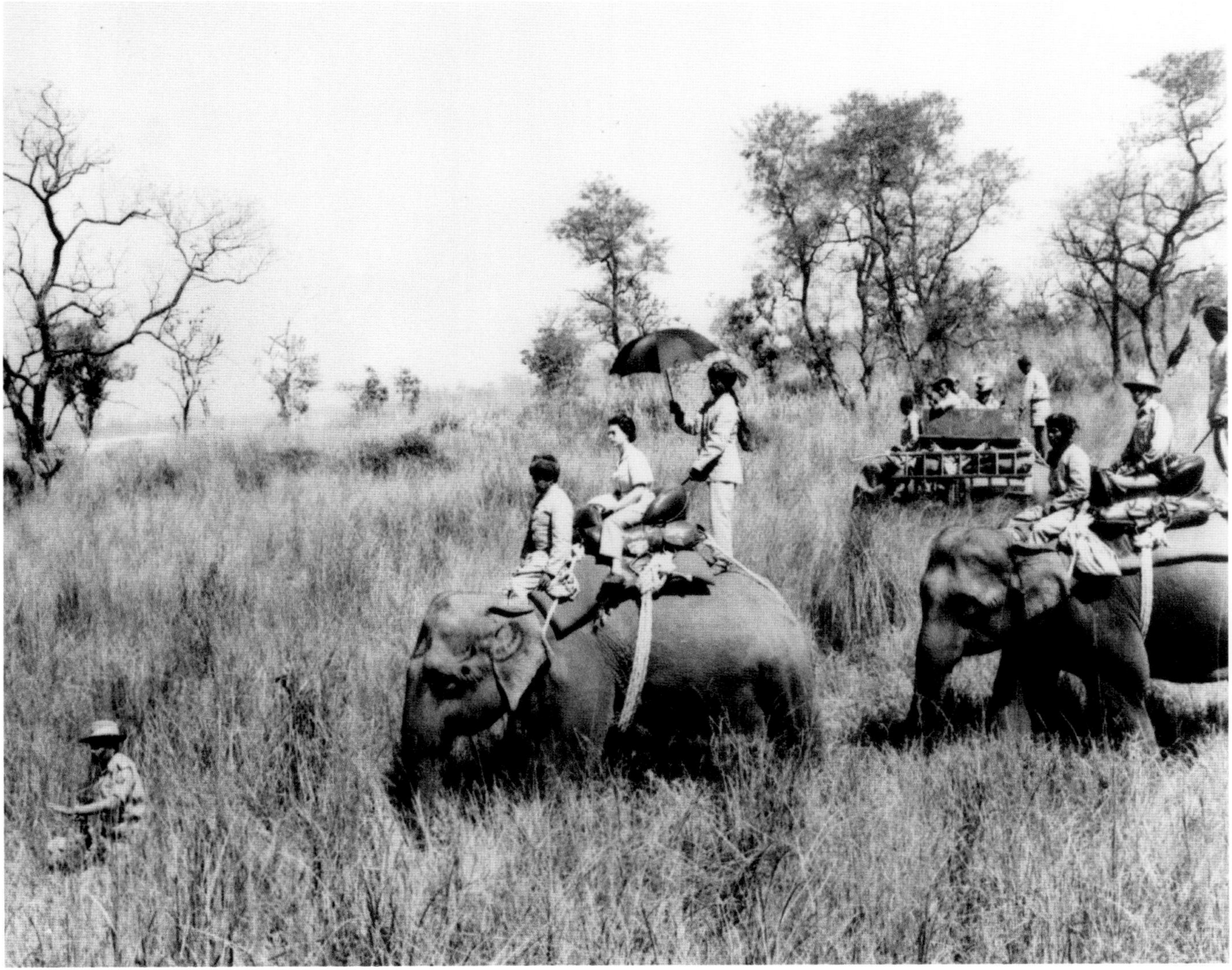

ON THE PLATFORM

By Dennis Edward Risley

August 10, 1962

The start of the summer royal getaway to Scotland was often marked with a photograph at the train station. The Queen holds the hand of her son Andrew, aged two, as she prepares to board a service at London Euston station. She is talking to Mr HC Johnson, general manager, London Midland Region of British Railways. In the background are Prince Charles and, out of sight, Crown Prince Carl Gustaf of Sweden.

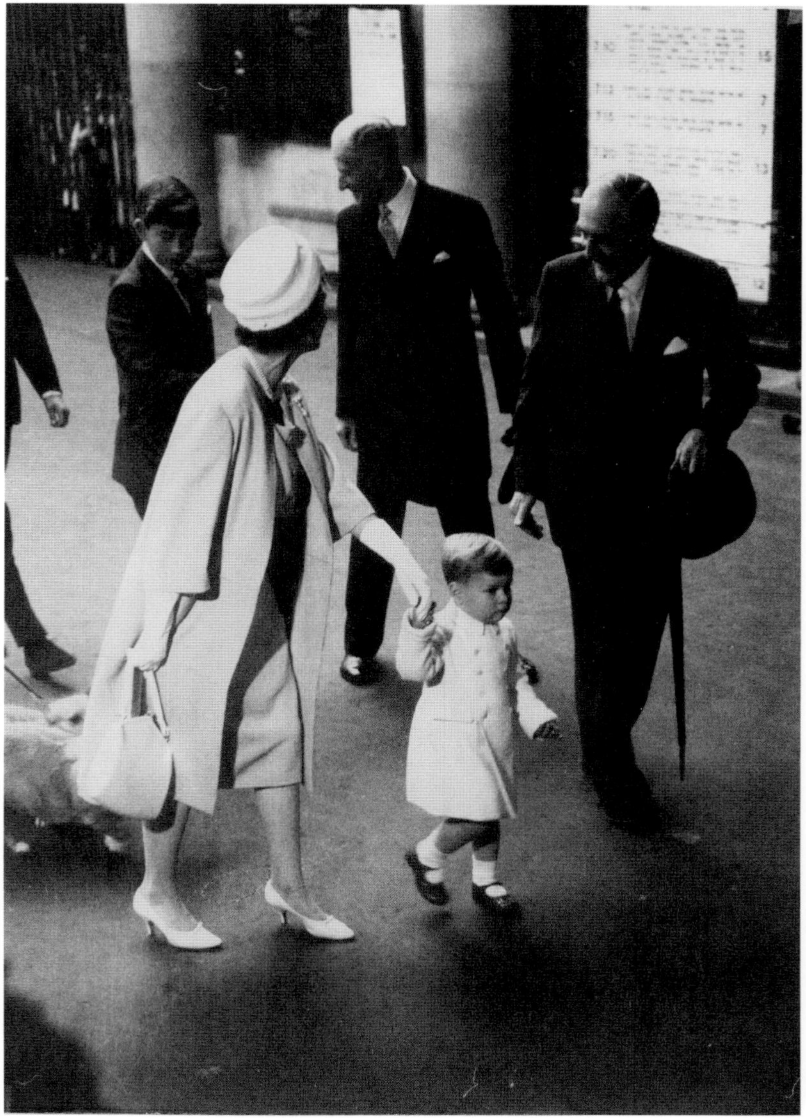

PORTRAIT FOR BANK NOTES

By Douglas Glass

1963

Happy and glorious: this portrait shows Queen Elizabeth II resplendent in the Diamond Diadem. Made for the Coronation of George IV, the crown was adopted by Elizabeth II for state occasions, such as the state opening of parliament. It became a well-recognised sign of the monarchy as the Queen was depicted wearing it on bank notes and stamps issued cross the Commonwealth. Featuring 1,333 brilliant-cut diamonds, a 4-carat yellow diamond, and 169 pearls, it pulls together the different nations of the United Kingdom in a design that alternates between four crosses and four floral bouquets of roses, thistles and shamrocks.

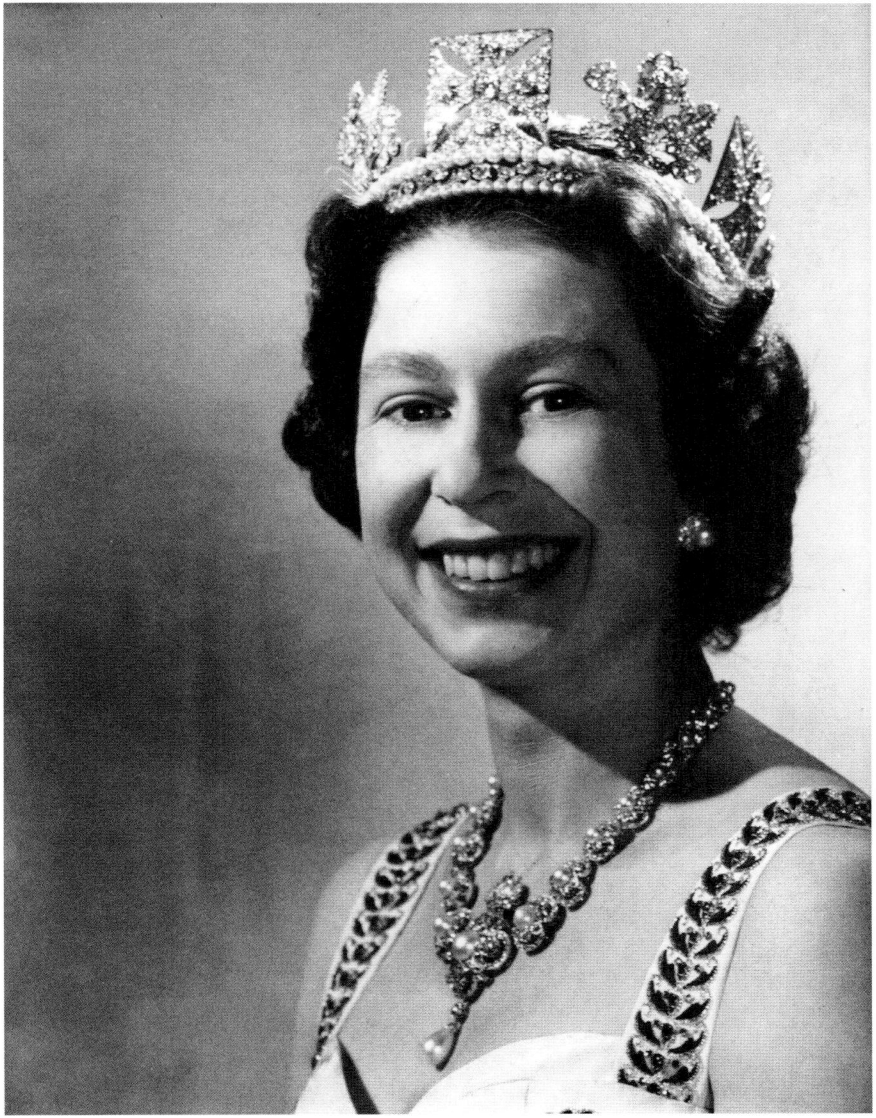

WINSTON CHURCHILL'S FUNERAL

By Alfred Harris

January 30, 1965

A sombre moment for the nation as the Queen and Duke of Edinburgh ascend the steps of St Paul's Cathedral for the state funeral of Sir Winston Churchill. While tradition stipulates that the monarch should always be the last to arrive at a church service, the Queen on this occasion broke with royal protocol to arrive before his family as an act of respect. The gesture was read as a sign of the close bond between the monarch and her first prime minister.

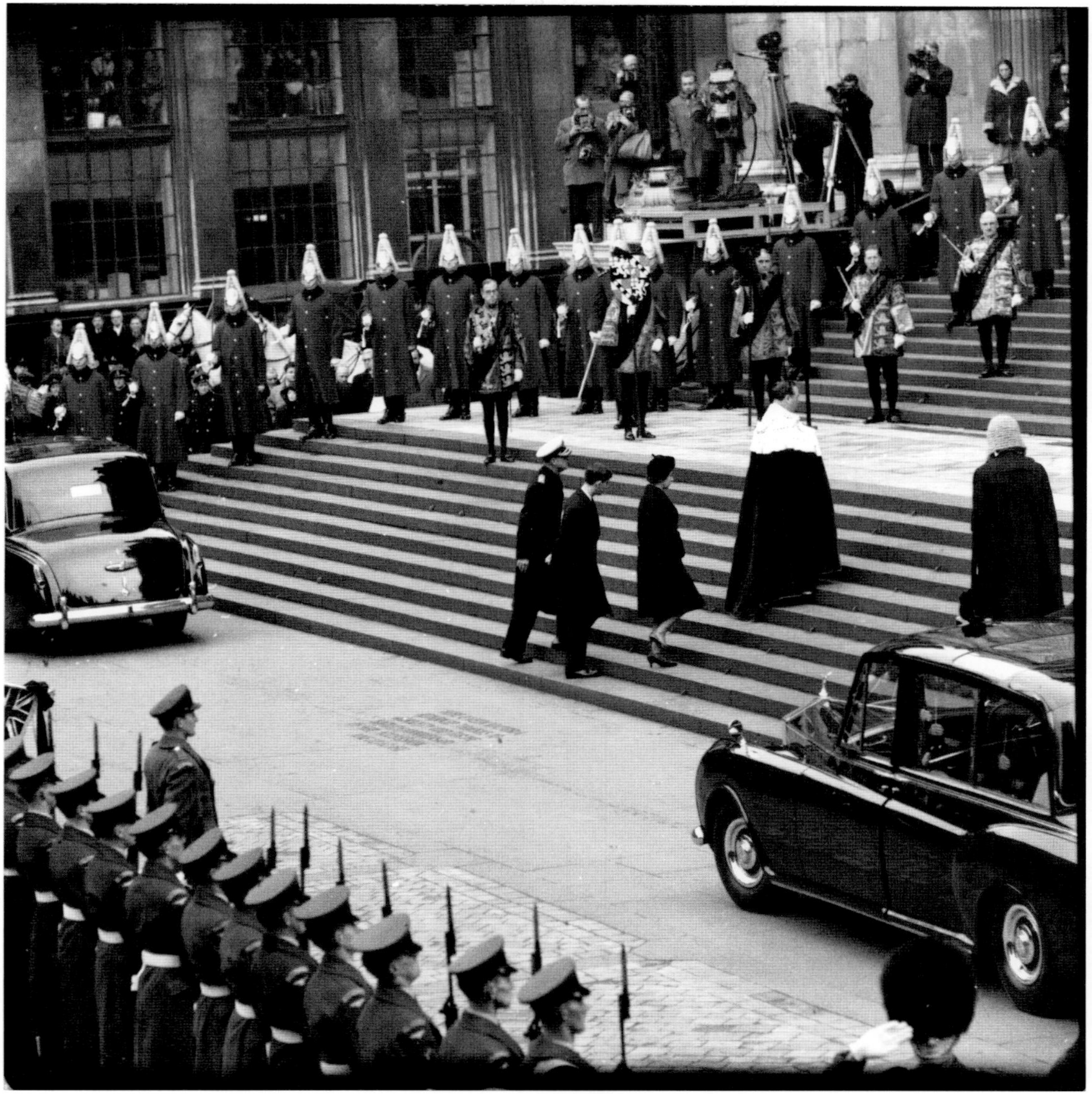

ROYAL WAVE

By Peter Trievnor

December 29, 1965

Looking uncertainly out of the window of the carriage, a young Prince Edward gives a tentative royal wave. Edward, the fourth child of the monarch, was born in March the previous year and completed the Queen's young family. The family was leaving Liverpool Street station en route to Sandringham.

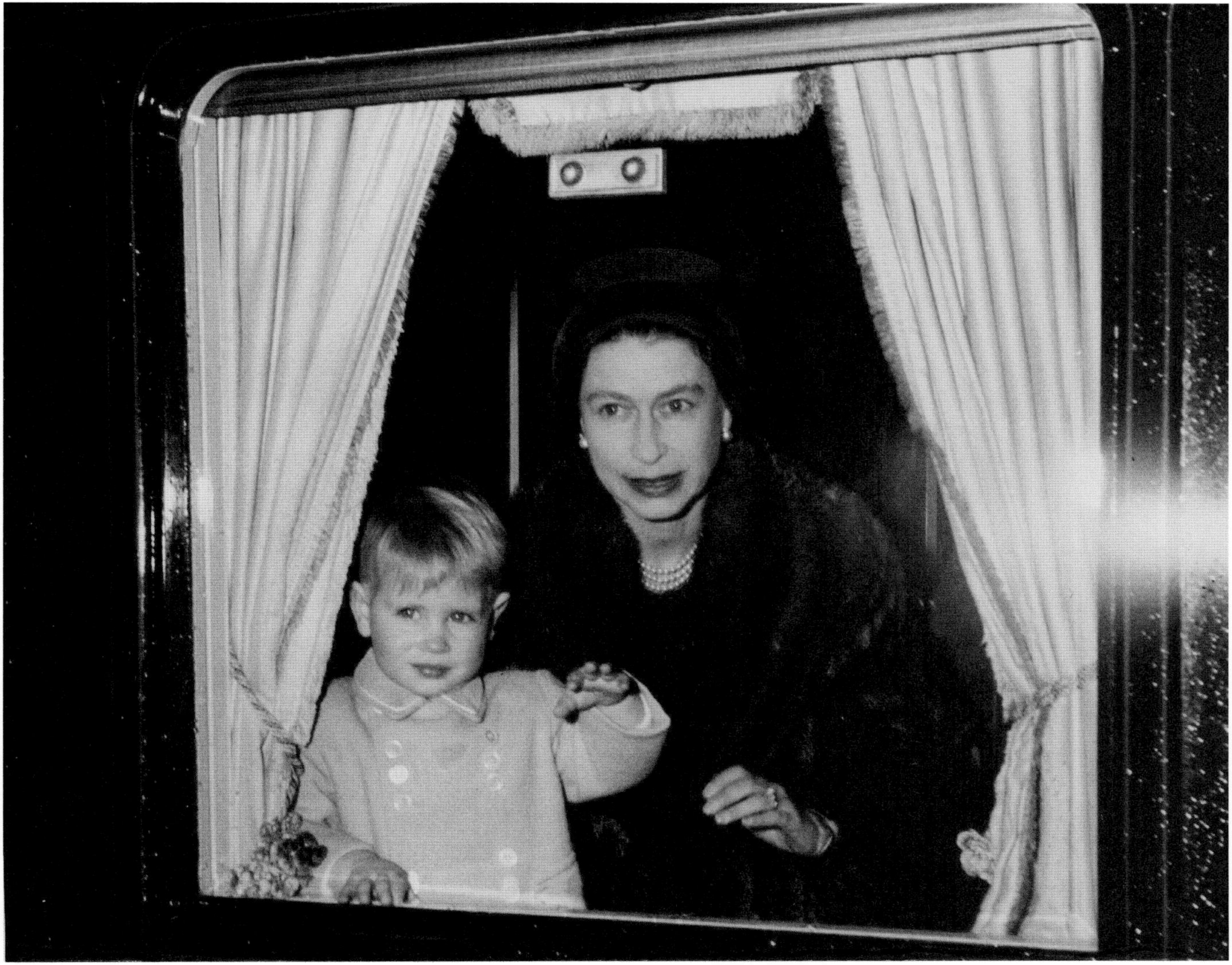

WORLD CUP OPENING CEREMONY

By Bryan Wharton

July 11, 1966

It was an auspicious start for what became one of the most celebrated sporting triumphs. Queen Elizabeth II attends the opening ceremony of the 1966 football World Cup and while England's first match against Uruguay was to result in a 0-0 draw, the team went on to win the tournament. Her Majesty presented the Jules Rimet trophy to England captain Bobby Moore after his team beat West Germany 4-2 in the final at Wembley Stadium. Bobby Moore famously cleaned his hands on his shorts before accepting the trophy from the Queen.

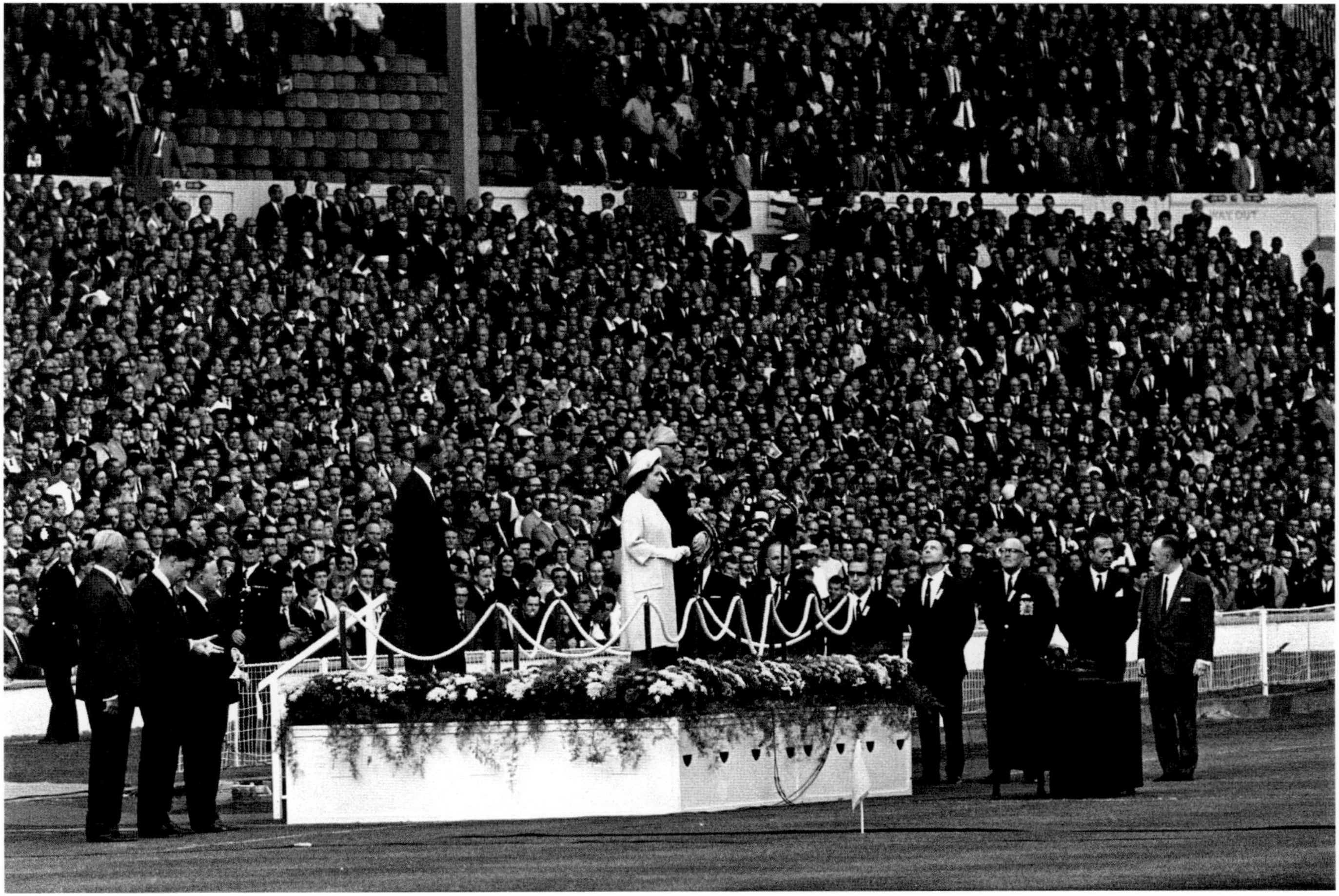

ABERFAN

By Frank Hermann

October 29, 1966

One of the darkest days in the nation's history and a bleak moment in the reign of Queen Elizabeth II. Following the disaster where 116 children and 28 adults were killed when a colliery spoil tip collapsed, engulfing a primary school and surrounding houses, the Queen visits the village of Aberfan in Wales. Although Prince Philip and Lord Snowdon had joined Prime Minister Harold Wilson at the scene the day after the catastrophe, the Queen was criticised for waiting eight days before travelling to the village near Merthyr Tydfil.

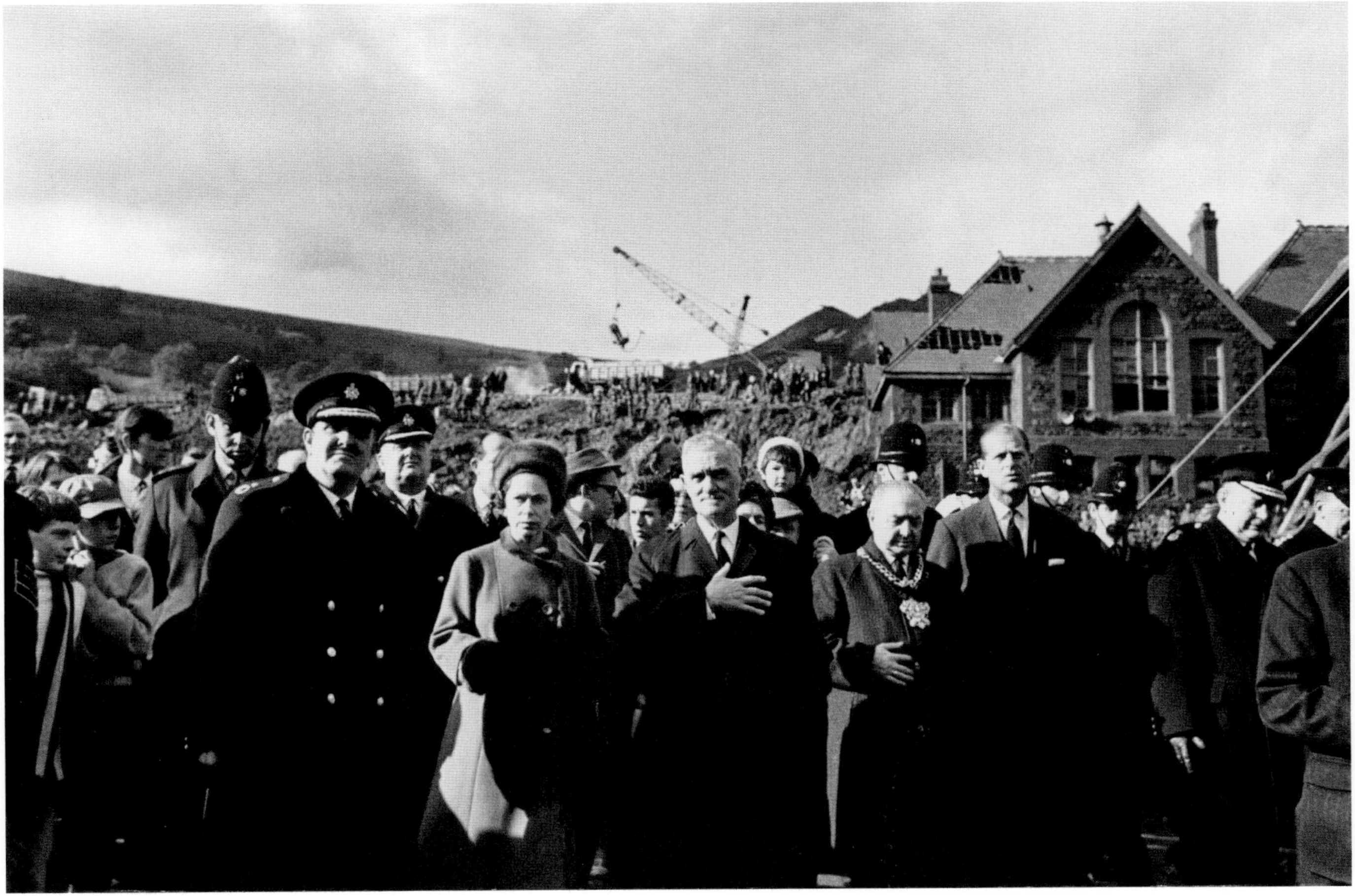

KNIGHTHOOD

By Peter Trievnor

July 7, 1967

Within the setting of the Royal Naval College in Greenwich, South East London, Francis Chichester receives his knighthood from the Queen, an honour for becoming the first person to sail solo around the world by the clipper route through the Southern Ocean. It took him nine months and one day to complete the voyage in 1966-67 aboard his yacht, Gipsy Moth IV. In recognition of his extraordinary achievement, the Queen used the same sword that Queen Elizabeth I had used to knight Sir Francis Drake.

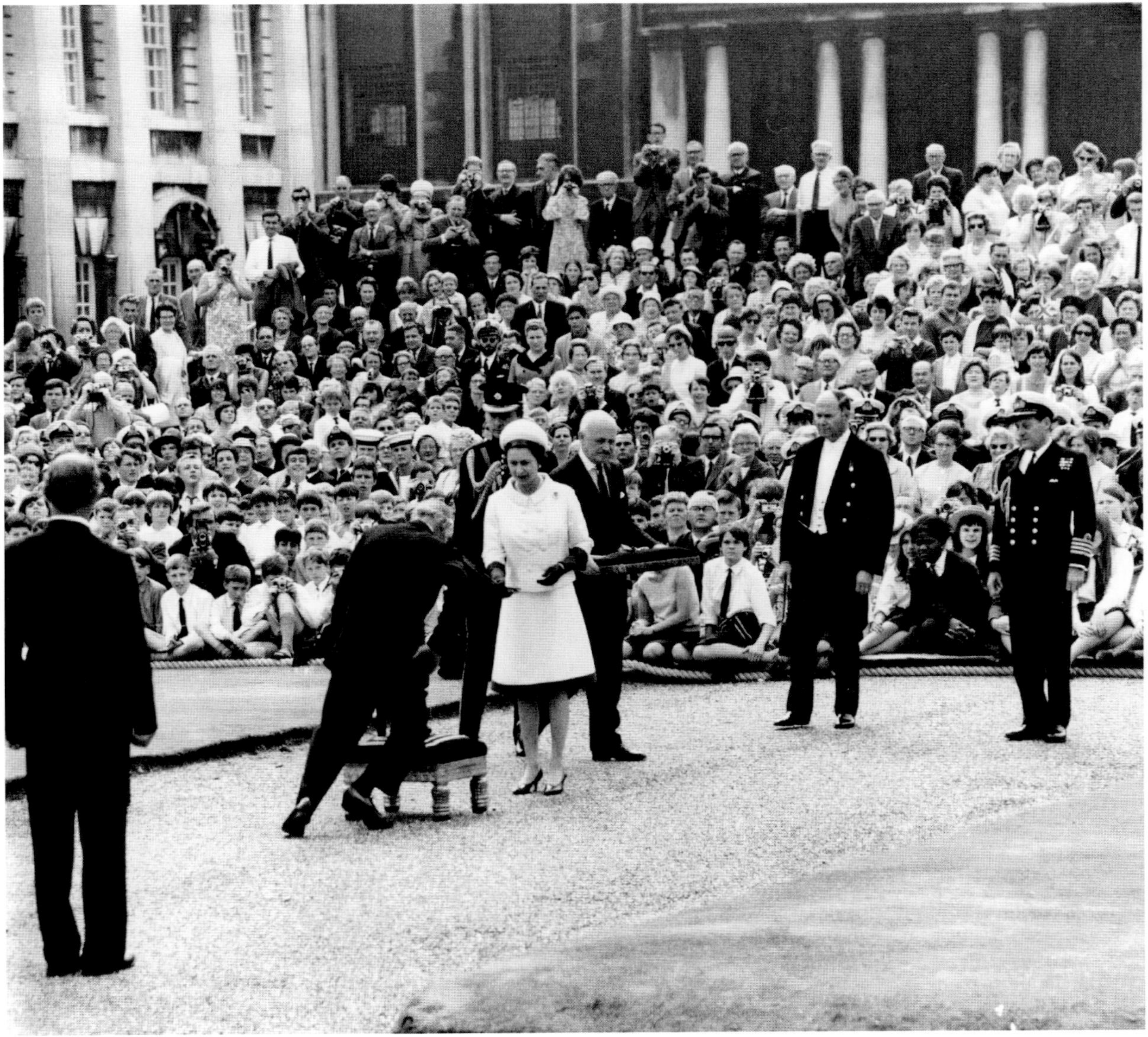

THE QUEEN AND DOCTOR DOLITTLE

Photographer unknown

December 12, 1967

In a glittering black tie ceremony, English actor Rex Harrison is presented to Her Majesty at the Odeon cinema in Marble Arch, before a screening of his performance as Doctor Dolittle. Wearing the Girls of Great Britain and Ireland tiara, the Queen outshone the film stars at a charity event for the British Empire Cancer Campaign. Harrison, who began his career on the stage before moving to the big screen, was later knighted by the Queen in 1989 for his services to acting.

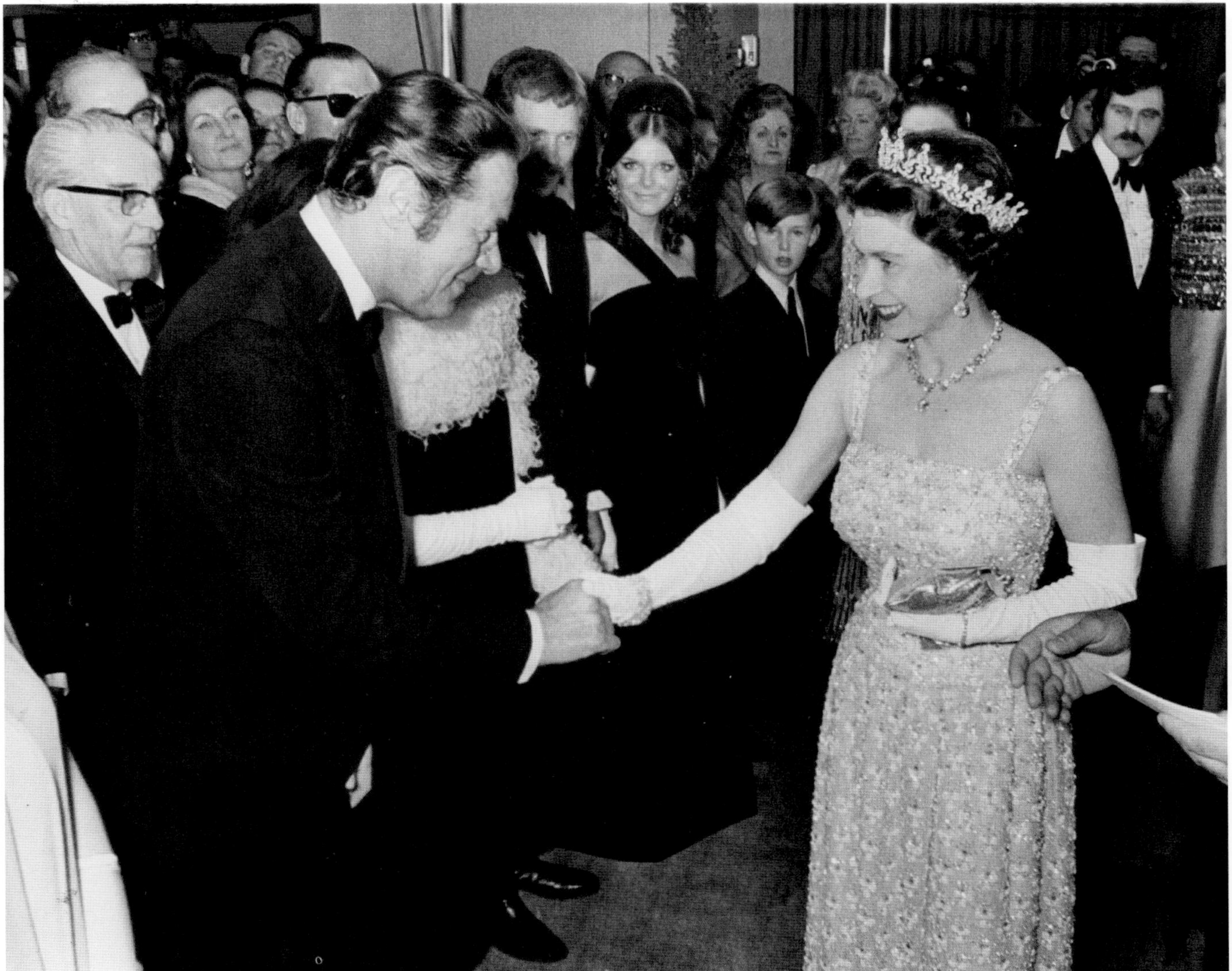

PRINCE OF WALES INVESTITURE

By Gerrard Herbert "Bill" Warhurst

July 1, 1969

A true moment of royal splendour and history, the likes of which may never be seen again. Prince Charles has just been invested of the title Prince of Wales in a grand ceremony at Caernarfon Castle, Gwynedd, Wales, by his mother Queen Elizabeth II. During his time at Cambridge University, Prince Charles spent a term learning Welsh at Aberystwyth University. Charles wears the Investiture Coronet which was specially designed for the ceremony by the architect and goldsmith Louis Osman, and given to Queen Elizabeth II by the Goldsmiths' Company in 1969. Made of Welsh 24-carat gold reinforced with platinum, it features four crosses patées and four fleurs-de-lys, and is decorated with diamonds and emeralds.

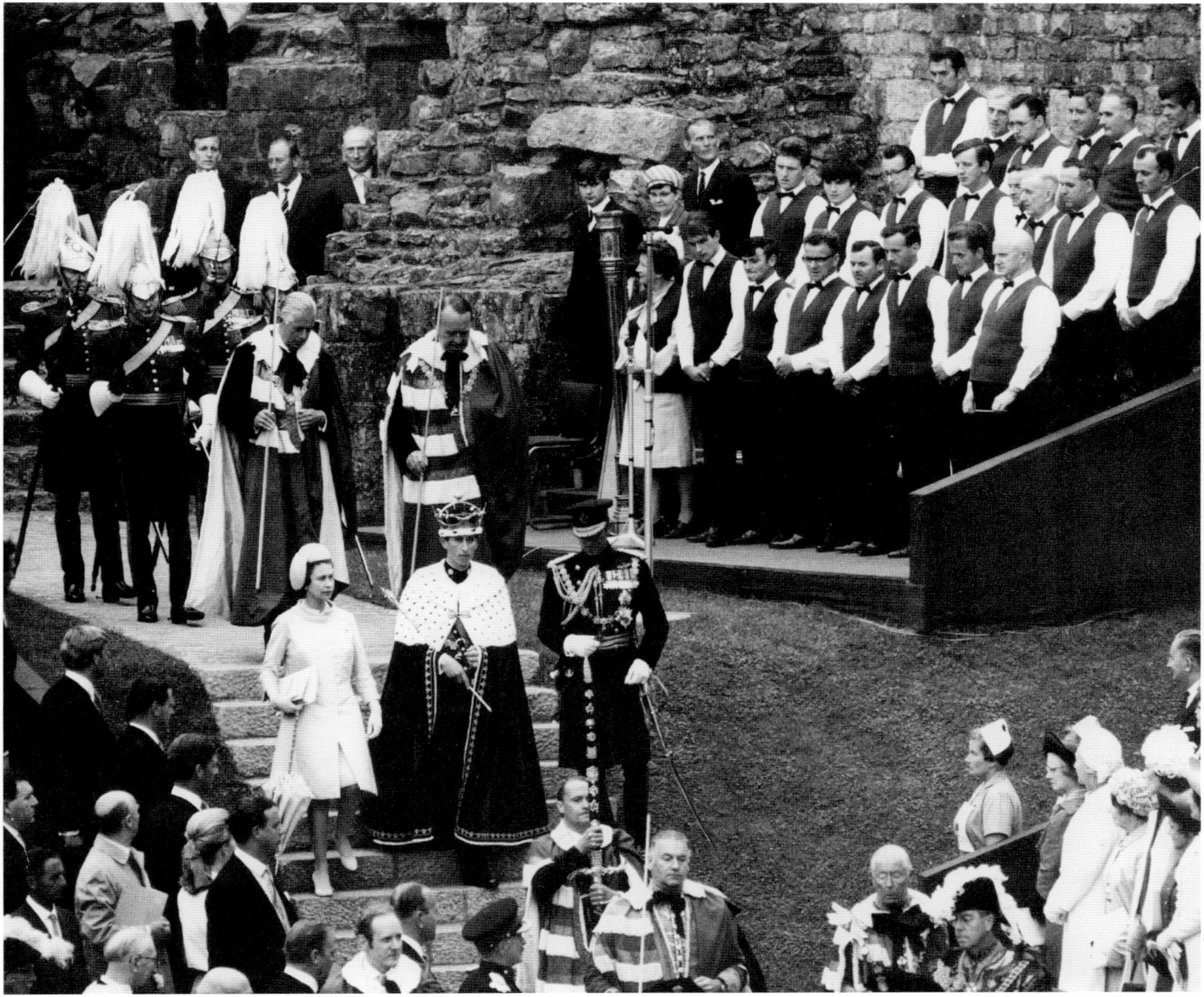

FAMILY HOSPITAL VISIT

By Chris Travis

July 8, 1971

The Queen arrives at King Edward VII's Hospital following the admission of her daughter, Princess Anne. Later known as The Princess Royal, Anne had undergone an operation by the Queen's gynaecologist Sir John Peel, to remove an inflamed ovarian cyst. With a smile, the Queen gives an unspoken message of reassurance to the waiting photographers that there is nothing to worry about.

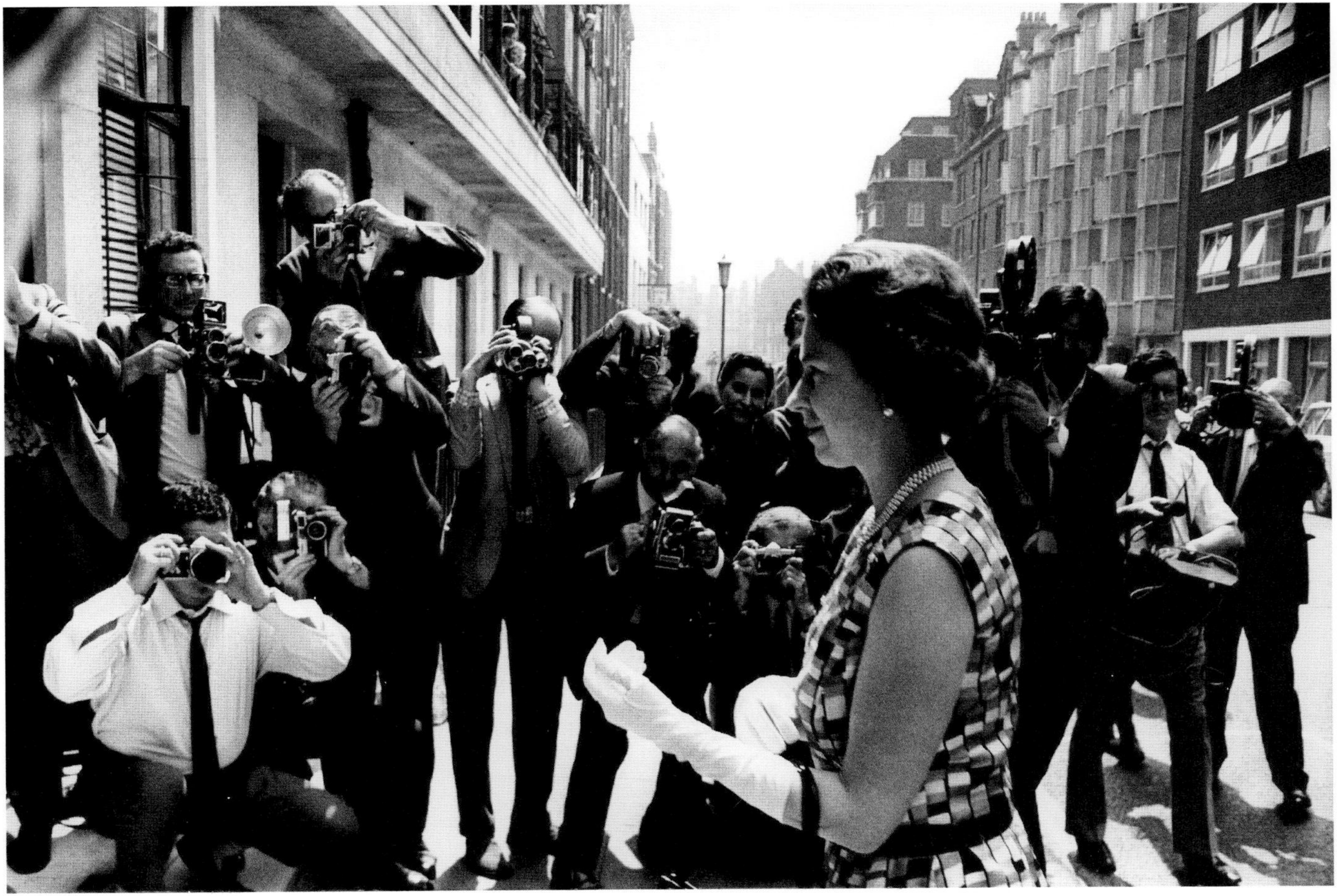

LONDON BRIDGE REOPENS

By Gerrard Herbert "Bill" Warhurst

March 16, 1973

Thousands of flag-waving school children turned out on a sunny spring day to catch a glimpse of the Queen as she opened the new London Bridge. The monarch, who created the modern notion of the royal "walkabout", spent time speaking to members of the public who had turned out to experience the excitement of a royal visit. Young children were seen craning their necks over the barriers to get a better view. The new bridge, which was created with concrete and steel, took five years to complete.
It replaced the 19th-century stone structure that had been built by John Rennie, which itself replaced a medieval bridge over the River Thames.

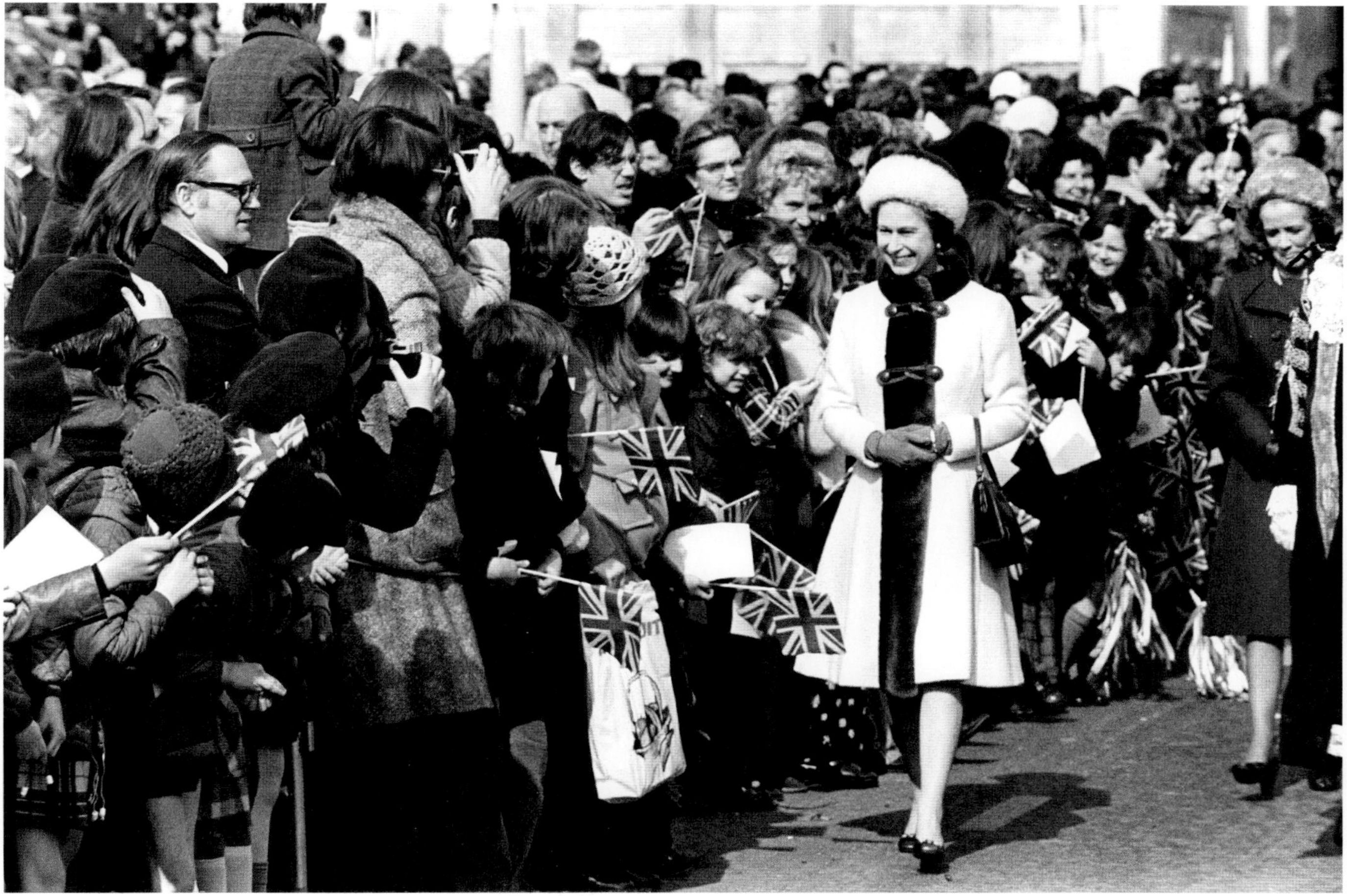

AT THE RACES

By Peter Trievnor

June 1, 1977

Smiling proudly at her daughter, the Queen Mother enjoys a day at the races with the Queen. The women are seen studying the form of horses in the Paddock during the parade of the Derby runners at the Epsom races. The festival was held during Queen Elizabeth II's Silver Jubilee year, in which she marked 25 years on the throne. Celebrations and street parties were held throughout June to mark the occasion and during the year the Queen and Prince Philip travelled extensively throughout the UK and the wider Commonwealth to greet as many people as possible.

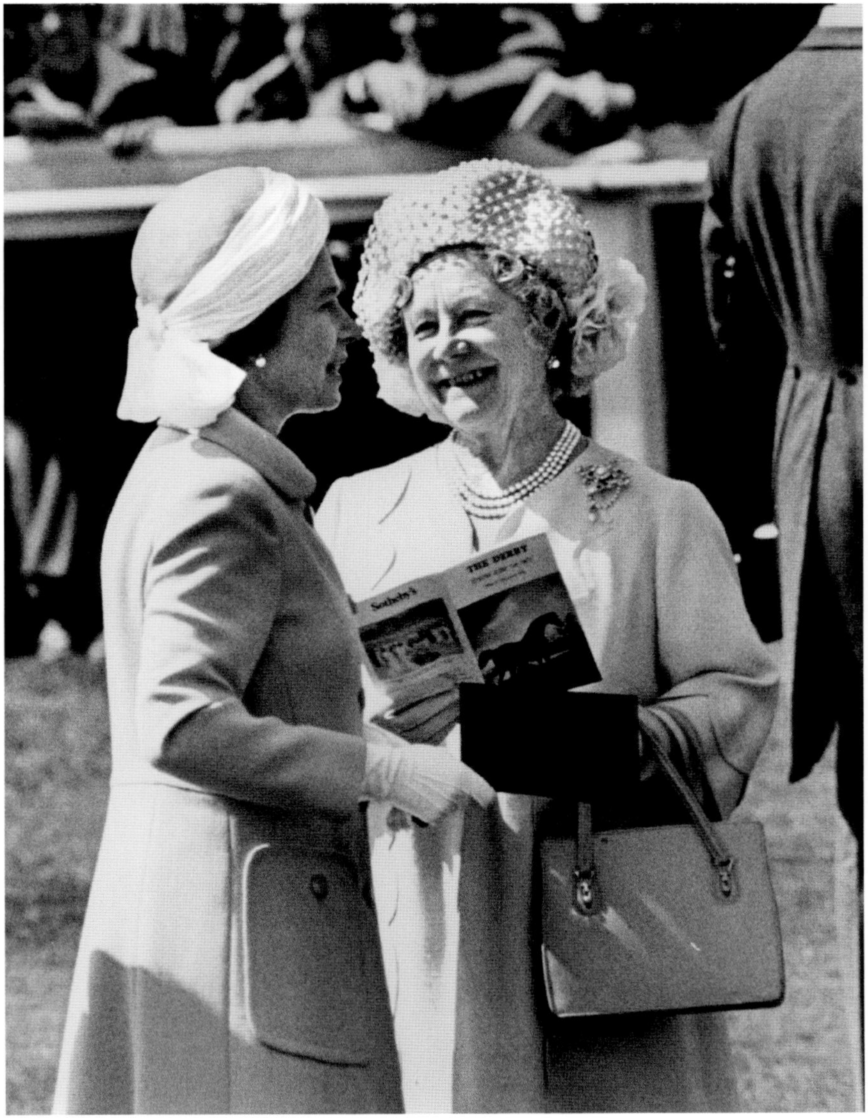
Sotheby's
THE DERBY

THE QUEEN MOTHER'S 80TH BIRTHDAY

By Chris Ball

August 4, 1980

There is rarely a picture of the Queen Mother in which she isn't wearing a broad smile, and this is no exception. A source of near-constant support and encouragement to Elizabeth II during her reign, the Queen Mother took centre stage on her 80th birthday. She is seen here receiving a posy of flowers from a child, while members of her family, joined by a curious corgi, look on. In public recognition of the birthday, celebratory coins were issued by the Royal Mint featuring a portrait of the Queen Mother with a design of bows and lions, a nod to her maiden name, Bowes-Lyon.

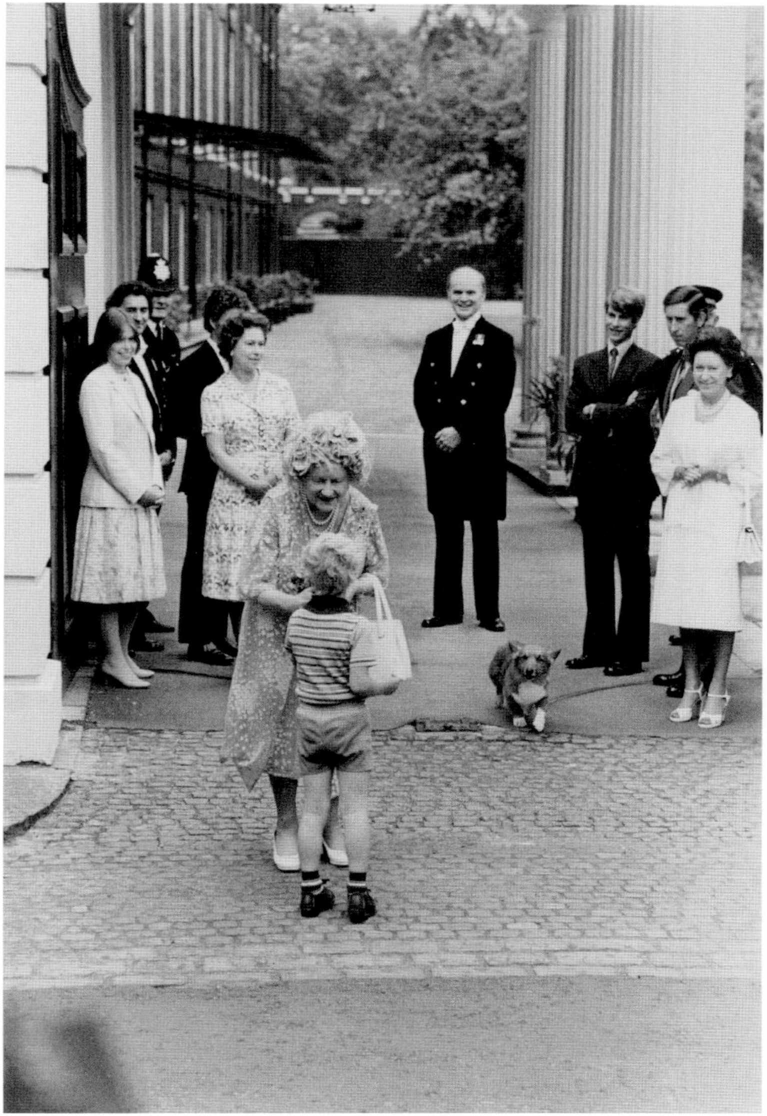

THE ROYAL WEDDING OF CHARLES AND DIANA

Photographer unknown

July 29, 1981

The fairytale wedding of Prince Charles and Lady Diana Spencer was watched by an estimated global television audience of 750 million viewers in 74 countries. The worldwide spectacle saw the new Princess of Wales, aged 20, formally welcomed into the royal family as the wife of the heir to the throne. The ceremony was held at St Paul's Cathedral, with carriage processions through the streets of London. After the service the bride and groom appeared on the balcony of Buckingham Palace alongside the Queen and Prince Philip. Following the wedding, the couple spent their honeymoon aboard the Royal Yacht Britannia.

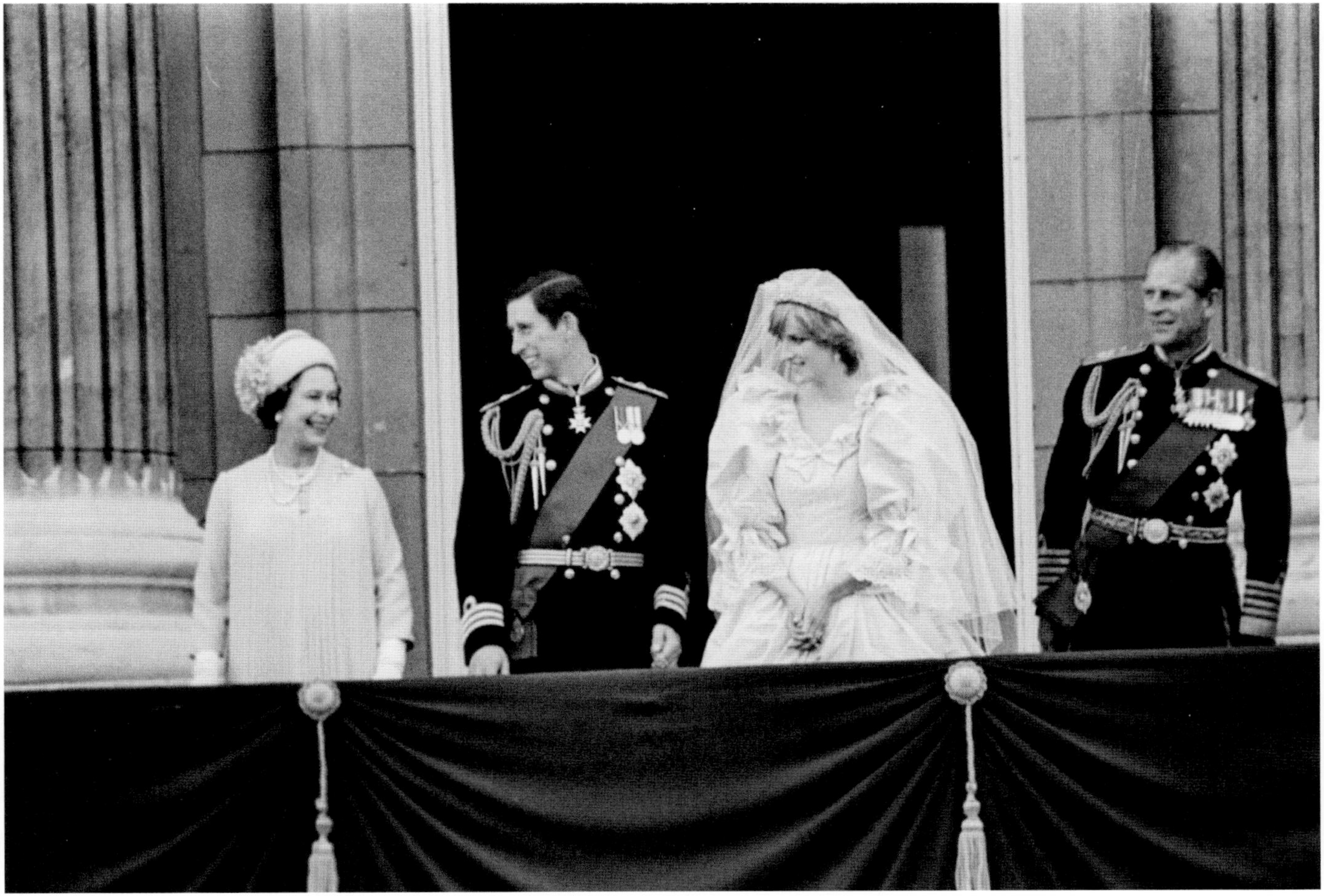

THAMES BARRIER

By Harry Kerr

May 8, 1984

Opening the new Thames Barrier, a vital flood defence for the capital, the Queen described it as an "engineering wonder of the world". Inspired by the catastrophic North Sea flood which killed more than 300 people in Britain in 1953, the project took eight years to build. In an official opening ceremony, the Queen described its construction as "a race against the tide" and said that without it the Thames Barrier flood defences would have to be as high as Victorian street lamps, thus "depriving Londoners of their river".

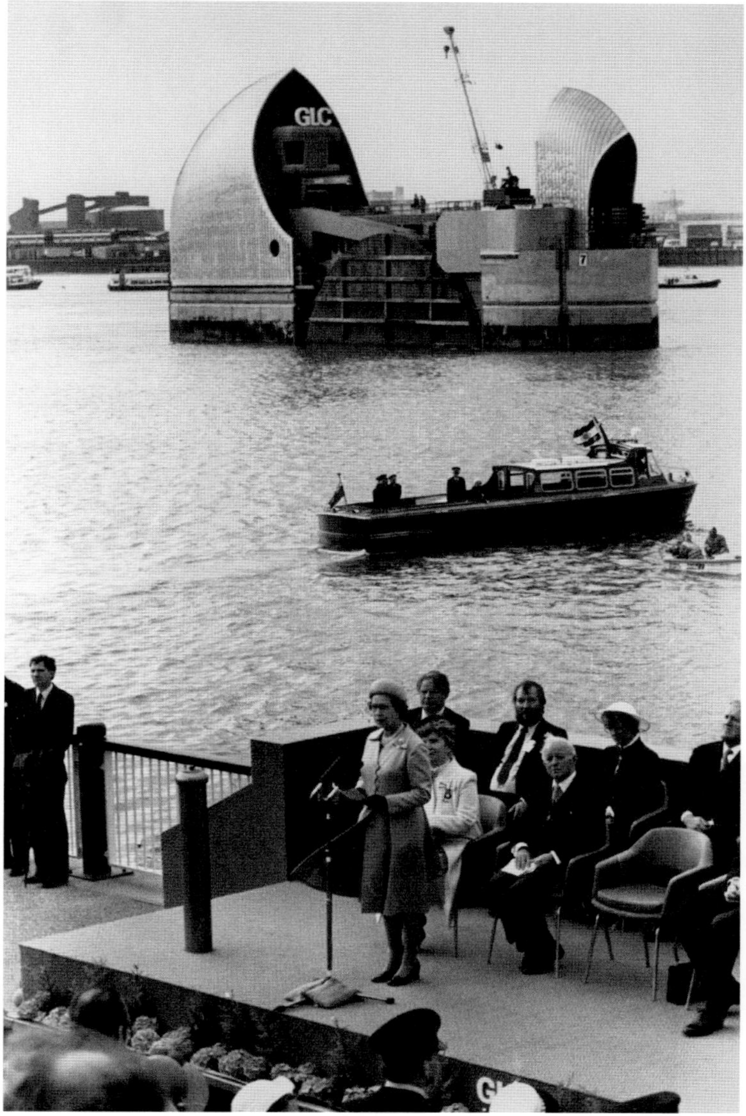
GLC
7

THE VIEW FROM GRANDMA'S LAP

Photographer unknown

June 28, 1984

There is always room on a grandma's lap for a little one and so it proves with Queen Elizabeth II. Zara Phillips, the daughter of Princess Anne, is seen sitting with the Queen at the Windsor Park Polo. With an attentive look on her face, Zara, aged three, takes in the sights and sounds of the event. Zara inherited a love of horses from her grandmother and mother and became an accomplished equestrian, winning a silver medal at the Olympics and a gold medal at the World Equestrian Championships.

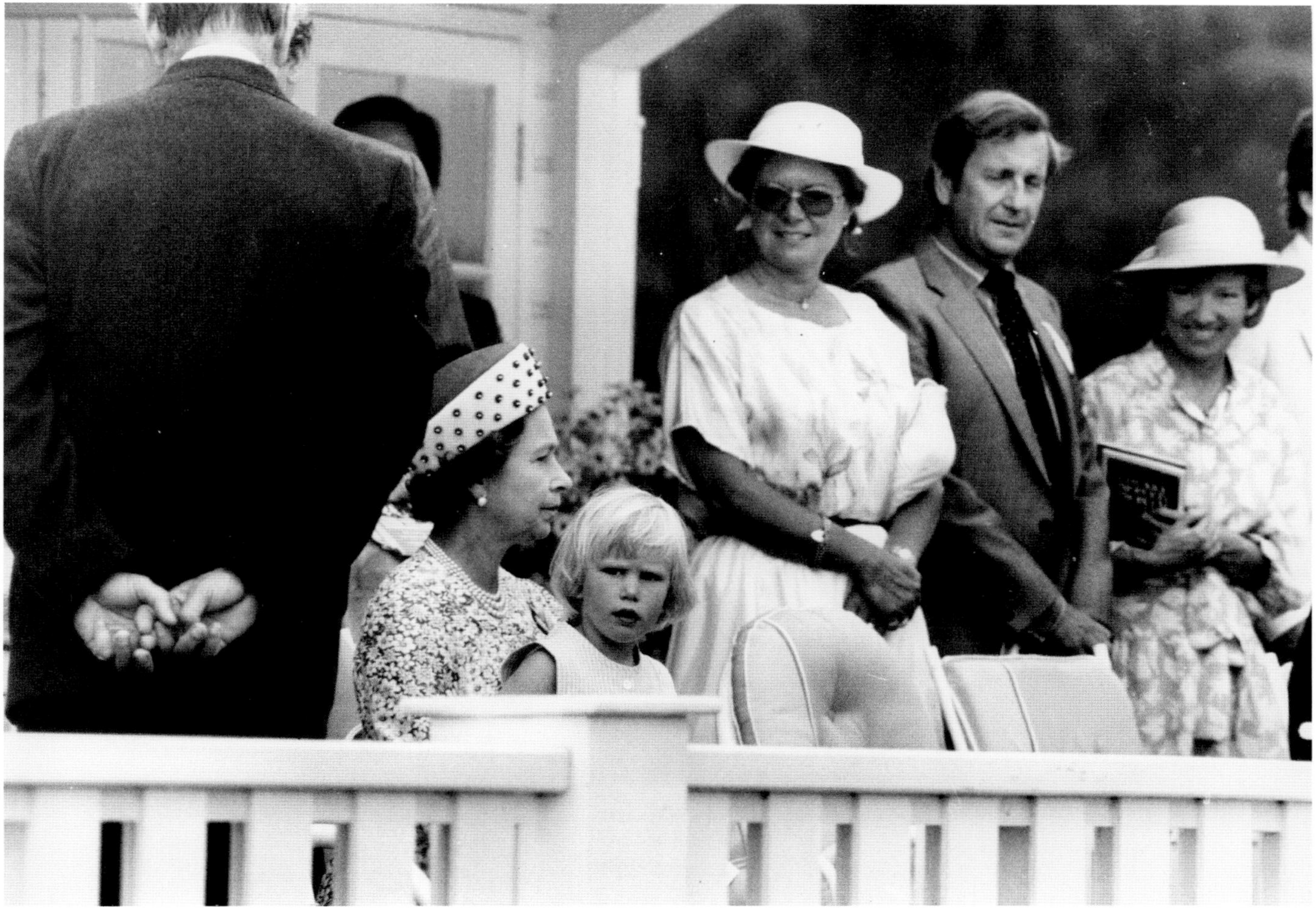

VISIT TO THE TIMES

By Gerrard Herbert "Bill" Warhurst

February 28, 1985

The Queen is seen enjoying her visit to the offices of The Times at Gray's Inn Road, London, where she was given a tour by proprietor Rupert Murdoch (right). The Times reported the highlight of the newspaper's bicentenary celebrations as "an occasion for fresh paint and crisp white shirts in the proudly grubby and chaotic world of journalism". Her Majesty, along with the Duke of Edinburgh, joined editorial meetings in the afternoon to see how the newspaper was created and returned at 8.30pm to see it being printed.

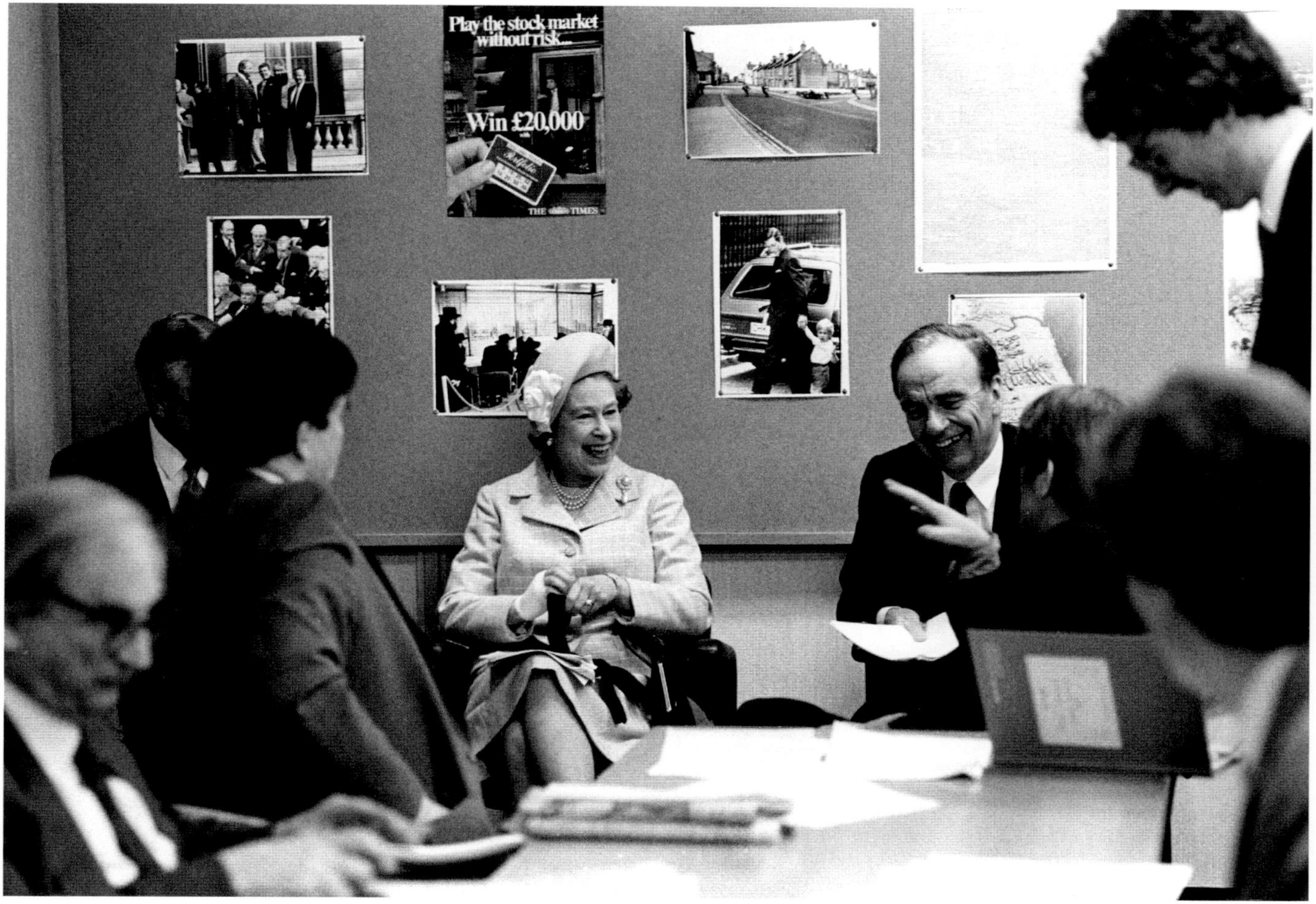
Play the stock market
without risk...
Win £20,000

ROYAL TOUR OF CHINA

By John Voos

October 14, 1986

With camera and handbag at the ready, the Queen makes history by becoming the first British monarch to visit China. Joined by Prince Philip, she toured the Great Wall of China, stopping at the Badaling path, 50 miles northwest of Beijing. A fort along the Great Wall can be seen in the distance behind the couple. The Queen and Prince Philip also visited the site of the Terracotta Warriors in Xian. The visit was of diplomatic significance as it came following the agreement to return Hong Kong to China in 1997.

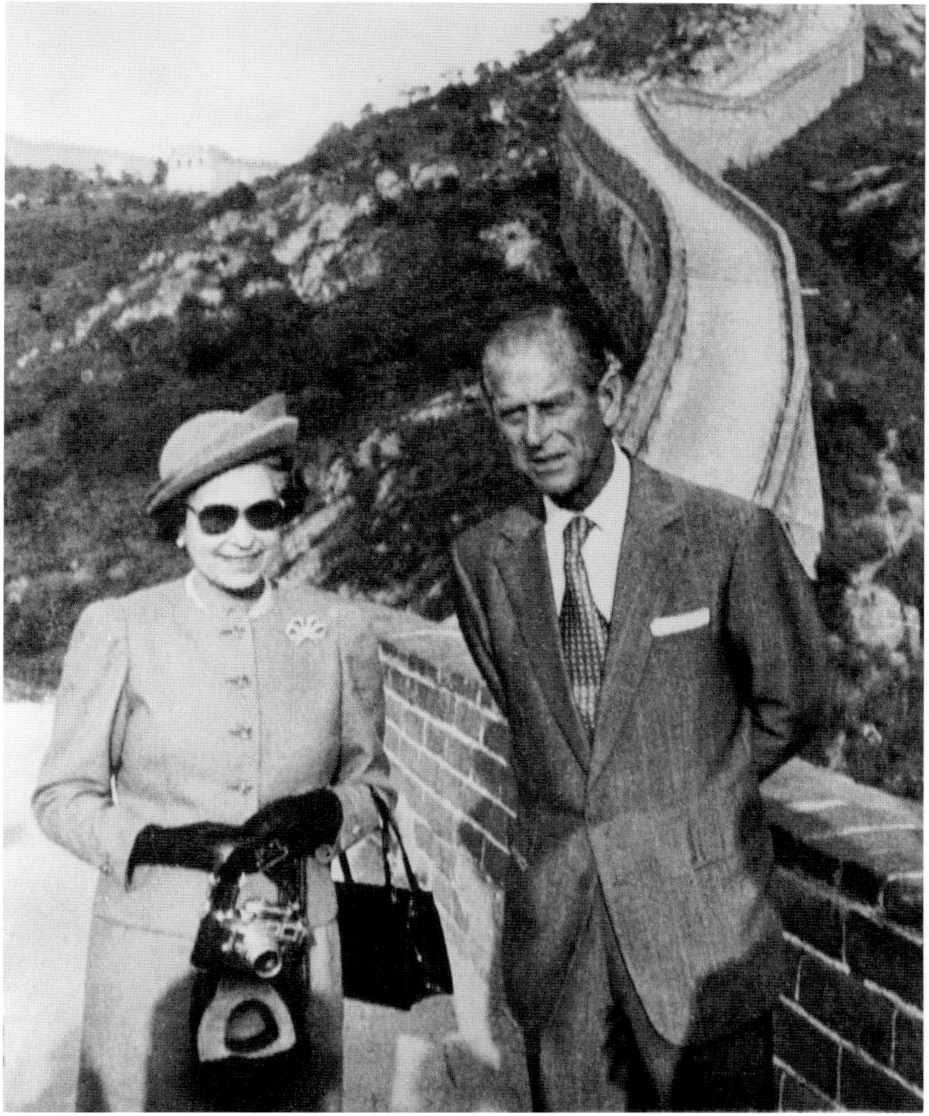

DOCKLANDS LIGHT RAILWAY

By Alan Weller

July 30, 1987

All aboard the new driverless trains! The Queen peers out from the front windscreen of a train on the Docklands Light Railway as the new, automated vehicles come into operation. Running through London's East End to the City, the commuter line was officially opened by the monarch at Poplar station. Seen as a major step in the development of the East End, the service linked 15 stations across an eight-mile stretch of track and opened to passengers the month after the Queen's test drive.

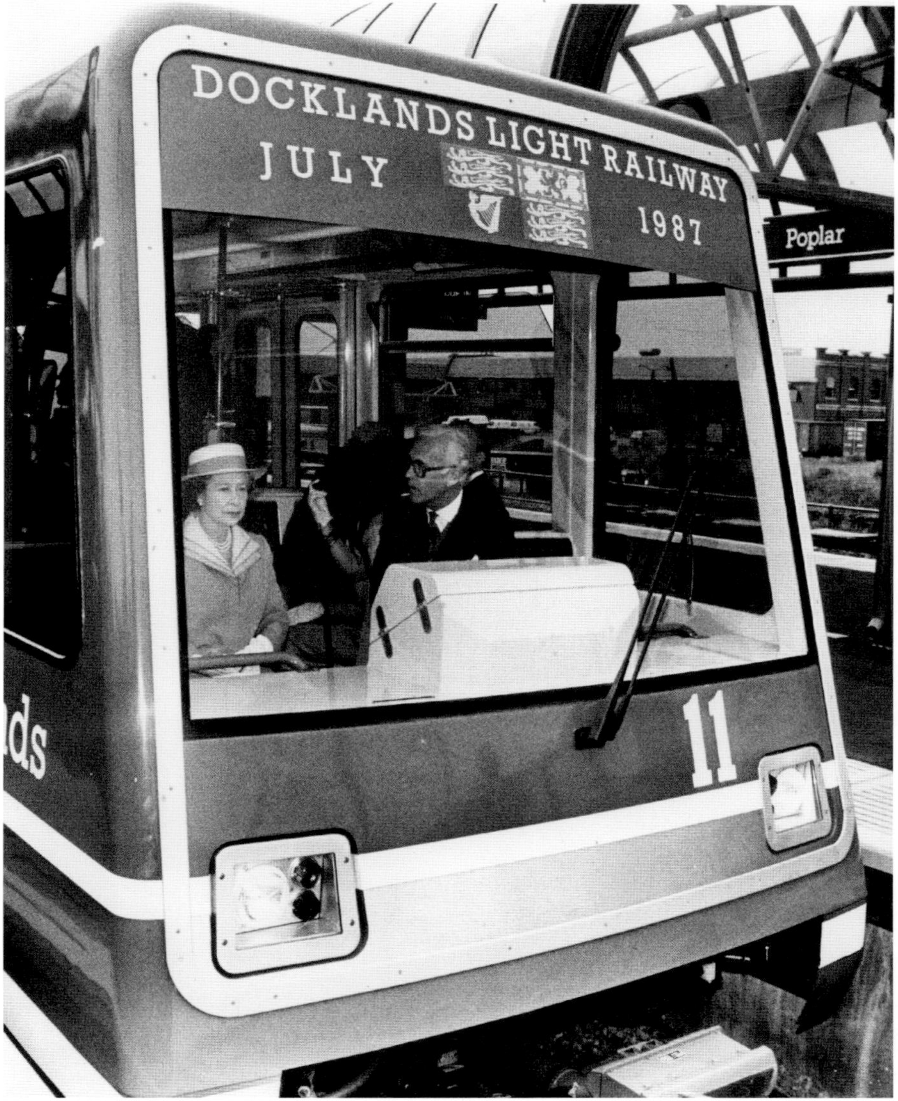
DOCKLANDS LIGHT RAILWAY
JULY
1987
Poplar
11

MEDAL FROM MOTHER

By James Gray

1988

There is a chuckle and a kiss on the hand for his dear mama as the camera captures a charming moment between the Queen and her eldest son. Following a polo match, Charles is thrilled to be awarded a medal by his mother, which the Queen is clearly delighted to present. Sporting events such as this often show the royal family at their most human, whether in the exhilaration of a win or the misery of defeat. Charles played in the defensive number 4 position but later retired from the sport after several injuries.

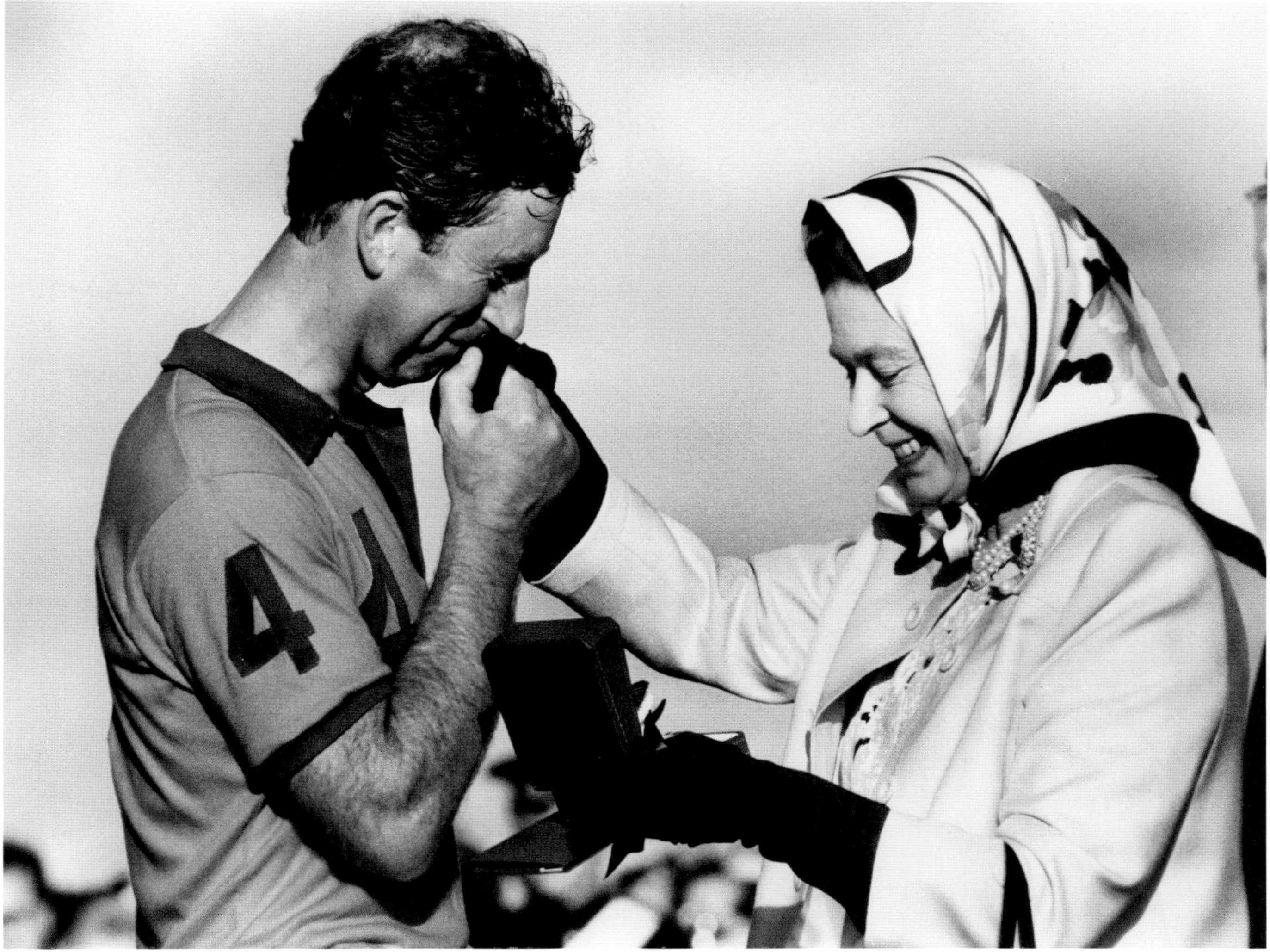
4

FLORAL TRIBUTES FOR DIANA

By Peter Nicholls

September 5, 1997

A sea of floral tributes greeted the Queen and Duke of Edinburgh when they returned from Balmoral to be faced with the public outpouring of grief following the sudden death of Diana, Princess of Wales. Diana's sons Princes William and Harry had been in Scotland with the Queen when they learned the news. What was a family tragedy became a source of extraordinary public grief. After receiving criticism for not returning to London earlier, the Queen made one of her most memorable speeches when she addressed the nation. Her Majesty described Diana as "an exceptional and gifted human being" who "never lost her capacity to smile and laugh, nor to inspire others with her warmth and kindness".

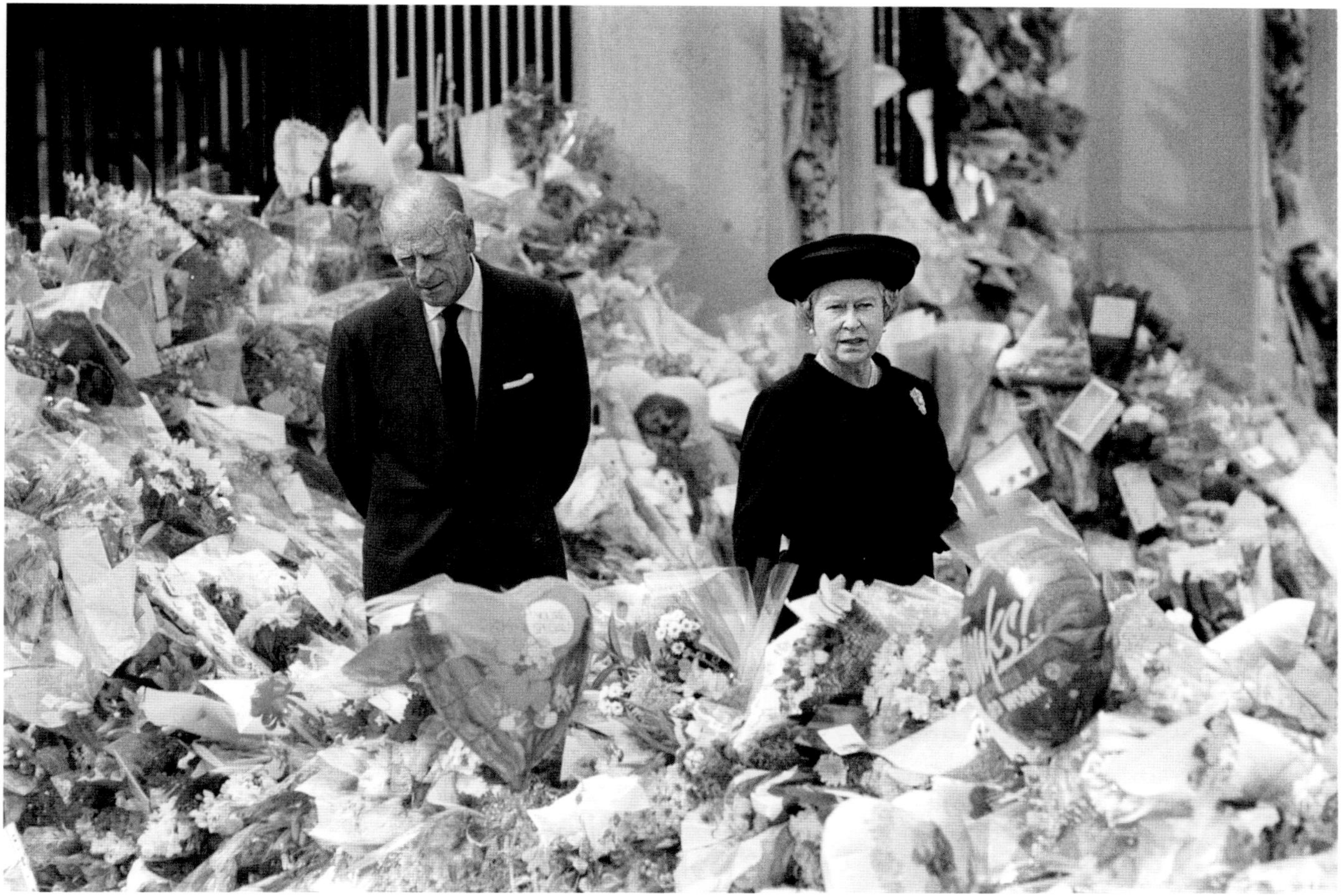

MILLENNIUM NEW YEAR

By Peter Nicholls

December 31, 1999

Ringing in the New Year with a celebration unlike any other, the Queen and Prince Philip have joined Prime Minister Tony Blair, his wife Cherie Blair (both seen here behind the Queen) and other dignitaries at the Millennium Dome. The monarch was seen joining hands with the prime minister and singing *Auld Lang Syne* at midnight, although critics at the time described the event as "excruciating" and "a disaster", reporting that the Queen would have preferred to mark the turn of the century privately.
Now known as the O2 arena, the white dome-shaped structure with yellow support towers was constructed in Greenwich to host The Millennium Experience exhibition.

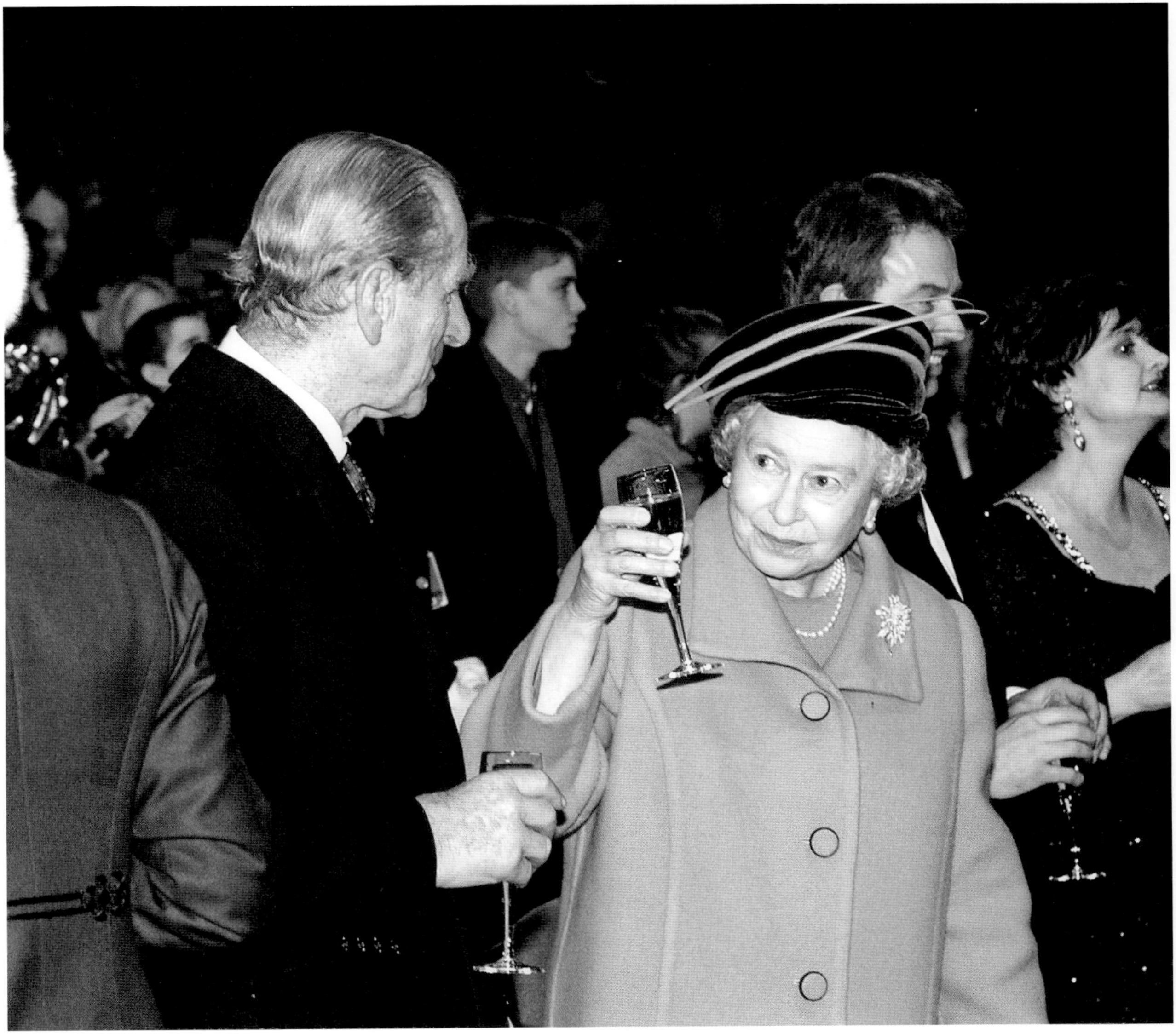

IMPERIAL WAR MUSEUM

By Simon Walker

June 6, 2000

With smiles, flowers and a deep desire to herald a brighter future, the Queen met Holocaust survivors as she opened a new exhibition at the Imperial War Museum in London that had taken four years to assemble. The Queen's cousin, the Duke of Kent, president of Imperial War Museum Trustees, described the exhibition which details the Nazi persecution of the Jews as one of its "most important developments". "Accurate information is needed to prevent myths and misconceptions from proliferating, and to ensure that the important lessons that need to be learned from the Holocaust are not distorted or derailed," he said.

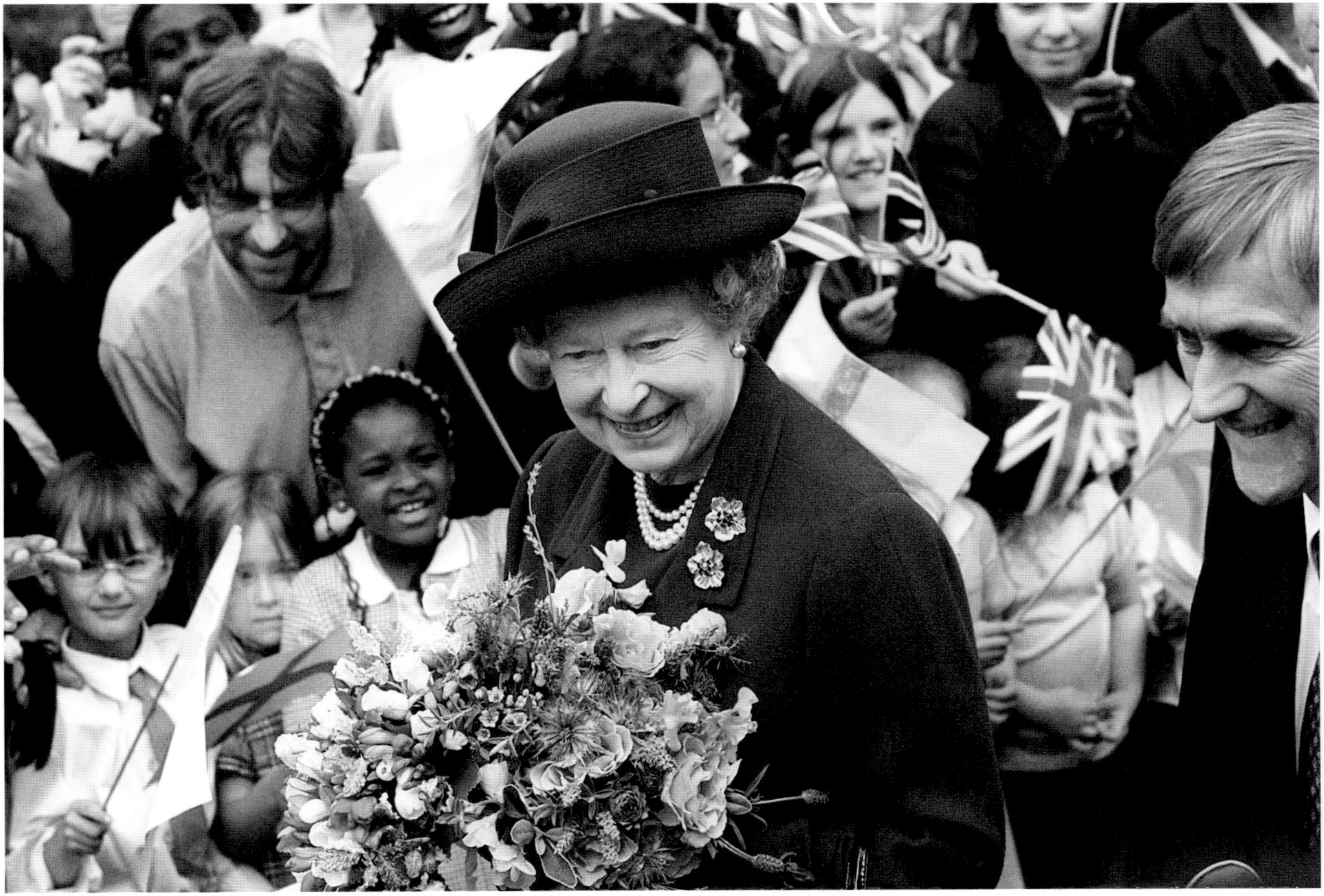

LOOK UP!

By Richard Pohle

October 17, 2000

Looking up with wonder, the Queen admires the ceiling of the Sistine Chapel during a visit to the Vatican. The official state visit to the Holy See in Italy saw Elizabeth II, head of the Church of England, hold a private audience with Pope John Paul II. During the historic meeting the Queen, accompanied by Prince Philip, discussed the peace process in Northern Ireland and exchanged gifts. The trip marked the 20th anniversary of the monarch's first official visit to the Vatican.

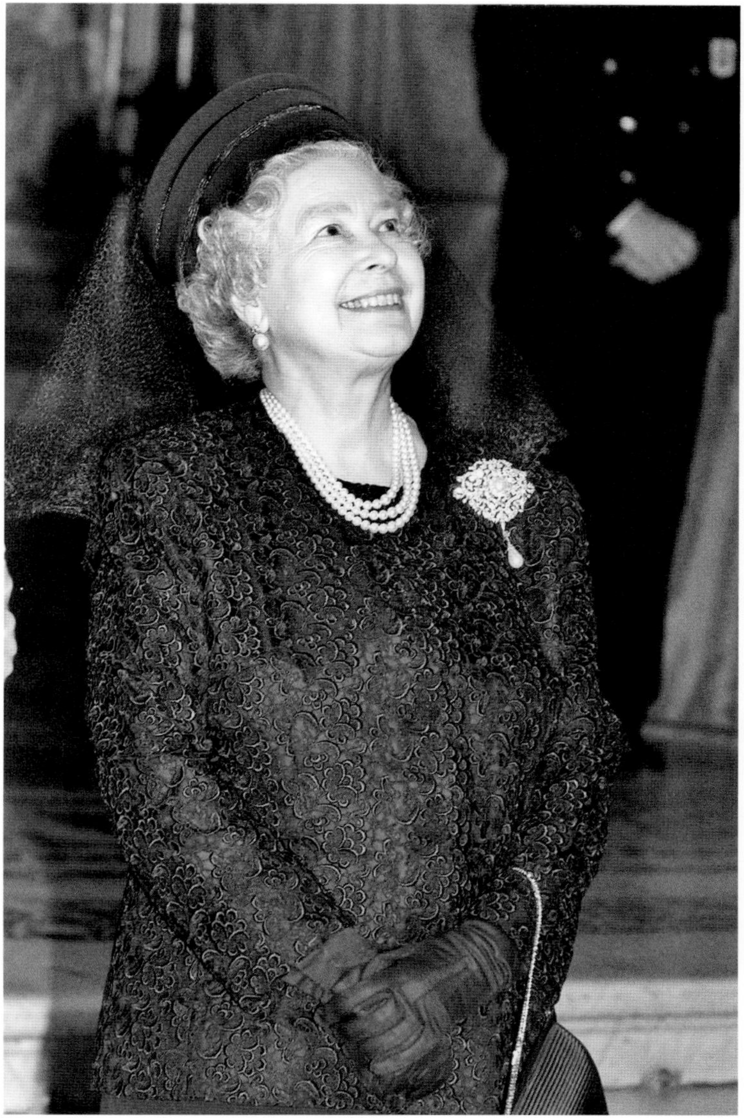

MAUNDY SERVICE

By Richard Pohle

March 28, 2002

Showing her wit and sense of fun, the Queen meets members of the cathedral choral choir at Canterbury Cathedral and pretends to conduct their singing. The visit came as part of the traditional Maundy service at the cathedral. Later, in 2015, statues of the Queen and Prince Philip wearing their Garter robes were unveiled at the cathedral, which were commissioned in honour of the Diamond Jubilee in 2012.

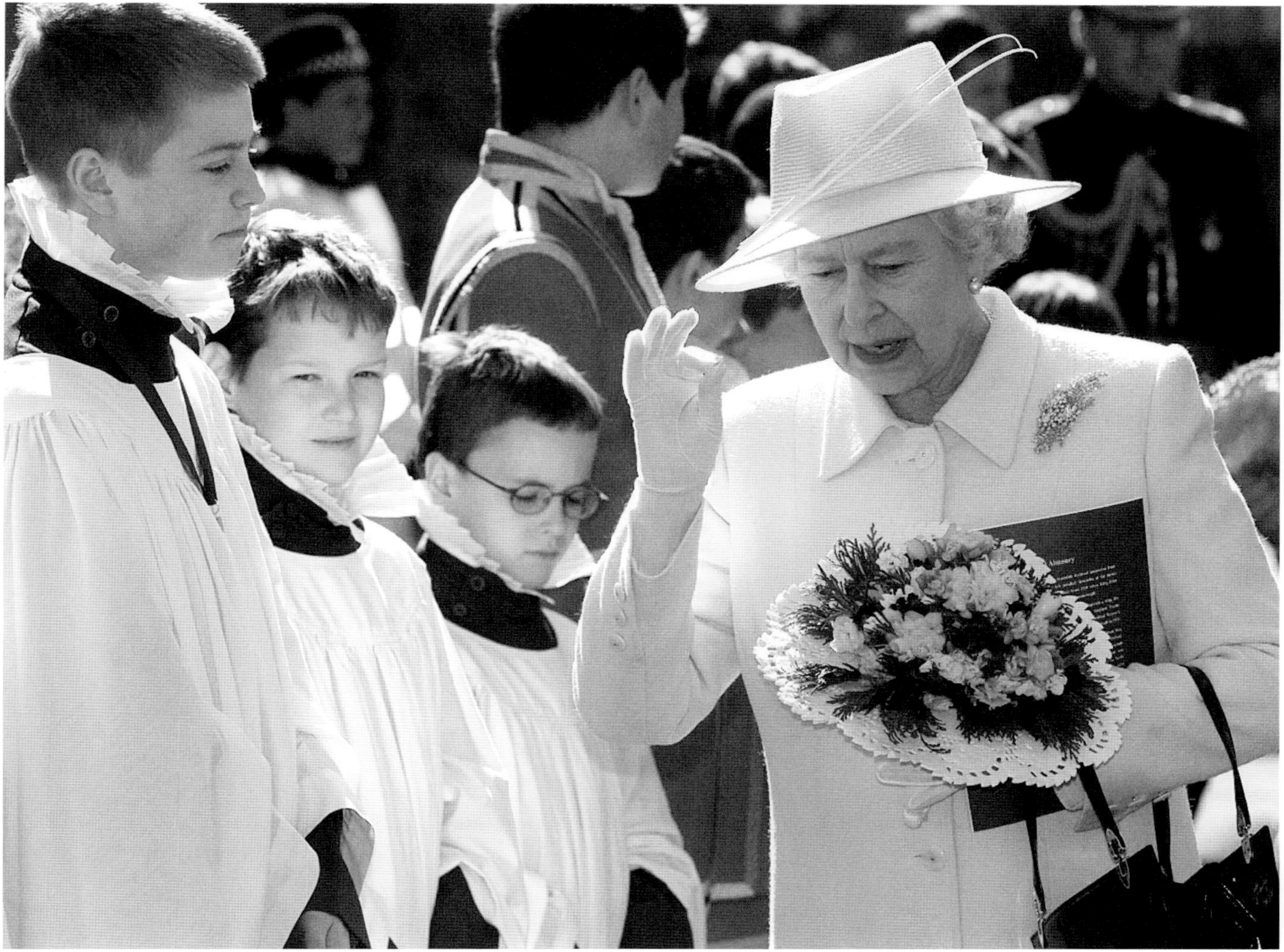

QUEEN MOTHER'S FUNERAL

By Chris Harris

April 9, 2002

After the state funeral of the Queen Mother at Westminster Abbey, the Queen and Prince Charles follow behind the coffin as it is taken out to the royal hearse. With a sombre look of grief etched on the monarch's face, she stares straight ahead as if lost in thought. The death of her mother came just two months after that of her younger sister, Princess Margaret, who died on February 9. In her Christmas broadcast later that year, she said: "Many of you will know only too well from your own experience the grief that follows the death of a much-loved mother or sister."

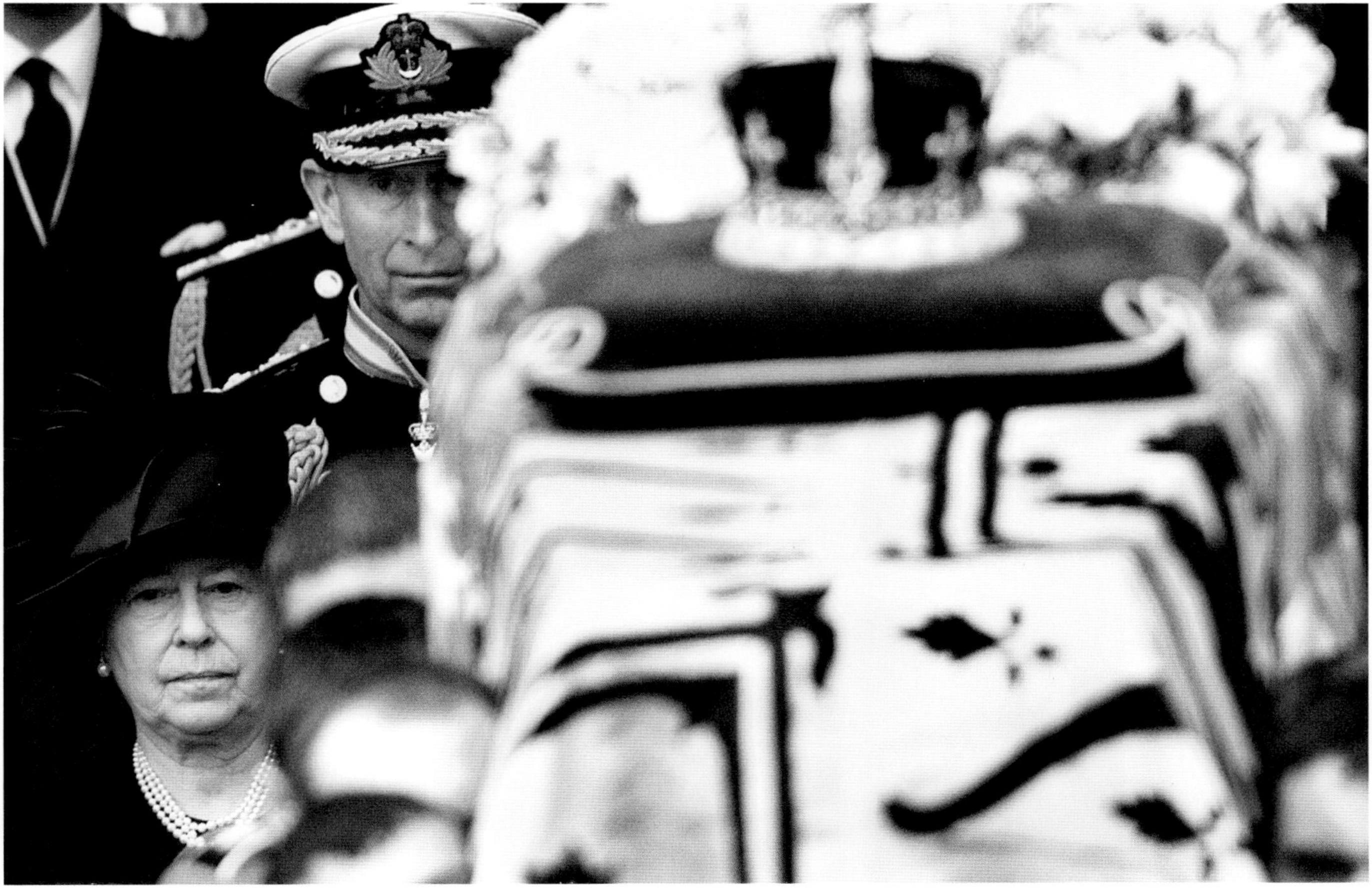

GOLDEN JUBILEE

By Ben Gurr

June 4, 2002

After half a century on the throne, the Queen celebrated her Golden Jubilee with a spectacular weekend of events. A flypast, featuring 27 aircraft including Concorde and the Red Arrows, proved to be a spectacular finale to the celebrations. Members of the royal family crowded onto the balcony of Buckingham Palace to watch the display as it passed overhead. Down on the Mall, an estimated one million people thronged the streets, joining together with one voice to sing renditions of *Land of Hope and Glory* and the national anthem.

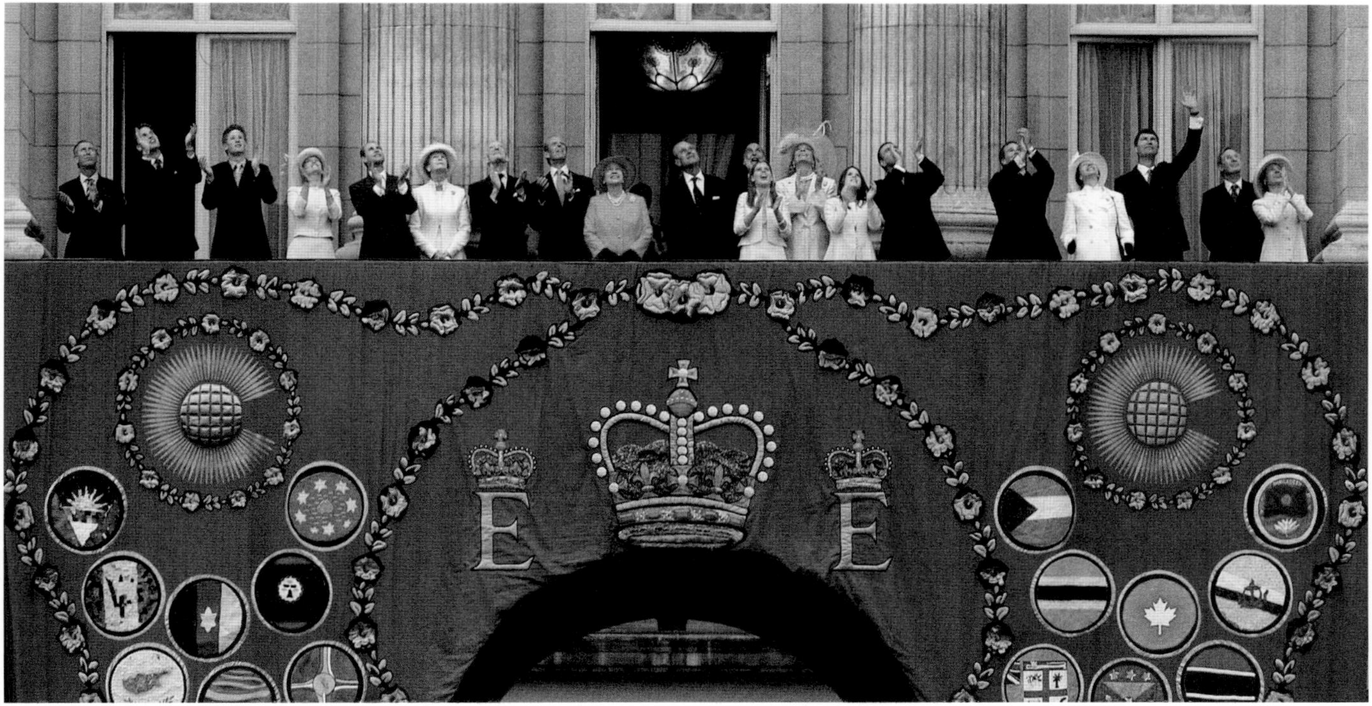
E
E

ROYAL ALBERT HALL

By Richard Pohle

March 30, 2004

Peering round a pillar at the Royal Albert Hall, the Queen visits the concert venue to herald the completion of an eight-year restoration project. New facilities were built by excavating the basement, and more legroom was created for the audience. Synonymous with Queen Victoria's consort, Prince Albert, the concert hall is intrinsically linked to the royal family and performs a central role in Remembrance Day events and other important social occasions.

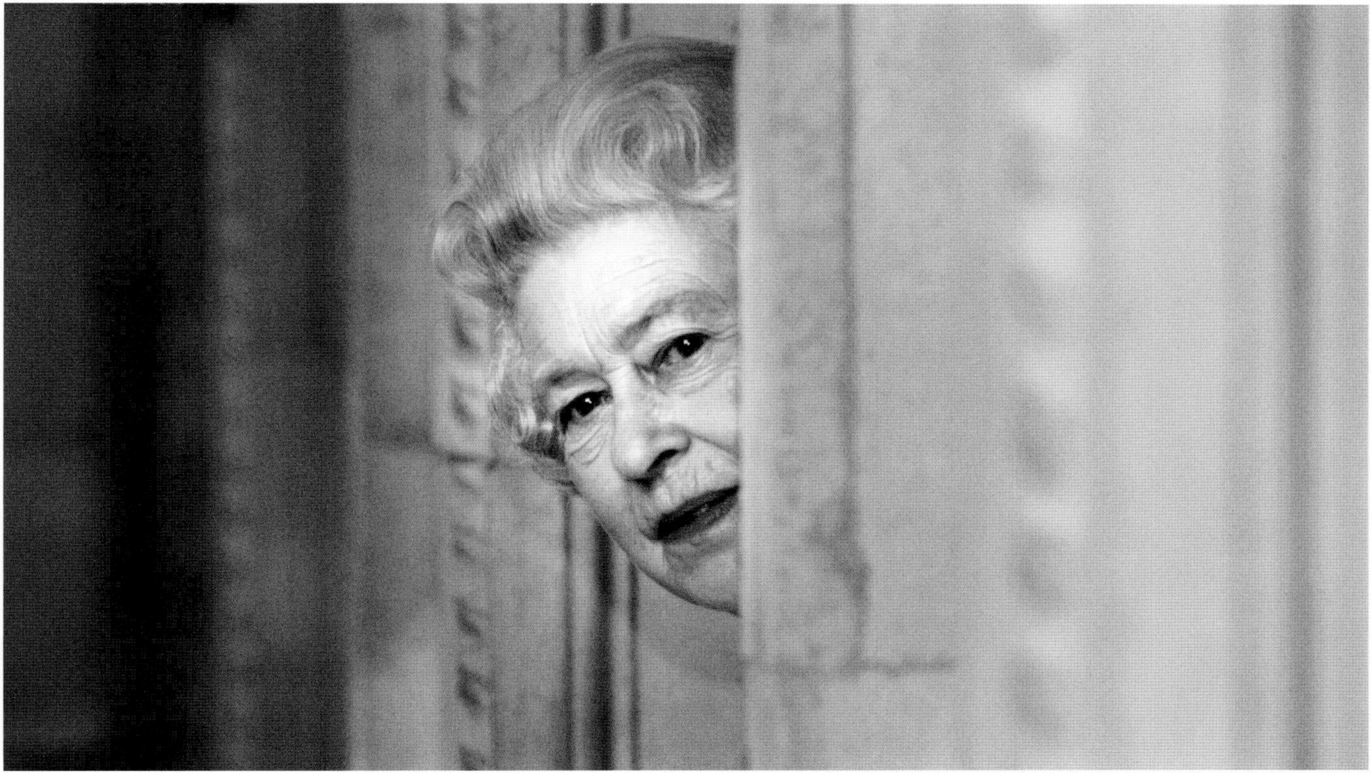

SECOND WORLD WAR VETERANS' MARCH

By Gill Allen

July 10, 2005

Commemorating 60 years since of the end of the Second World War, the Queen and Prince Philip wave to the public from an open-topped Range Rover. On July 10, a national event was held at Horse Guards Parade in central London. The Queen, accompanied by Prince Philip, was the focal point of the day as she took part in a procession featuring the Massed Bands of the British Army, RAF and Royal Navy. Afterwards, the royal family joined together on the balcony of Buckingham Palace in a scene reminiscent of the VE Day celebrations in 1945.

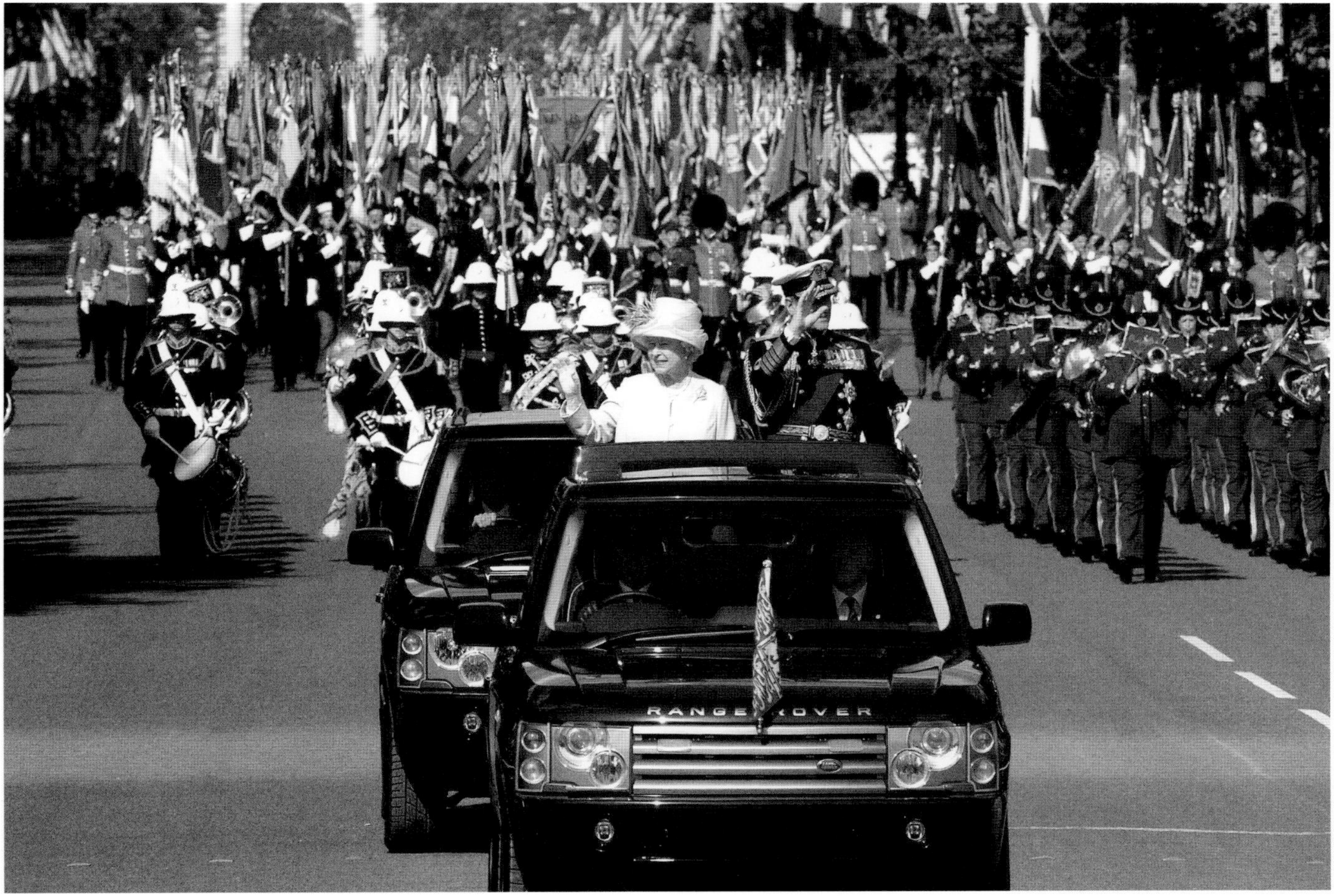
RANGE ROVER

HARRY ON PARADE

By Richard Pohle

April 12, 2006

I'm sure I recognise that face! We may never know what has just been said but the Queen's remark is enough to make Prince Harry's face crack into a broad grin as his grandmother inspects the troops. Trying unsuccessfully to hide his smile, the Prince, at the age of 21, is taking part in his passing out ceremony at Sandhurst military academy. Harry was commissioned into the Household Cavalry after completing his course. The Queen addressed the newly qualified military recruits before following the parade into the college.

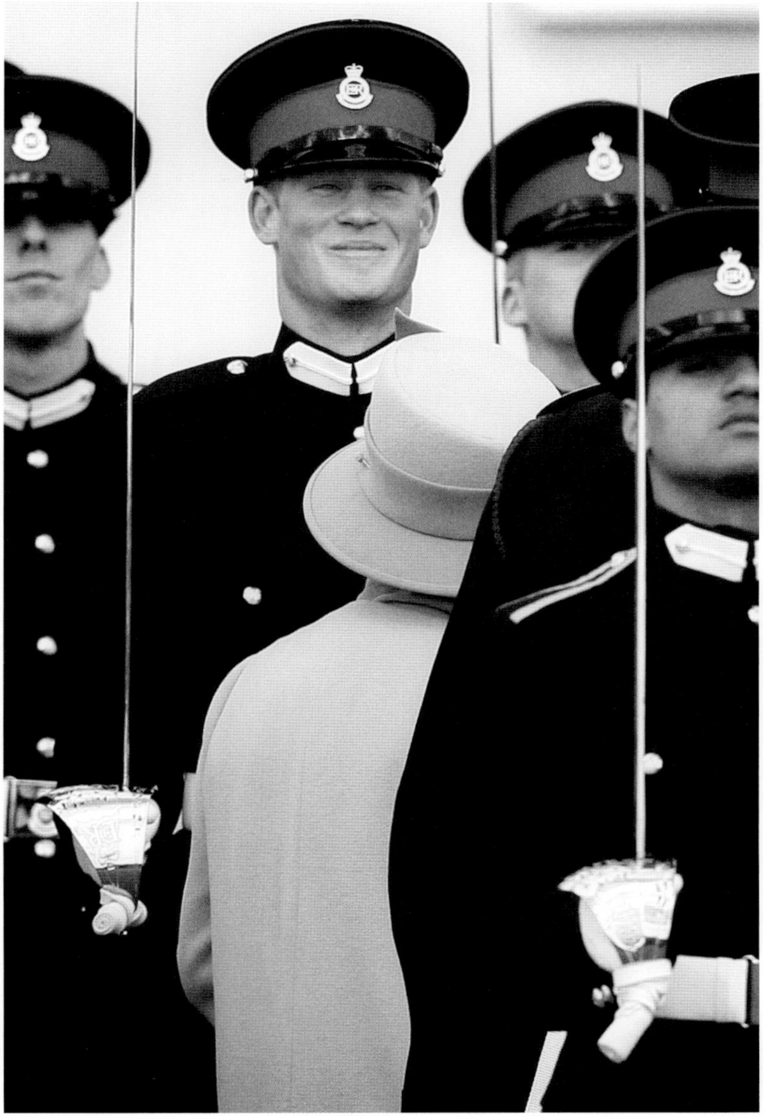

80TH BIRTHDAY CELEBRATIONS

By Chris Harris

April 21, 2006

With a joyful smile and a royal wave, the Queen greets the public in Windsor town centre on her 80th birthday. The monarch, dressed in red, spent time walking around the town, stopping to shake hands and speak to members of the public who had turned out to wish her a happy birthday. To mark the landmark birthday, events were held at Windsor Castle and Buckingham Palace, where the Queen hosted a lunch for other people who were celebrating their 80th birthday on the same day. Services of thanksgiving were held at St Paul's Cathedral and St George's Chapel, Windsor.

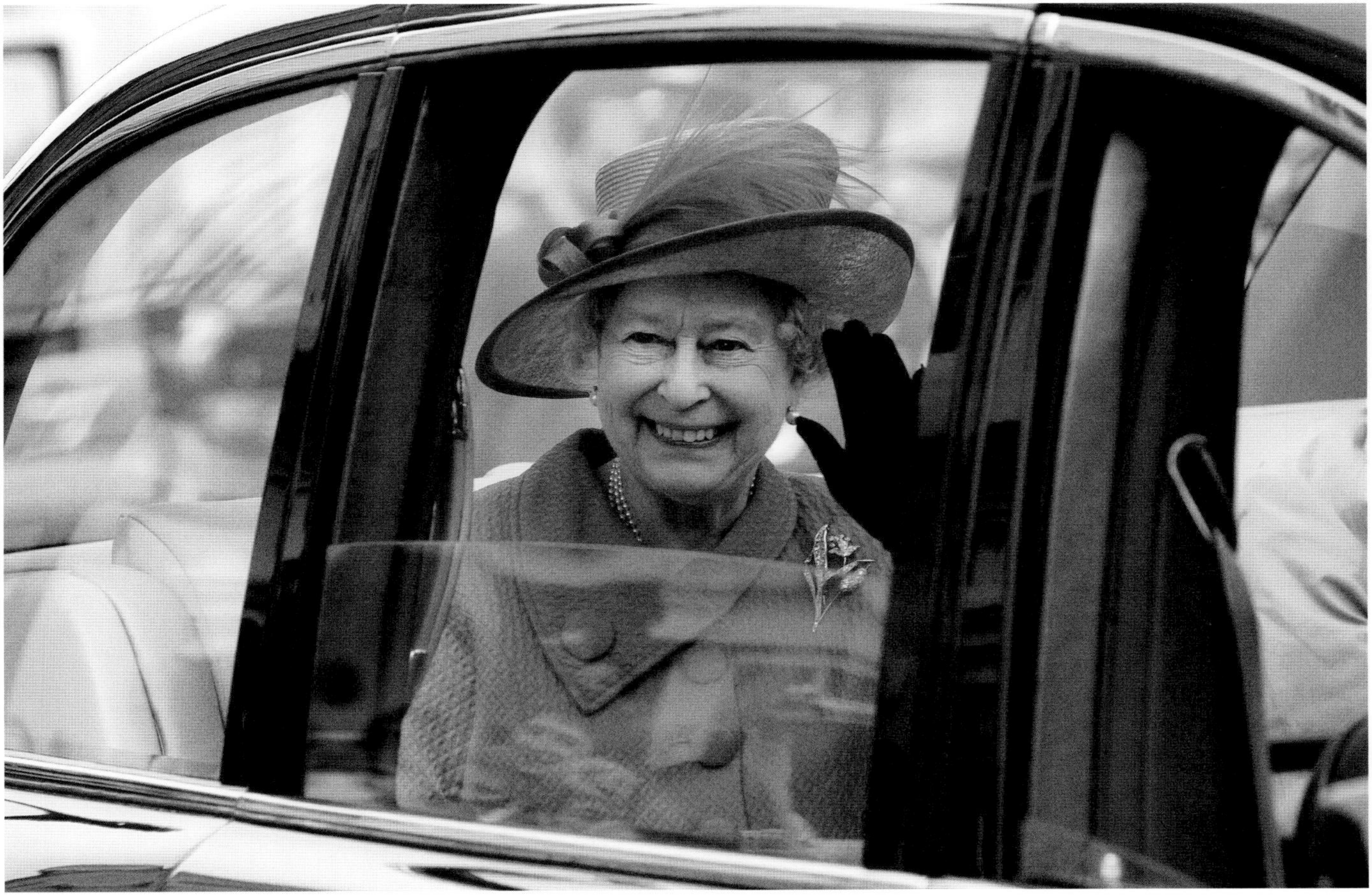

THE DIAMOND COUPLE

By Richard Pohle

November 19, 2007

The Queen and Prince Philip return to Westminster Abbey for a service of thanksgiving on the occasion of their diamond wedding anniversary. Six decades after their wedding at the abbey, a special service was designed for the royal couple. They were joined by 2,000 guests for a celebration in which they renewed their vows in a blessing. It was a historic moment for the monarchy as well as a time for personal reflection, because Elizabeth II was the first monarch to reach this milestone.

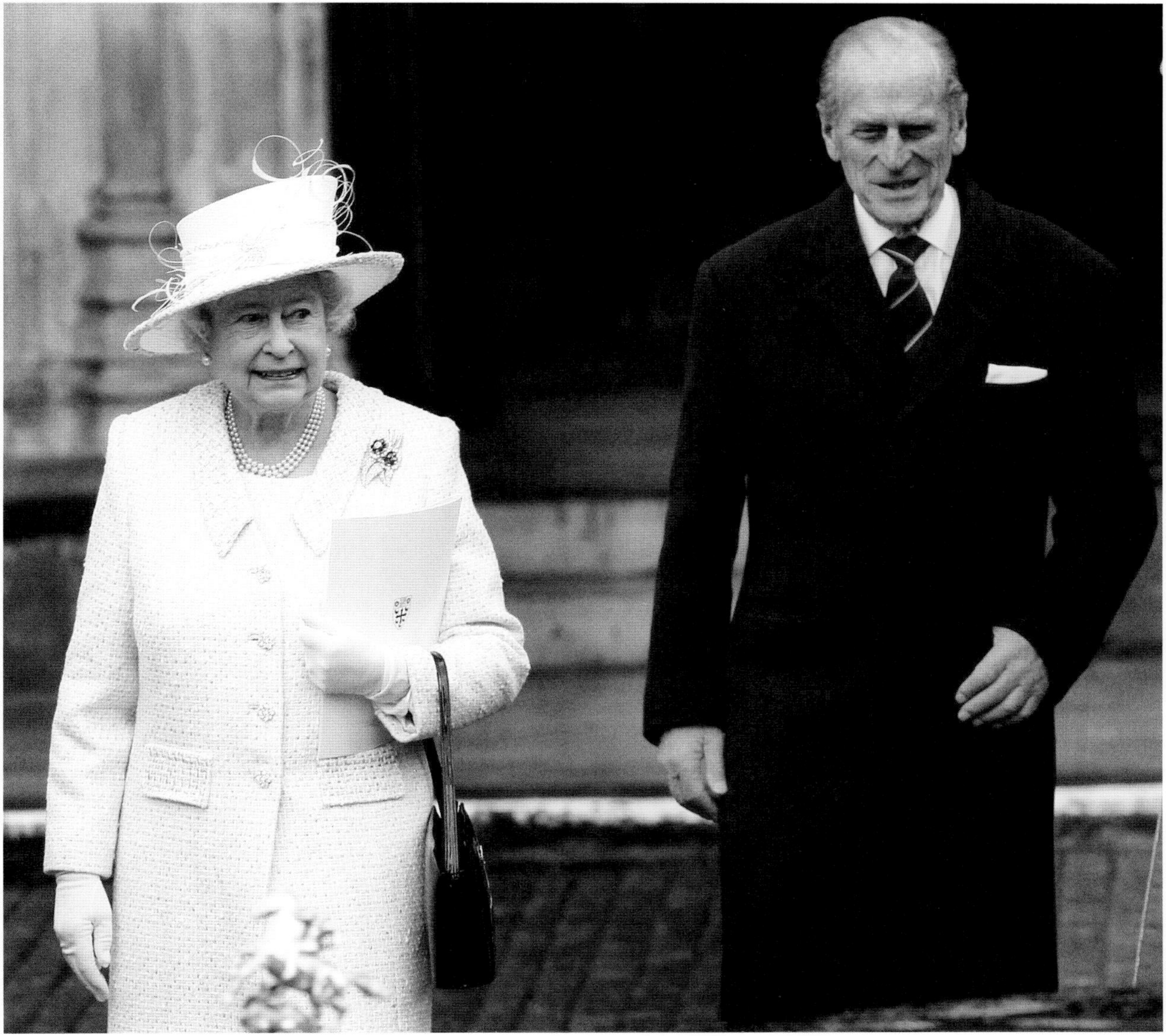

INSPECTING THE TROOPS

By Peter Nicholls

November 21, 2007

Arriving in Uganda, the Queen inspects a guard of honour comprised of soldiers from the African nation's army. The Queen was in the country for a state visit ahead of the biannual Commonwealth Heads of Government Meeting. In a speech to acknowledge the "transforming societies" theme of the conference, the Queen said that "recognising that each one of us is made up of layer upon layer of identity and that each of our unique personalities has ties to culture, religion, community, country and beyond, is the essence of open and tolerant communities."

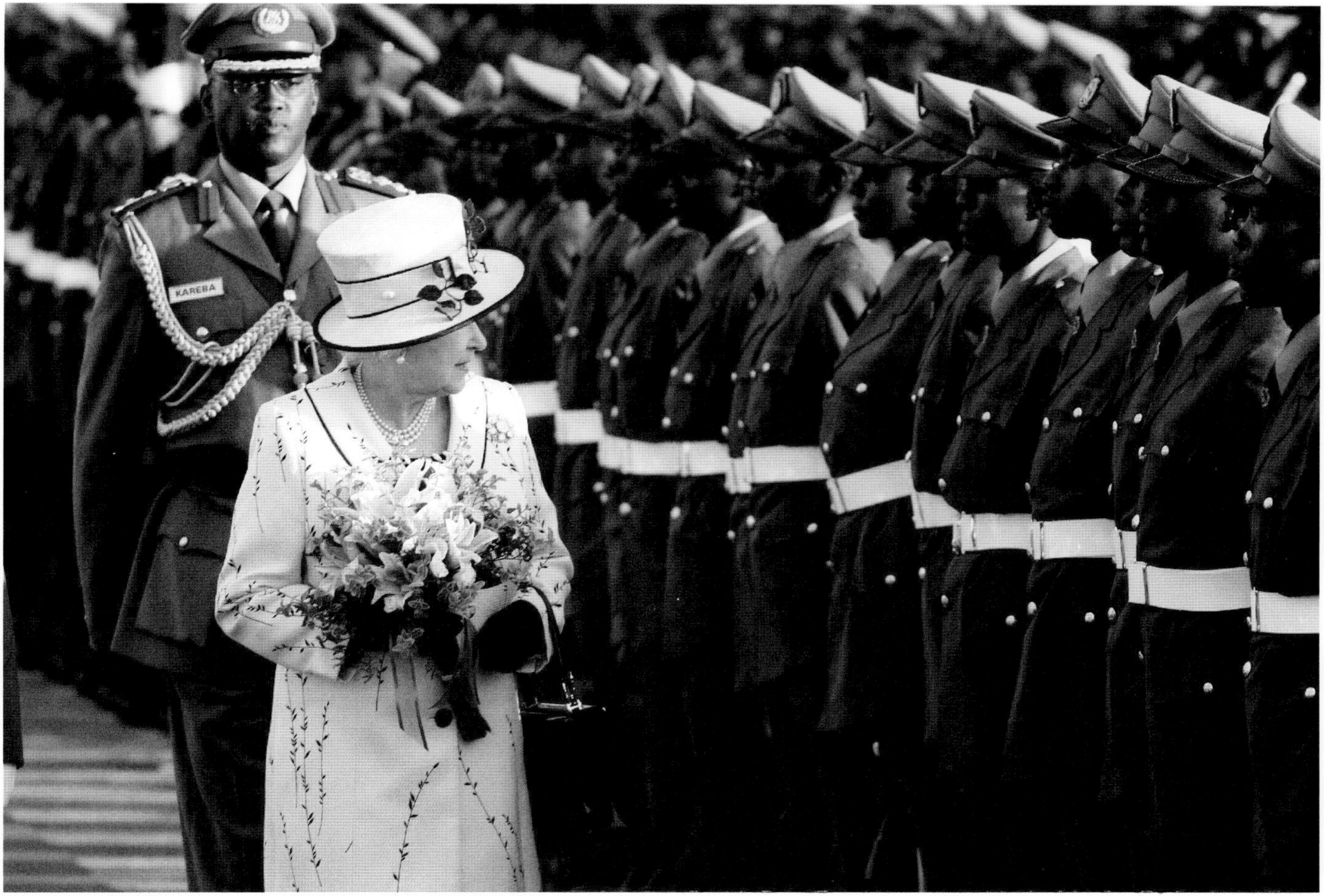
KAREBA

SEABIRD CENTRE

By James Glossop

July 2, 2009

Say cheese! A small child raises a camera to capture the moment that the Queen and Prince Philip pass by in the royal car. The Duke lifts a hand to wave while the Queen looks towards the crowds on the other side of their vehicle. The royal couple had just departed the Scottish Seabird Centre in North Berwick, Scotland. It was the first visit to the region by a reigning monarch since 1902 and their arrival brought crowds of well-wishers out onto the streets to witness the occasion in the bright summer sunshine.

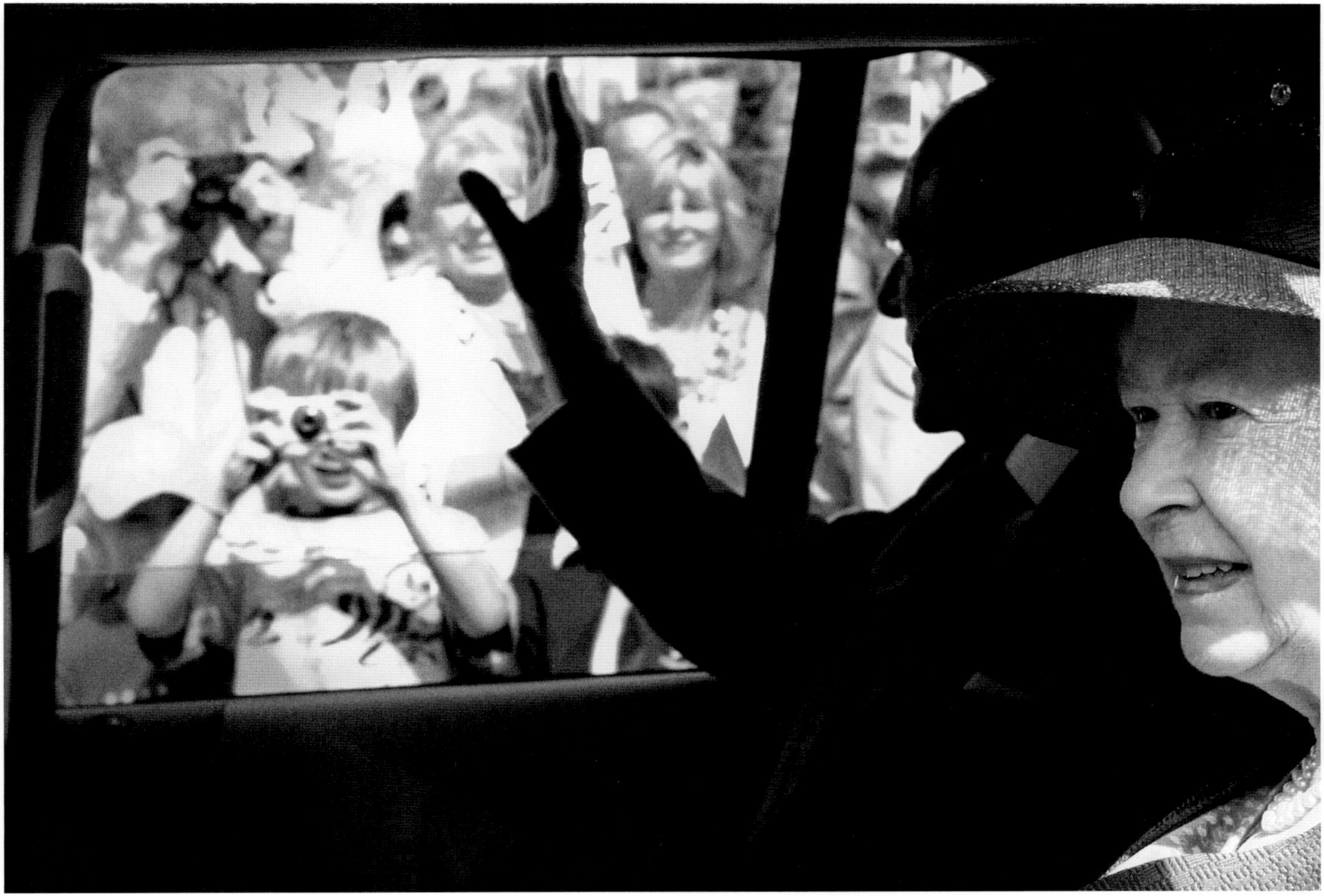

ARMISTICE DAY

By Richard Pohle

November 11, 2009

When the Queen and Prince Philip marked Armistice Day in 2009, the few had undoubtedly become the fewer. Gathering in Westminster Abbey, the Queen and Prince Philip paid tribute to the passing of the First World War generation by singing hymns. The last surviving British veterans of the war had died earlier that year, making the service particularly poignant. The image captures a moment of sombre reflection for the Queen who is wearing a cluster of poppies.

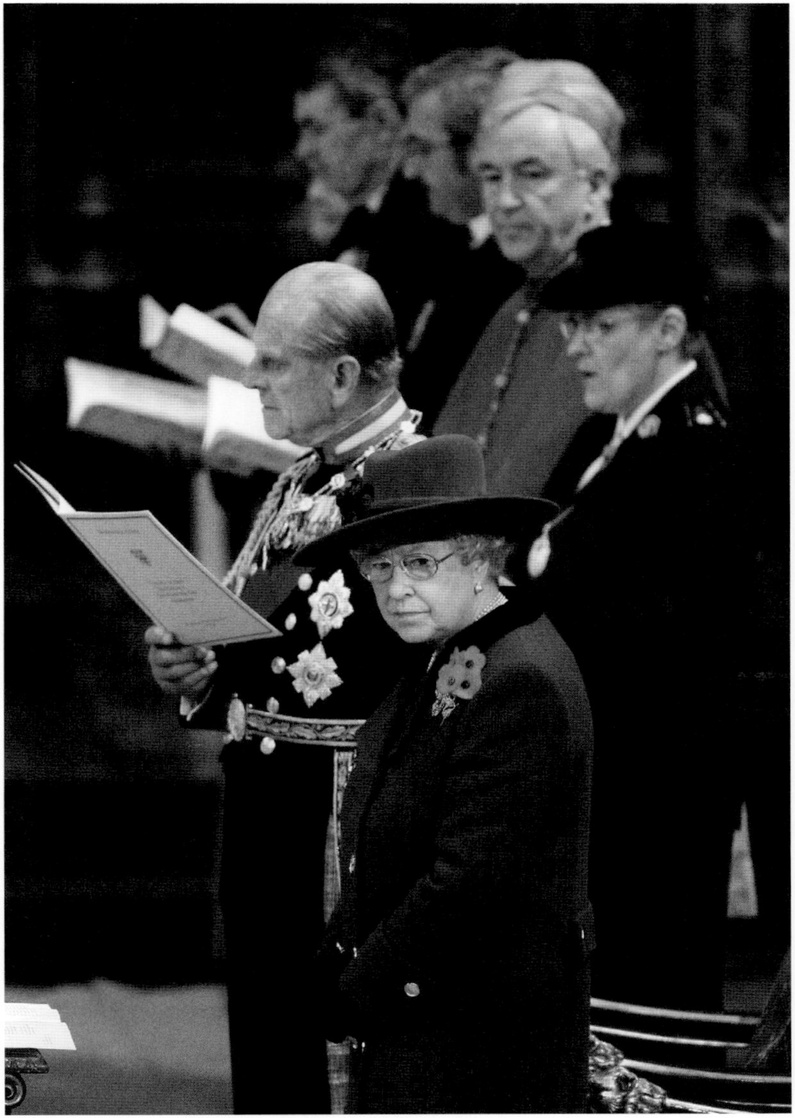

HMS ARK ROYAL

By Richard Pohle

November 5, 2010

Quite what has just been said to elicit such a mischievous grin on the Queen's face is anyone's guess. But there's no doubt that the moment not only captured the monarch's sense of humour but also her deep affection for the Senior Service of the British Armed Forces as she sat beside Captain Jerry Kyd, commanding officer of HMS Ark Royal (on the Queen's left) and Admiral Sir Trevor Soar (on Her Majesty's right). The Queen boarded the Ark Royal to celebrate the aircraft carrier's 25th anniversary. The month beforehand, it was announced that the ship would be scrapped as part of a defence review.

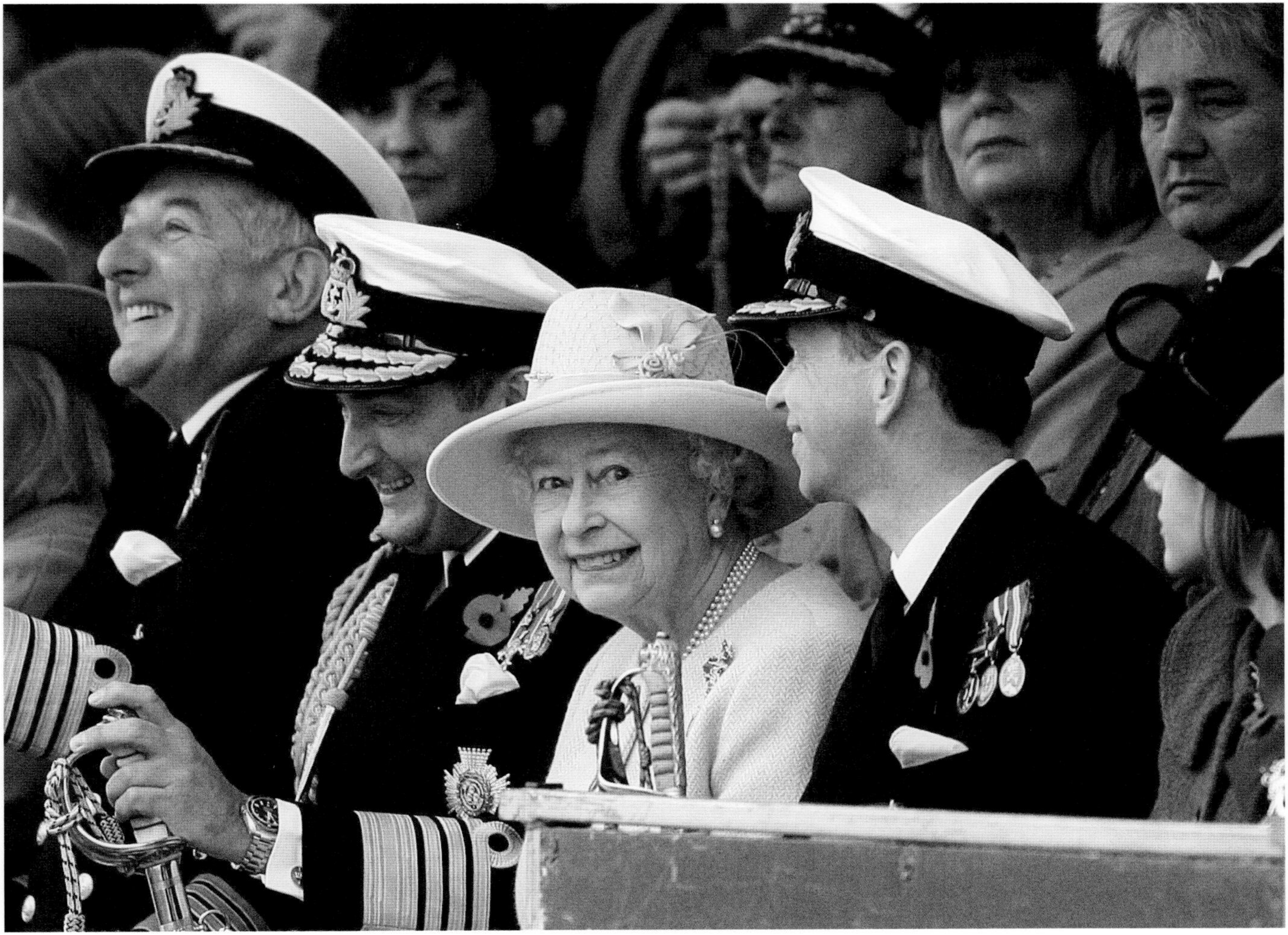

ROYAL WEDDING OF PRINCE WILLIAM AND KATE MIDDLETON

By Marc Aspland

April 29, 2011

Newlyweds Prince William and Kate Middleton kiss on the Buckingham Palace balcony after marrying at Westminster Abbey. The Queen, who had conferred upon them the titles of Duke and Duchess of Cambridge, looks on proudly as the public applaud the couple. On the left of the picture, Charles and Camilla, then the Duke and Duchess of Cornwall, take part in the happy day. As the crowds on the Mall cheer with approval and a flypast roars overhead, little bridesmaid Grace van Cutsem clamps her hands over her ears to cover the din.

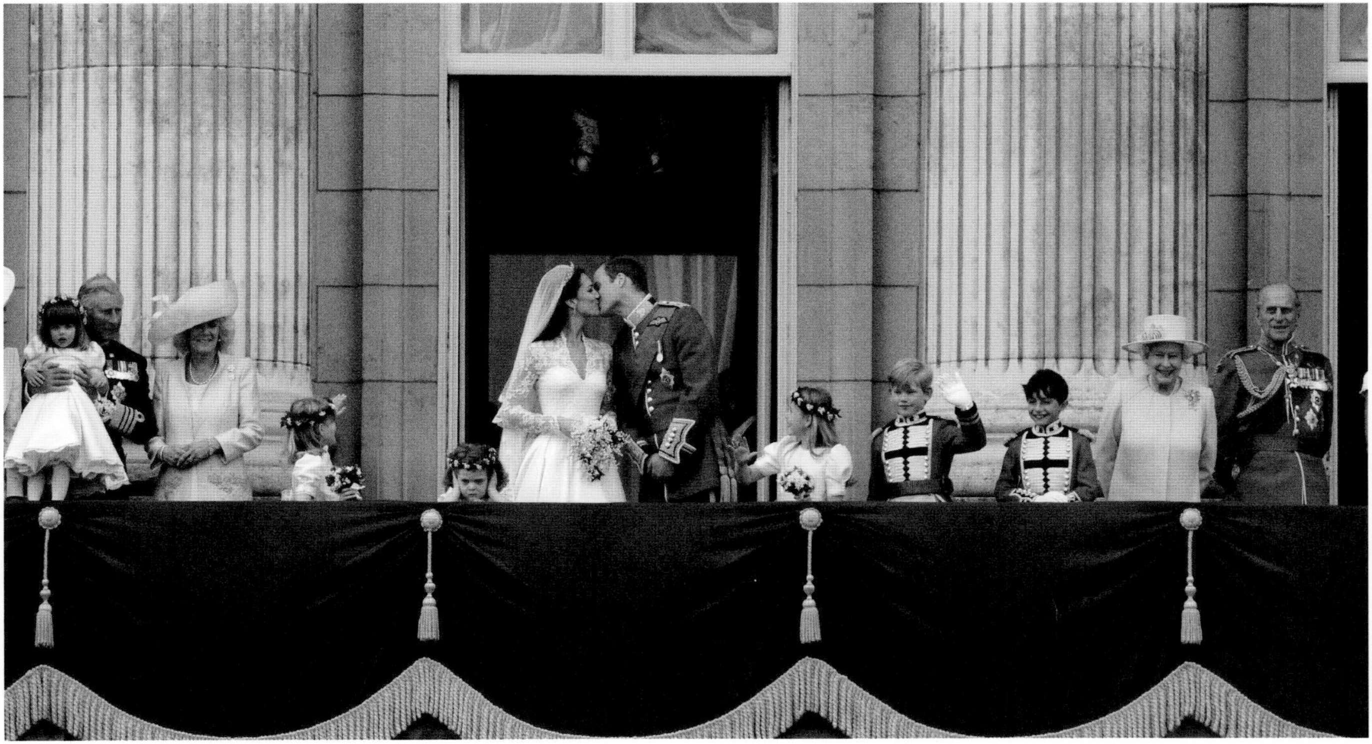

PASSING THE BATON

By Richard Pohle

October 8, 2013

The Queen places a sealed, secret message into the Commonwealth Games baton in the forecourt of Buckingham Palace, watched by Prince Imran of Malaysia and Lord Smith of Kelvin, chairman of Glasgow's 2014 games. Elizabeth II's handwritten note to the Commonwealth travelled more than 100,000 miles across all 70 competing nations and territories over 288 days before arriving in Scotland for the Games. At the opening ceremony on July 23, 2014, the Queen said: "To you, the Commonwealth athletes, I send my good wishes for success in your endeavours. Your accomplishments over the coming days will encourage us all to strengthen the bonds that unite us."

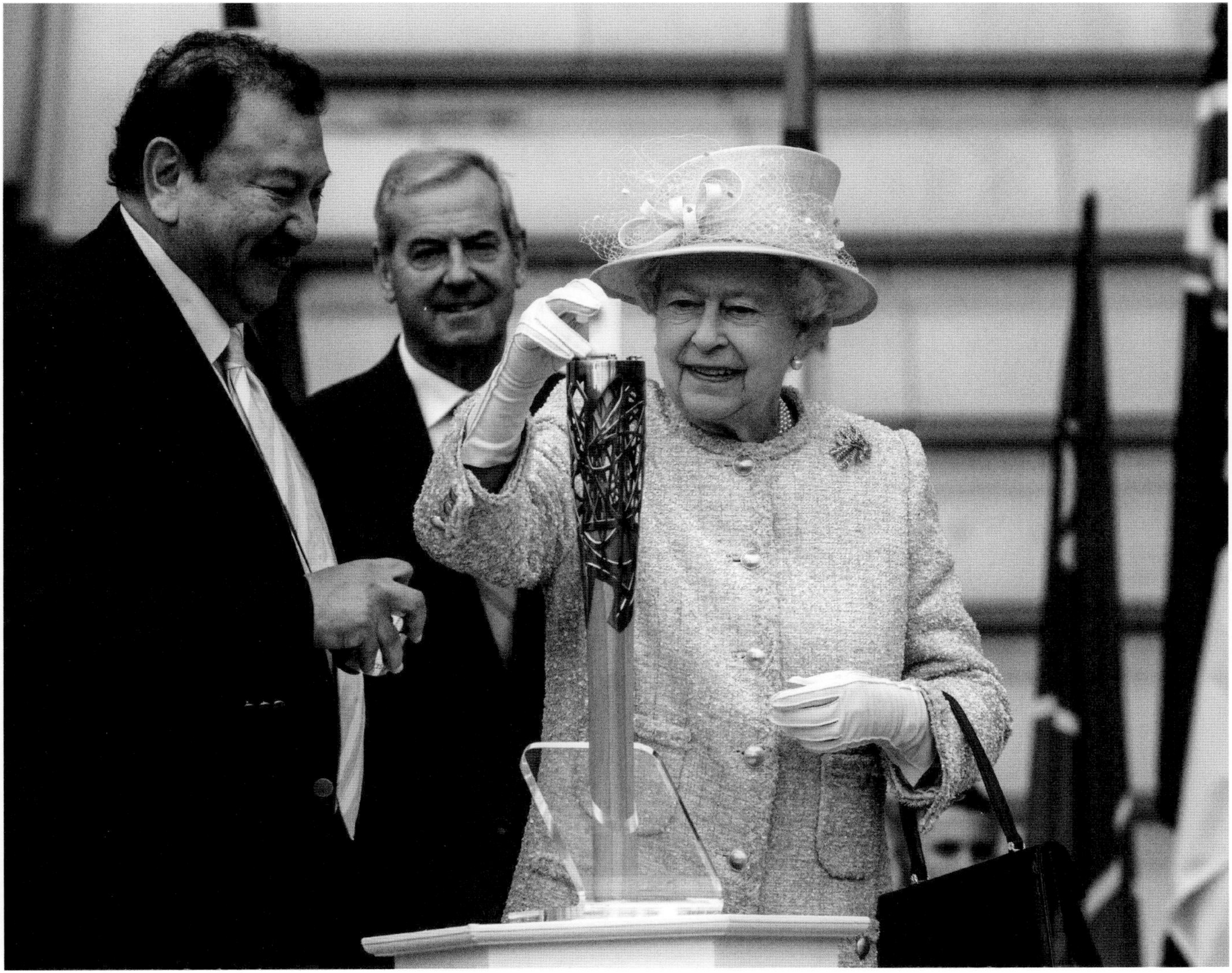

POPPIES AT THE TOWER OF LONDON

By Jack Hill

October 16, 2014

Walking through a river of poppies, the Queen and Prince Philip view the "Blood Swept Lands and Seas of Red". The installation at the Tower of London to mark the centenary of the outbreak of the First World War filled the moat of the Tower with 888,246 ceramic poppies, representing one for every British and Colonial military life lost during the war. It was the product of a collaboration between artist Paul Cummins and designer Tom Piper in which they paid tribute to the fallen.

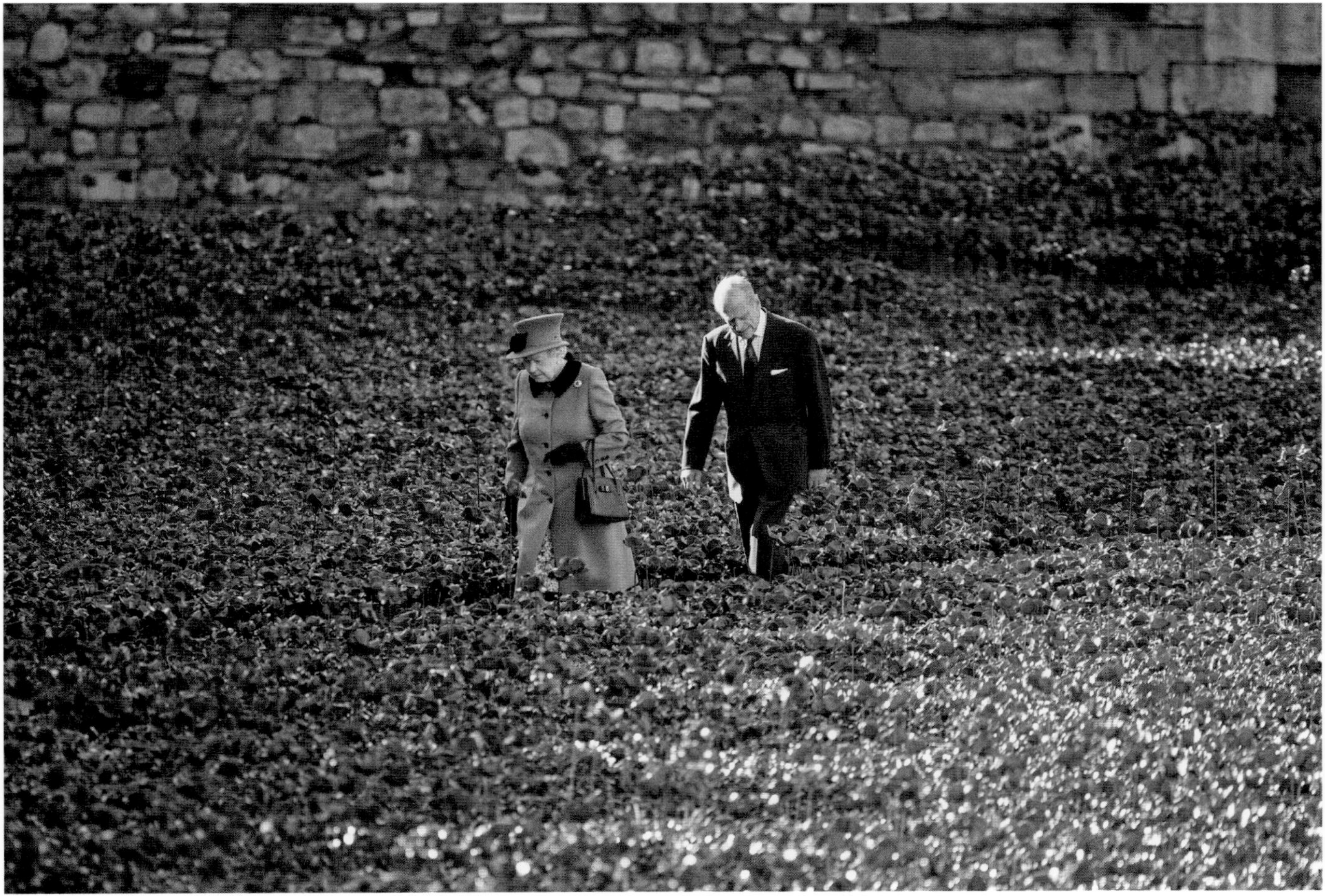

THE ELIZABETH LINE

By Richard Pohle

February 22, 2016

After the Jubilee Line, there was another London transport link named in honour of Britain's longest-serving monarch: the Elizabeth Line. Running right across London, the Crossrail project was renamed during the Queen's visit to the construction site at Bond Street station, where she is seen holding a commemorative plaque.
Her Majesty officially opened the line on May 18, 2022.

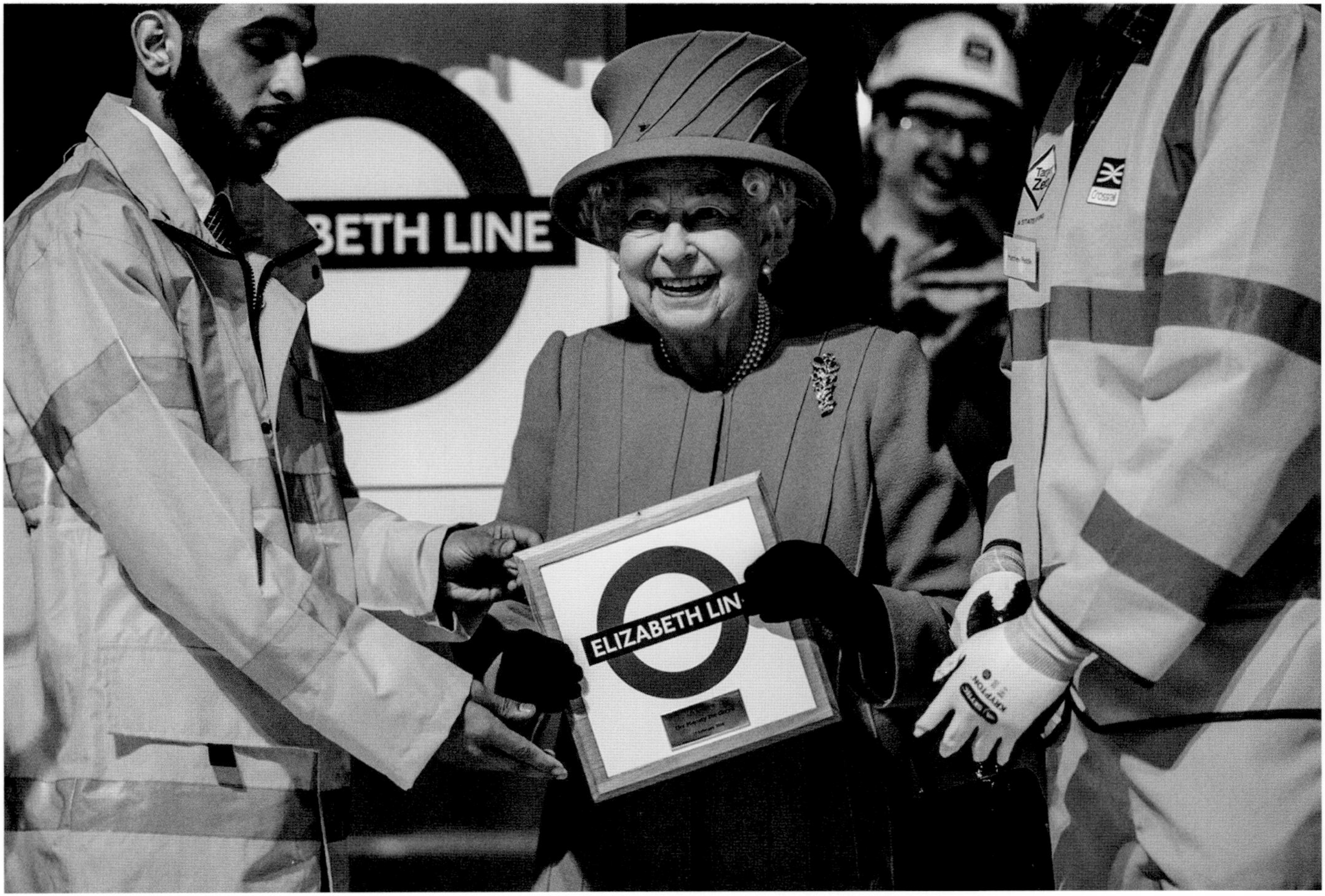
BETH LINE
ELIZABETH LIN

90TH BIRTHDAY CELEBRATIONS

By Richard Pohle

April 21, 2016

Becoming the first British monarch to turn 90, the Queen greets crowds lining the streets outside Windsor Castle. Wellwishers arrived in their thousands, waving flags and offering posies to the nonagenarian sovereign on her landmark birthday. Gun salutes were fired in London and Windsor to acknowledge the special day.

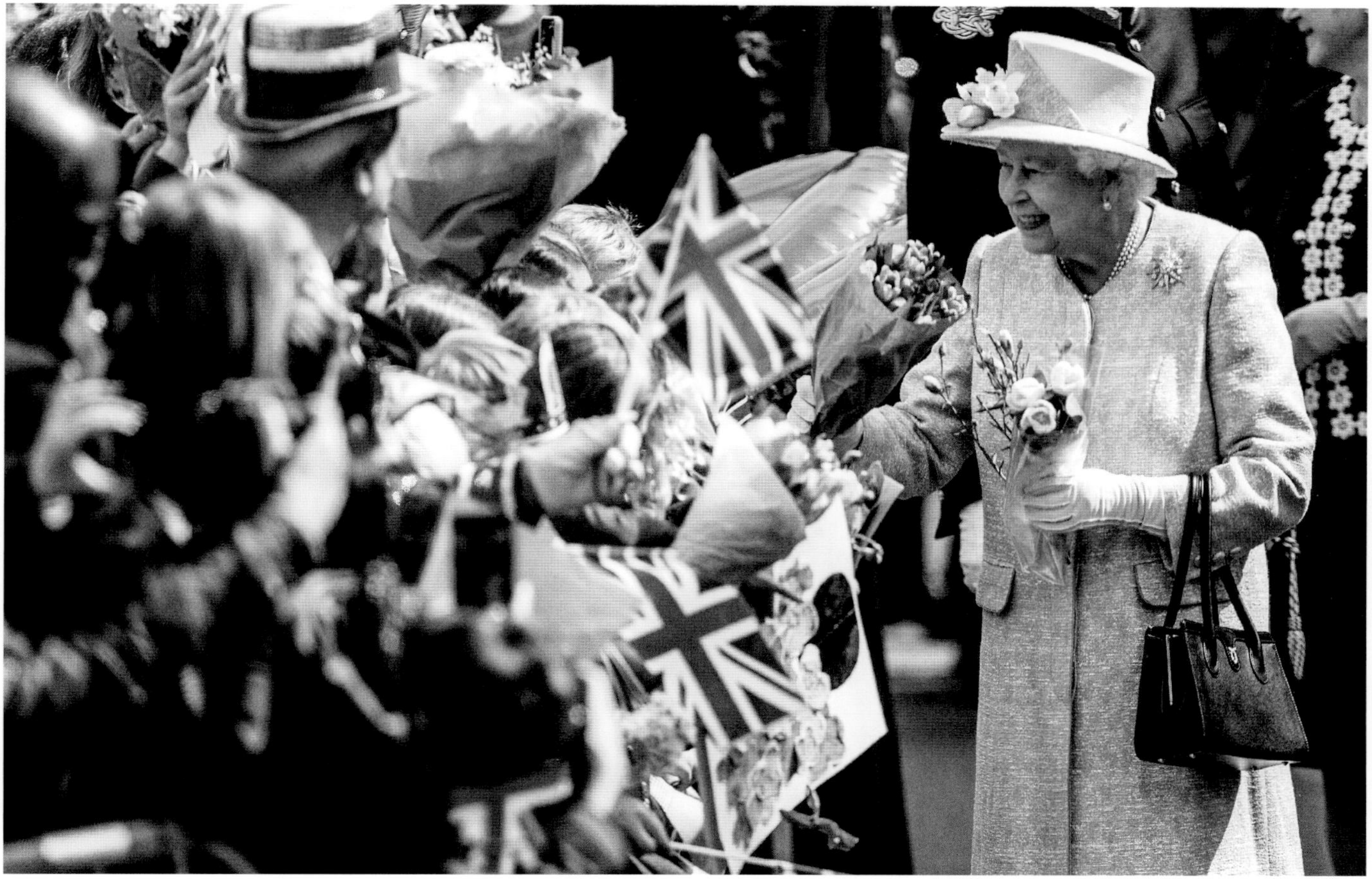

CHARTERHOUSE

By Richard Pohle

February 28, 2017

The Queen smiles as she bends down to accept a posy from four-year-old Daisy Cox, on a visit to the Charterhouse in London. The royal visit saw the Queen unveil a plaque to mark the completion of a major redevelopment project. In the background the Latin motto Deo dante dedi, or "God having given, I gave", is seen on a gate at the historic site. Its message of dedication and duty is one with which the Queen, still carrying out official engagements at the age of 90, would surely be associated.

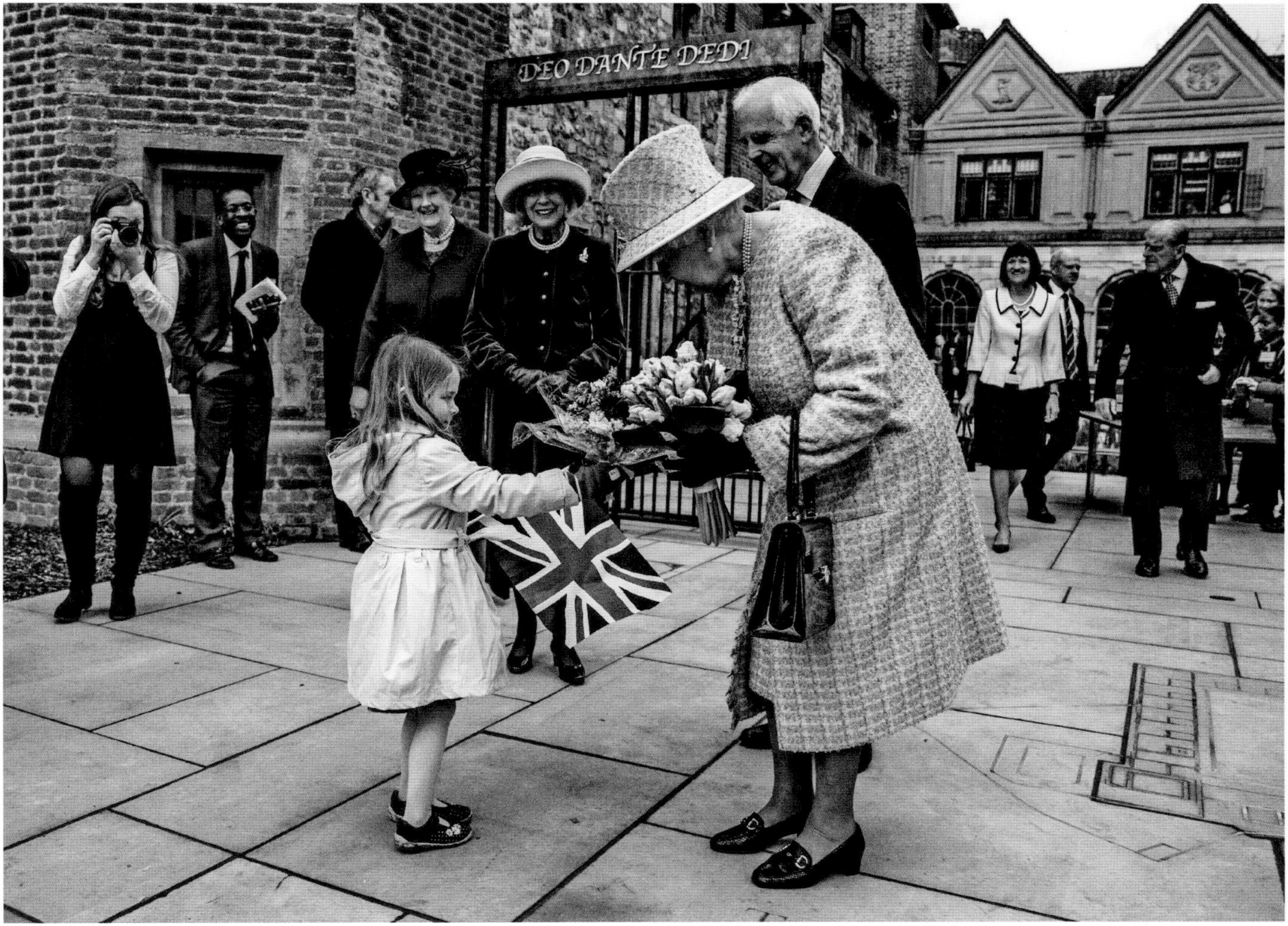
DEO DANTE DEDI

A VISIT FROM PRESIDENT TRUMP

By Richard Pohle

May, 2019

It was a moment which solidified the "special relationship" between the US and UK, although even then there was a moment of controversy. When President Donald Trump made an official visit to Windsor Castle, he joined the Queen to inspect the troops of the Coldstream Guards. Some commentators said that the President had broken palace etiquette by stepping in front of the monarch, however palace aides denied that there was any wrongdoing. Trump said as much himself and described the Queen as "a fantastic woman". He returned to the UK and to Buckingham Palace the following month for a state visit, an honour which would be repeated during his second presidency in 2025.

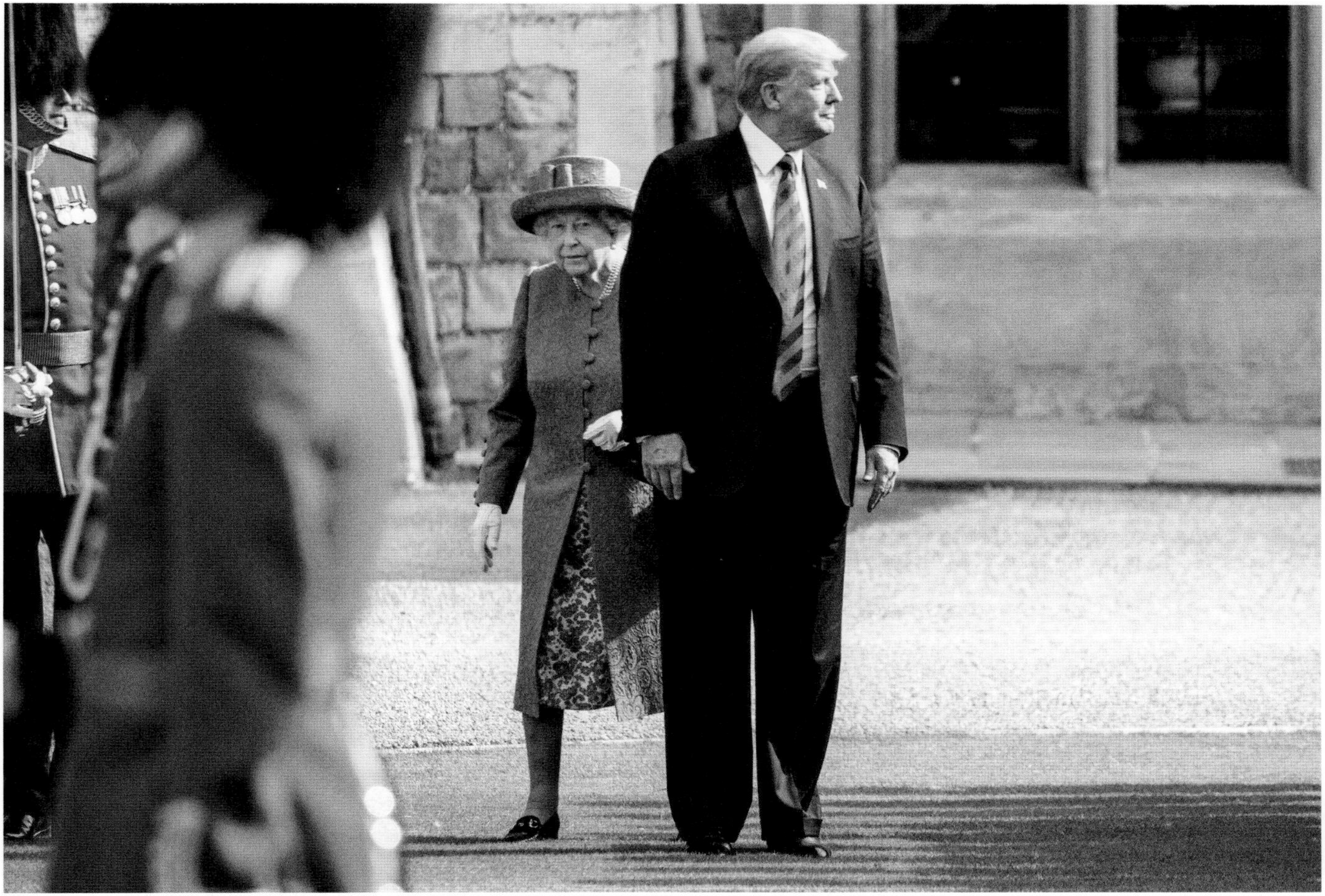

A RAINY DAY AT THE RACES

By Richard Pohle

June 19, 2019

Despite the inclement weather, the Queen raises a smile, and an umbrella, against the rain during a visit to Royal Ascot. Never happier than when she was at the races, the Queen attended every day of Royal Ascot, delighting in seeing the horses and spending time with her family and guests.

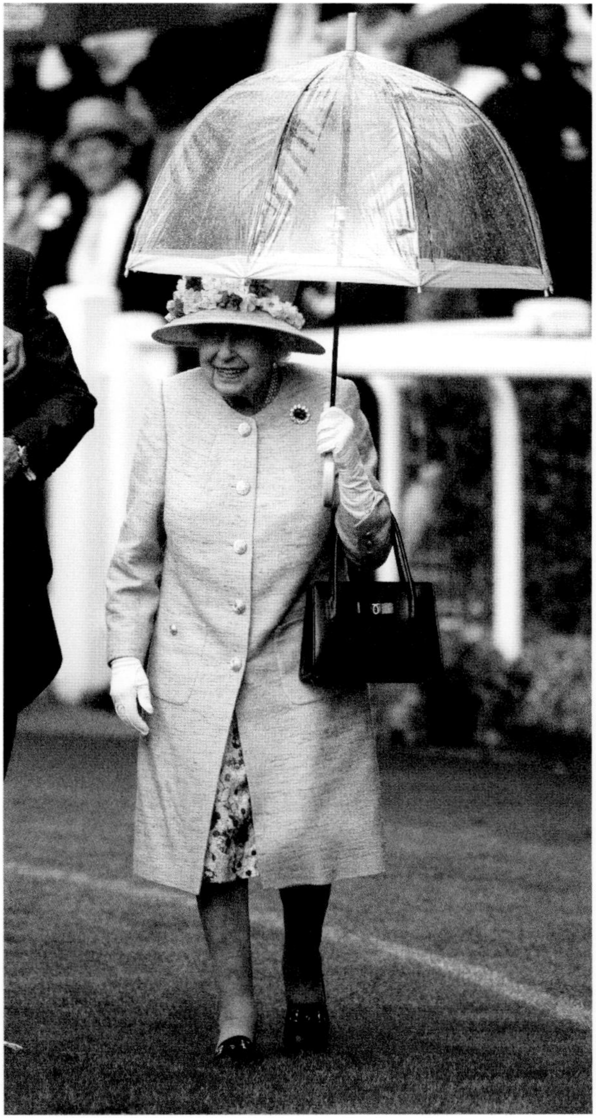

REMEMBRANCE

By Richard Pohle

November 10, 2019

Lest we forget: with every passing year, the poignancy of the debt we owe to those who sacrificed their lives never failed to move the Queen. With a gloved hand, she is seen wiping away a tear as she looks down from a balcony over the Cenotaph for the annual Remembrance Day service. The Queen led the nation at the service but stopped laying a wreath herself in 2017, watching instead while other members of the family participated on her behalf.

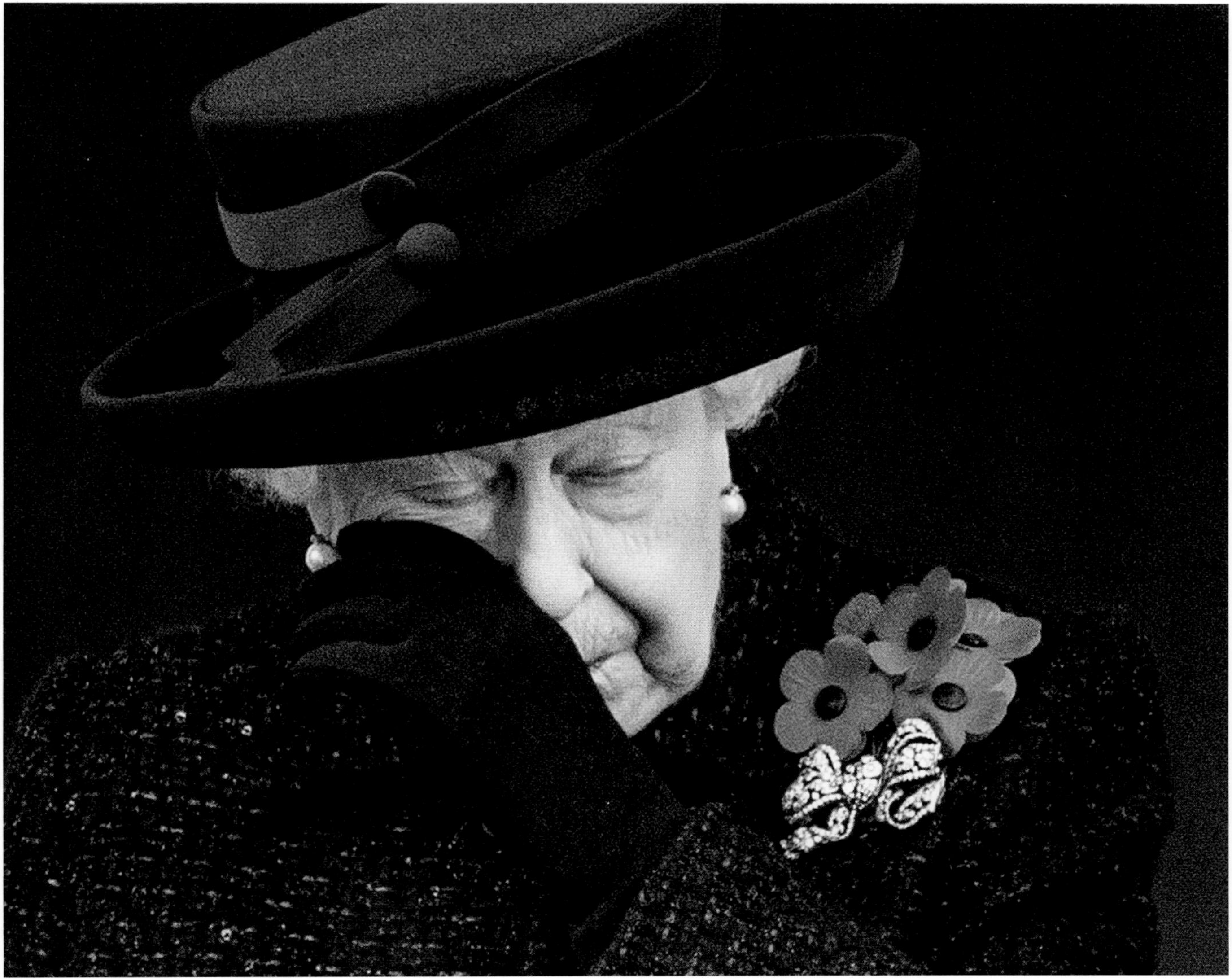

STATE OPENING OF PARLIAMENT

By Richard Pohle

December 19, 2019

Happy and glorious: in a shaft of light the Queen dazzles in the Diamond Diadem and a diamond necklace at the state opening of parliament. Speaking to two members of the military after delivering the Queen's speech, she gives them a broad smile.

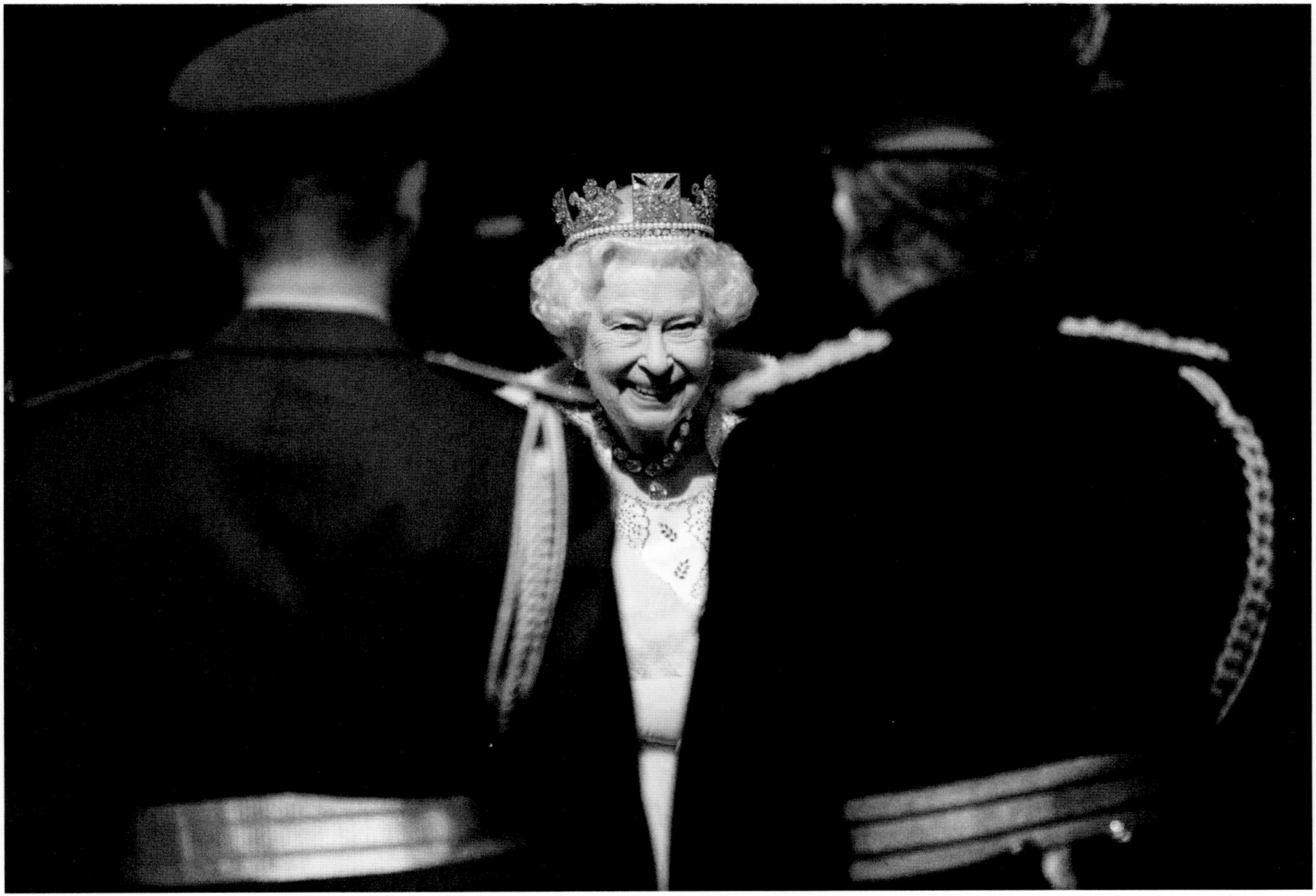

G7 AT THE EDEN PROJECT

By Jack Hill

June 11, 2021

Just two months after the death of her husband Prince Philip, the Queen is at the Eden Project in Cornwall where she hosted a reception during the G7 summit.
As world leaders including US President Joe Biden jetted in, the Queen was joined by Prince Charles, the Duchess of Cornwall and the Duke and Duchess of Cambridge.
At a photocall, the Queen, known for her quick wit, asked the politicians:
"Are you supposed to be looking as if you're enjoying yourselves?"
Prime Minister Boris Johnson raised a laugh when he replied:
"Yes. We have been enjoying ourselves in spite of appearances."

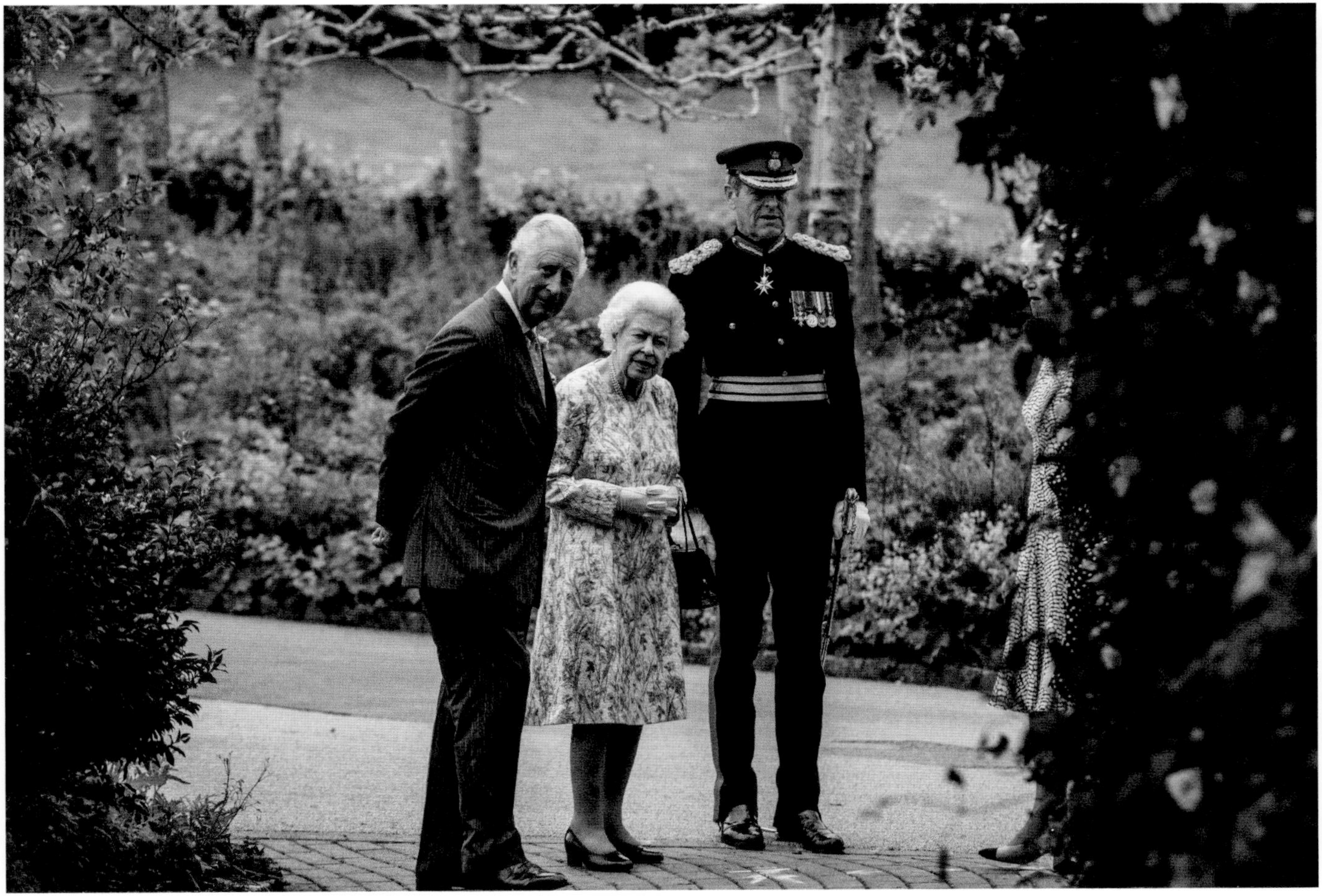

PLATINUM JUBILEE

By Richard Pohle

June 5, 2022

Holding onto a walking stick, the Queen waves to the public from the balcony of Buckingham Palace during the Platinum Jubilee celebrations. It was to be her last major public occasion before her death a little over three months later. Determined to continue with her duties until the last, the Queen took part in several events that weekend but did not attend the Platinum Party pop concert held on the Mall.

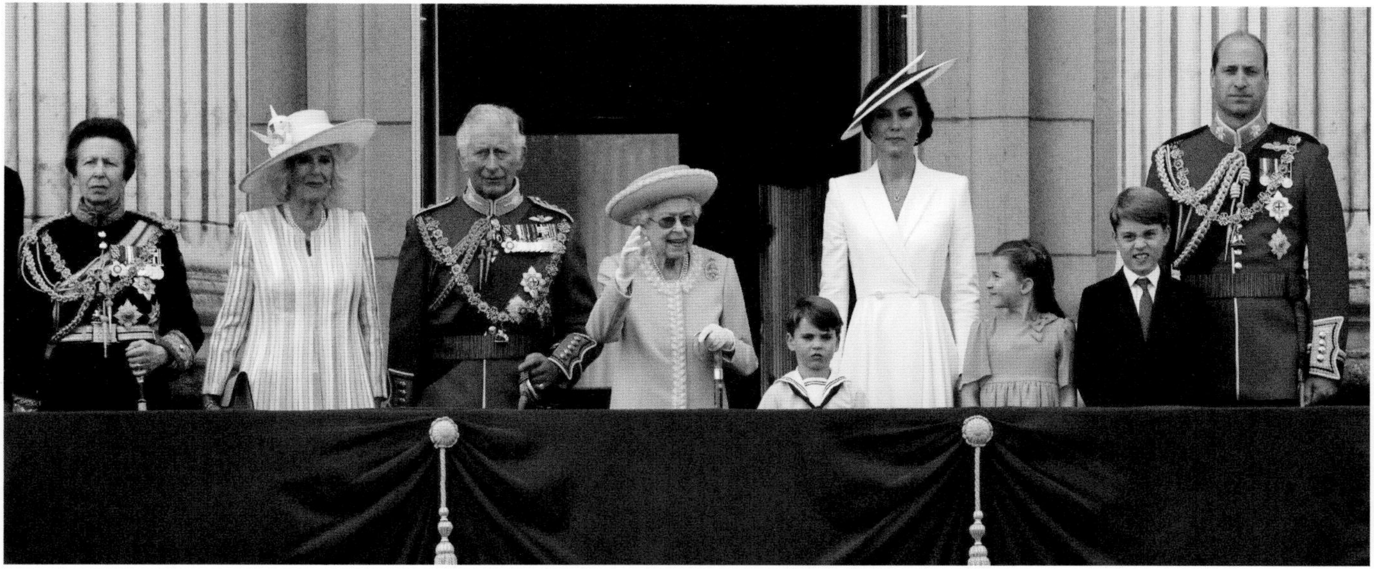

THE FINAL JOURNEY

By Jack Hill

September 13, 2022

The coffin of Her Late Majesty Queen Elizabeth II arrives at RAF Northolt in West London after being flown from Scotland. Following her death at Balmoral on September 8, the Queen's coffin was taken to St Giles' Cathedral in Edinburgh where a vigil and service were held. The coffin was then flown to London when it was accompanied on its final journey by the late Queen's only daughter, the Princess Royal. Amid overcast skies, heads were bowed as the royal hearse arrived in London. The royal hearse, seen here, transported the coffin first to Buckingham Palace and then to Westminster Abbey for the state funeral.

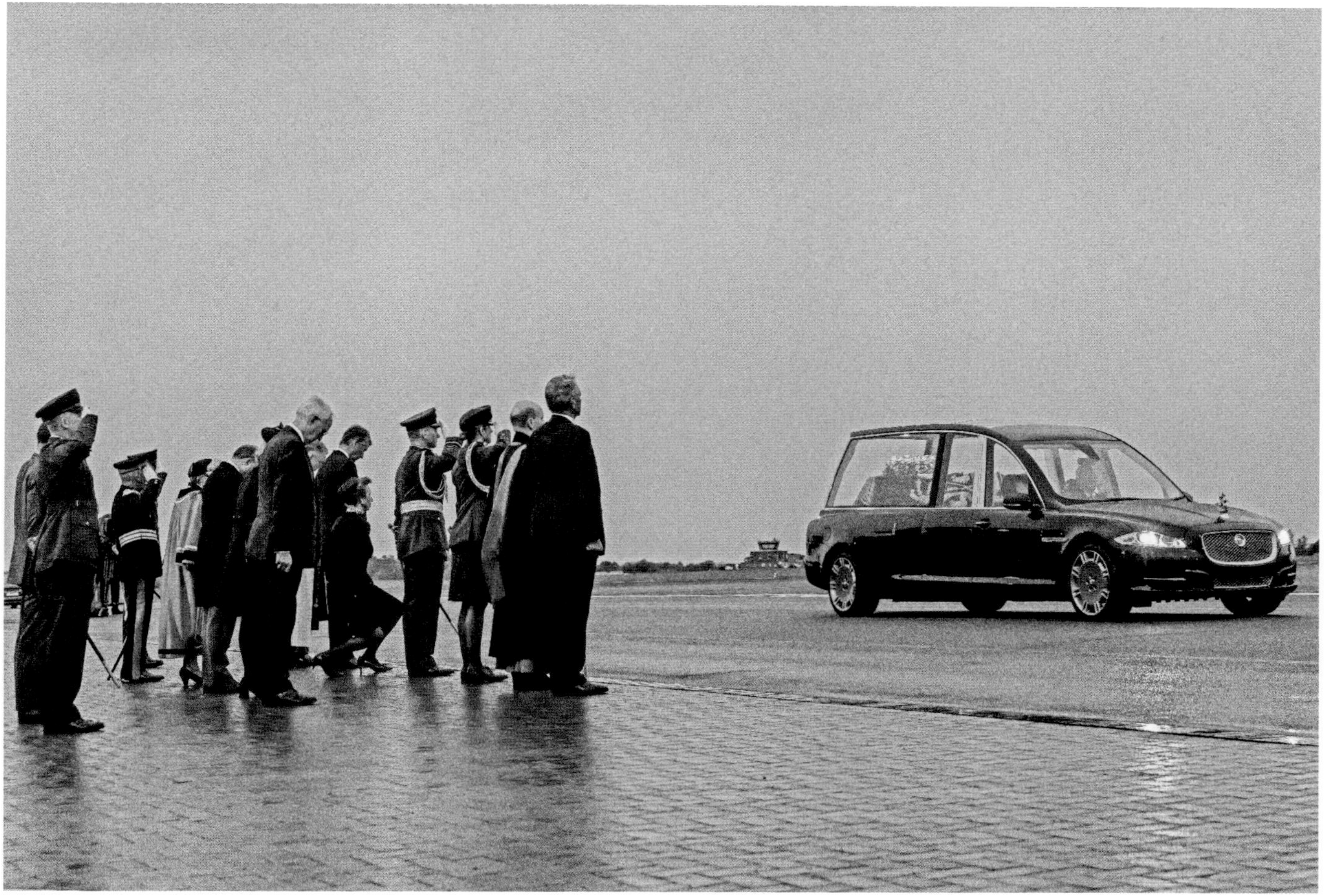

LYING IN STATE

By Peter Tarry

September 14, 2022

If Britain had known anything like it before, few were alive to remember it. Mourners and members of the public queued overnight, some waiting for more than a day to file past the Queen's coffin during the lying-in-state at Westminster Hall. Queen Elizabeth II lay in state for four days from September 14 until her state funeral on Monday, September 19. During that time, eight of the Queen's grandchildren, including Princes William and Harry, held a historic vigil around her coffin while it was lying in state. Much of the lying-in-state was broadcast live on television for the first time so that people around the world could pay their respects to the monarch.

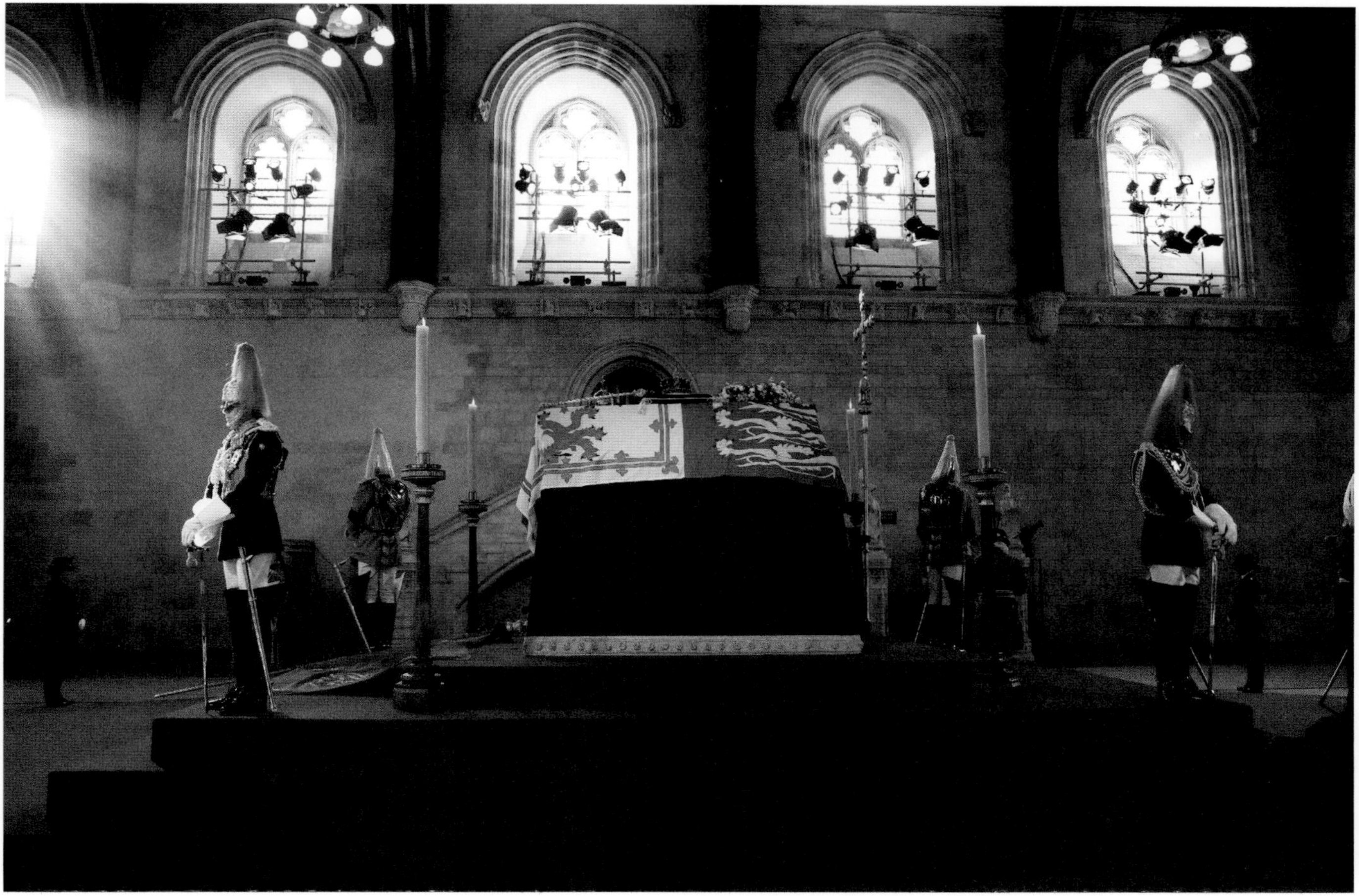

INDEX

Published by Times Books
An imprint of HarperCollins Publishers
1 Robroyston Gate
Glasgow
G33 1JN
www.harpercollins.co.uk

HarperCollins Publishers
Macken House
39/40 Mayor Street Upper
Dublin 1
D01 C9W8
Ireland

First edition 2026

Thanks and acknowledgements go to Joanne Lovey and Robin Ashton at News Licensing and, in particular, at The Times, Ian Brunskill and, at HarperCollins, Lauren Murray, Sarah Woods, James Hunter and Sophie Waeland. With special thanks to News UK Archives.

A catalogue record for this book is available from the British Library.

ISBN 978-0-00-880670-5

10 9 8 7 6 5 4 3 2 1

If you would like to comment on any aspect of this publication, please contact the Publishers at the above address or online.

e-mail: times.books@harpercollins.co.uk
www.timesbooks.co.uk

Printed in India

FSC
www.fsc.org
MIX
Paper | Supporting responsible forestry
FSC™ C016779

Published by Times Books
An imprint of HarperCollins Publishers
1 Robroyston Gate
Glasgow
G33 1JN
www.harpercollins.co.uk

HarperCollins Publishers
Macken House
39/40 Mayor Street Upper
Dublin 1
D01 C9W8
Ireland

First edition 2026

Thanks and acknowledgements go to Joanne Lovey and Robin Ashton at News Licensing and, in particular, at The Times, Ian Brunskill and, at HarperCollins, Lauren Murray, Sarah Woods, James Hunter and Sophie Waeland. With special thanks to News UK Archives.

A catalogue record for this book is available from the British Library.

ISBN 978-0-00-880670-5

10 9 8 7 6 5 4 3 2 1

If you would like to comment on any aspect of this publication, please contact the Publishers at the above address or online.

e-mail: times.books@harpercollins.co.uk
www.timesbooks.co.uk

Printed in India

FSC
www.fsc.org
MIX
Paper | Supporting responsible forestry
FSC™ C016779

Published by Times Books
An imprint of HarperCollins Publishers
1 Robroyston Gate
Glasgow
G33 1JN
www.harpercollins.co.uk

HarperCollins Publishers
Macken House
39/40 Mayor Street Upper
Dublin 1
D01 C9W8
Ireland

First edition 2026

Thanks and acknowledgements go to Joanne Lovey and Robin Ashton at News Licensing and, in particular, at The Times, Ian Brunskill and, at HarperCollins, Lauren Murray, Sarah Woods, James Hunter and Sophie Waeland. With special thanks to News UK Archives.

A catalogue record for this book is available from the British Library.

ISBN 978-0-00-880670-5

10 9 8 7 6 5 4 3 2 1

If you would like to comment on any aspect of this publication, please contact the Publishers at the above address or online.

e-mail: times.books@harpercollins.co.uk
www.timesbooks.co.uk

Printed in India

FSC
www.fsc.org
MIX
Paper | Supporting responsible forestry
FSC™ C016779